VACHERON CONSTANTIN

ARTISTS OF TIME

EDITORIAL MANAGEMENT
Suzanne Tise-Isoré
Style & Design Collection

PUBLICATION MANAGER AT VACHERON CONSTANTIN
Anne-Marie Bubanko Belcari

GRAPHIC DESIGN
Cakedesign
Thibaut Mathieu
Clément Prats
Tiphaine Massard

TEXT ADAPTATION
François Chaille

EDITORIAL ASSISTANCE
Sarah Rozelle
Boris Guilbert

TRANSLATED FROM THE FRENCH BY
Datawords

COPYEDITING AND PROOFREADING
Datawords

PRODUCTION
Corinne Trovarelli
Angélique Florentin

COLOR SEPARATION
Les Artisans du Regard, Paris

PRINTING BY
Musumeci, Italy

Simultaneously published in French as *Vacheron Constantin artistes du temps*

English-language edition

Flammarion, SA
87, quai Panhard et Levassor
75647 Paris Cedex 13
editions.flammarion.com
styleetdesign-flammarion.com
15 16 17 321

ISBN: 978-2-08-020224-6
Legal Deposit: October 2015

VACHERON CONSTANTIN
ARTISTS OF TIME

FRANCO COLOGNI

PHOTOGRAPHY BY
BRUNO EHRS

Flammarion

CONTENTS

Vacheron
Constantin
masse 1120

PREFACE

While I was writing *The Secrets of Vacheron Constantin,* the book that was published in 2005 to celebrate 250 years of the Manufacture, I set myself some simple yet ambitious objectives. By digging through its extraordinary archives, it was relatively simple to show that the spirit of Vacheron Constantin has always been linked to the spirit of the time, to progress, to beauty and to evolution in technology and the arts. What makes it simple is that this proposition has been beautifully demonstrated in each watch, each invention and each project created by Vacheron Constantin. To recount this authentic, deeply human story, I merely had to give a clear narrative to a series of achievements that have been nothing but exceptional for two and a half centuries.

My second objective, on the other hand, was more ambitious: to show that, while the Manufacture's archives and heritage reveal the past, it also has a vibrant heart that suggests a future with deep roots that can detect springs of pure water in the fertile ground of Swiss fine watchmaking.

Ten years after the book was published, the "secrets" of Vacheron Constantin are by no means buried behind the archive walls or hidden away in the workshops: fine watchmaking does not exist in an inaccessible world, like the Gods of Olympus, but in the here and now, right among us. It shares our hopes and ambitions, noting our desire for change and our search for beauty. In short, the real secrets of the Manufacture are its values. They are not secrets that must remain confidential, but secrets that infuse each Vacheron Constantin watch with an indelible identification. And these values have never varied throughout the course of history. This new book, which differs from its predecessor in both content and objectives, clearly conveys these values to the reader – values of passing down expertise that are demonstrated by the master watchmakers and masters of the associated arts still performing their crafts today.

The transmission of expertise is a continuous process in the Manufacture. From the watchmaker who masters the latest technology to the specialist whose art has evolved over the centuries, from the oldest to the youngest, from the expert to the beginner, from those who draw inspiration from the past to those whose eyes are fixed on the future... Everyone practices their own blend of discipline and intuition which is both a statement and a message: you will remember this. You will remember what I do, and you will do it even better. This is what the founder of Vacheron Constantin had in mind when he issued the delightful instruction: *Always do better if possible, and it is always possible.* Which has led to the title of this new book: *Artists of Time.*

At this point, I would like to reveal my own secret: I am not the sole author of this book. At most, I could be described as the librettist of an opera. As Lorenzo Da Ponte was for Mozart... But here the music has been written by Vacheron Constantin. And by the men and women in the Manufacture who perform and interpret it every day. Without the active participation of these artists, who employ their knowledge with such passion, this book would never have been produced. It is like a choral work that involves all those who have worked behind the scenes enthusiastically, skillfully and patiently. I would like to give my sincerest thanks to them all.

But, above all, I am grateful to the reader. It is for you that we present this opera, whether you are a passionate collector of fine watchmaking pieces, a connoisseur of objects with a soul, or a lover of beautiful books. Thank you.

Franco Cologni

LEFT-HAND PAGE
Vacheron Constantin sets itself apart in the watchmaking world with its distinct shallow Côtes de Genève.

AN UNINTERRUPTED STORY

1755–1819
THE CABINOTIERS AND THE FABRIQUE

From 1755 without interruption, three generations of Vacherons laid the foundations of a company that would become the world's oldest watch manufacturer in continuous operation: Jean-Marc, born in 1731; his son Abraham, born in 1760; and his grandson Jacques Barthélémi, born in 1787.

1755

DOUBLE PAGE 12–13
Silver pocket watch, 1926. The delicately hand-chiseled back represents the Tour de l'Île and the Quai des Moulins, based on an engraving prior to 1875. Inv. no. 10656

PREVIOUS LEFT-HAND PAGE
Christophe François von Ziegler, *Les cabinotiers au XVIIIe siècle*, 1879 (detail). Oil on canvas, 136 cm x 93 cm. Geneva, collection of the Watchmaking and Enamel Museum, Museum of Art and History.

On Wednesday, September 17, 1755, a 24-year old master watchmaker, a so-called *natif* of Geneva, was walking through the craftsmen's neighborhood, the borough of Saint-Gervais on the right bank of the Rhône. His name was Jean-Marc Vacheron. It was an important day for him because, like any self-respecting master watchmaker, he was about to take on an apprentice. He arrived at the office of Master Choisy, a well-known notary among watchmakers. The apprentice-to-be, Ésaïe Jean François Hetier, was already waiting there with his father, a master tailor. He would start work the very next day in his new master's workshop. For the next five years, the watchmaker would replace his father, teaching him his craft and providing food and accommodation. Two copies of the contract had been prepared a few days earlier; Ésaïe's father signed first, followed by the master, who then handed the quill to the boy. He carefully wrote out his full name: Ésaïe Jean François Hetier. The contract obliged the watchmaker to teach him the profession "hiding nothing from him," and to provide board and lodging, including "laundry and care of all things," in return for the sum of 1,050 florins paid by his father. The father also guaranteed that his son would serve the full term of his apprenticeship.

Young Jean-Marc Vacheron could certainly not have imagined that this simple agreement would leave a permanent mark on the history of watchmaking. The contract, dated September 17, 1755, is the earliest known reference to the master watchmaker who founded a prestigious dynasty. It was, in effect, the birth certificate of the company that grew to fame in every corner of the world and which, in the 1950s, became the world's oldest watch manufacturer still in operation.

It may be that Jean-Marc Vacheron had only started working for himself that very year, but it could have been the year before, which was also the year in which he married. Master watchmakers could only train one apprentice at a time so Ésaïe was indentured to a master who was still a young man himself. Jean-Marc was born in Geneva on July 12, 1731, so he was twelve years old when he began his own seven-year apprenticeship in March of 1744 with a well-respected Geneva watchmaker, Abraham Collomby. When he completed it in 1751, it is likely that he continued working as a watchmaker for Collomby before qualifying as a master and setting up his own workshop. To become a master craftsman it was required to make "a small clock with a morning alarm to be worn around the neck and a square clock to keep upon a table in two heights."

Jean-Marc was the sixth child of Jean-Jacques Vacheron, a master weaver born in Lugnorre, near Neuchâtel, who moved to Geneva where he became prosperous. From the 1650s onward, the "citizens" and tradespeople of the town fiercely protected their privileges with very restrictive laws: simple "inhabitants" or "residents" as well as their children born in Geneva, known as *natifs*, had no political rights of any kind. Jean-Jacques was only an "inhabitant" of Geneva and his son only a *natif*. These two classes were effectively excluded from the craft of watchmaking, and certainly from becoming master craftsmen. Regulations introduced through the second half of the seventeenth century were specifically designed to protect Genevans from having to compete with the new arrivals. No doubt Jean-Jacques Vacheron would have discouraged his son from becoming a watchmaker if these regulations had not been abolished in 1738 thanks to pressure from Geneva-born craftsmen. From that year, *natifs* had the right to become masters, a right that "inhabitants" and "residents" would only receive in 1782. The new law enabled at least two of Jean-Marc's brothers to work in watchmaking. The oldest, Jean Vacheron, born in 1715, was a master maker of watch cases and packaging. Jean Étienne, born in 1719, was also a master craftsman producing watchmaker files. A third brother, Paul-Vincent, was a bailiff of the Geneva Republic but his son Jean-Paul, born in 1758, became a master watchmaker; he had no successor. A fourth brother, Antoine, born a year before Jean-Marc, is known to have served an apprenticeship assembling watch cases.

Geneva had not always been so hostile to new arrivals. It was a small town of 12,000 people in the mid-sixteenth century but with the Reformation it became a haven of religious freedom that attracted thousands of persecuted protestants from Germany, Italy and, above all, France. Calvin warmly welcomed these foreigners, who increased the number of his supporters, and soon offered them full and complete citizenship. Geneva, the "Protestant Rome," also welcomed the wealth of knowledge and skills brought by these members of the intellectual and professional elite. The finest of France's watchmakers were Protestants and most of them moved to the town that had been famous for the quality of its jewelry since the thirteenth century. When Calvin banned all unnecessary ornamentation, he seriously damaged the Genevan jewelers' business and they converted to specializing in making what is known as *habillage* – the external parts of a watch – which was acceptable to the new Church. The arrival of excellent watchmakers at a time when jewelers were looking for work gave birth to a development that came to be called the *Fabrique*. Fabrique is an inclusive, symbolic word that does not indicate a factory, a production workshop, or any kind of company. It has a meaning specific to Geneva: the organization that brings together all the numerous technical and commercial skills involved in creating and selling jewelry, gold or silver objects, and timepieces. It was the dynamism and remarkable creativity of the Geneva Fabrique that led the town to make a unique impact on horological history.

The industry grew rapidly with its wealth of talent and determination to export, first to the original home countries of its members then to the oriental markets – notably Turkey and its empire. The Fabrique specialized in watches that were ornamental, complicated and refined. Many of them had cases boasting rich enameled decoration or could be classified as "fantasy" or shaped watches made in a wide variety of forms, including animals, flowers, fruit, and crosses. In 1601, the watchmakers founded their trade associations based on the goldsmith's model. It was open to all, newcomers included. Over the following decades, dozens of other trade associations were formed to reflect the division of labor within the Fabrique – such as those of engravers, case assemblers, hand makers, dial makers and spring manufacturers. At the same time, the growing number of new arrivals led the citizen artisans of the Fabrique to start restricting entry to their specialist crafts. However, in 1685 the Edict of Nantes was revoked and Protestant worship was permitted once again in France. This encouraged a wave of departures from Geneva and the protectionist measures were progressively relaxed at the start of the eighteenth century.

The majority of craftsmen and merchants in the Fabrique were located in the Saint-Gervais quarter of Geneva. This extended south to the river Rhône – which for a long time could only be crossed by a single bridge – and north to the line of

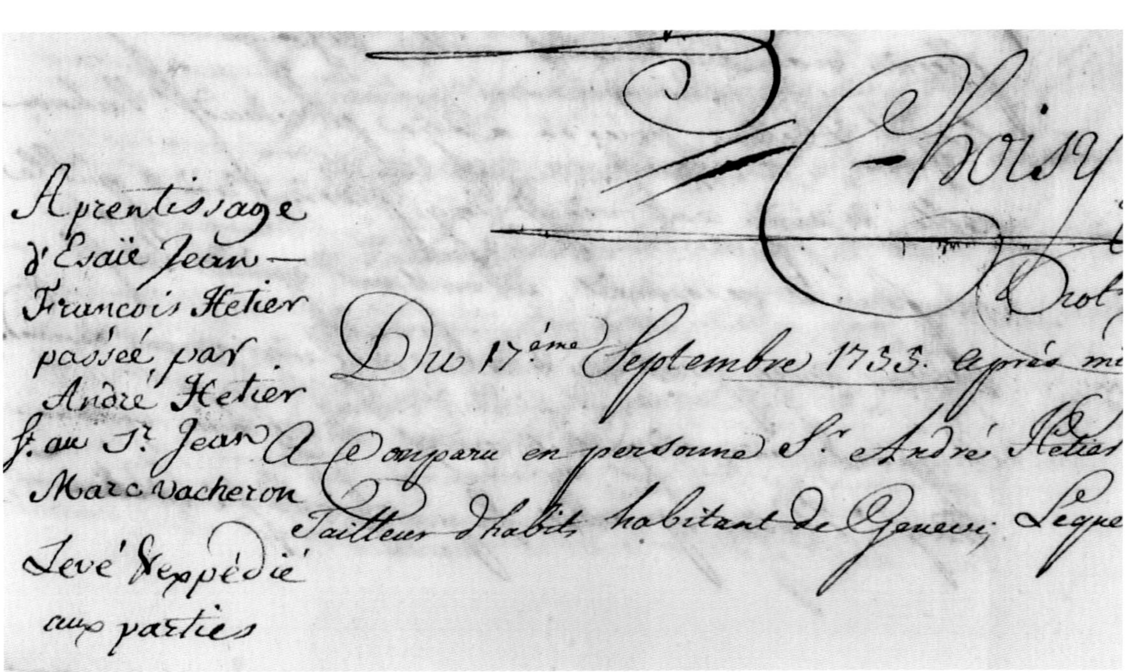
Aprentissage d'Esaïe Jean-François Hetier passée par André Hetier f. au Sr. Jean Marc Vacheron
Levé Expédiée aux parties

Choisy

Du 17ème Septembre 1755. après mi[di]
A comparu en personne Sr. André Hetier Tailleur d'habits habitant de Geneve, Lequel

BELOW
On September 17, 1755, Jean-Marc Vacheron hired his first apprentice, Ésaïe Jean François Hetier, as illustrated by this detail of the apprenticeship contract. This document signed before a notary is considered the founding act of Vacheron Constantin.

In an age when a woman was not considered to need to know the time and even less to ask for it in society, Vacheron Constantin dove into the design of genuine watchmaking jewels. Symbols of their owner's condition and status, these watches gradually became indispensable accessories: worn as necklaces, suspended on a châtelaine, pinned to a gown or concealed in a brooch, they satisfied the needs of privileged customers.

OPPOSITE
Rembrandt Harmensz Van Rijn, *Portrait of a Young Woman with a Fan*, 1633. Oil on canvas, 125 cm x 101 cm. New York, Metropolitan Museum of Art.

RIGHT-HAND PAGE
William Hogarth, *Miss Mary Edwards*, 1742 (detail). Oil on canvas, 126 cm x 101 cm. New York, Frick Collection.

fortifications that cut across the surrounding countryside. Its location made Saint-Gervais almost a self-contained world, although it remained open to the markets outside. Philosopher Jean-Jacques Rousseau spent part of his childhood there in the 1720s. At that time, the area was being extensively renovated: the old merchants' houses, with their overhanging storerooms along the first floor – which created a covered gallery at street level – were being replaced by solid buildings comprising five or six floors. Under the roof, the idea of an overhanging floor, called a "dome," was retained in order to capture the maximum amount of daylight, and it was there that the craftsmen called *cabinotiers* worked. At the start of the twentieth century, Genevan writer Philippe Monnier described these studios, or *cabinets*: "High up there in the attic, under the roof tiles, above the noise and the shadows, with a wonderful view of the blue sky and the blue lake, were the long lines of *cabinets*..."

This was the new world that young Ésaïe Hetier was positioned to discover: a watchmaker's *cabinet*, which at that time in Geneva, was not called a "workshop." Fifty years later, the name *cabinotier* came to denote the aristocrats among these craftsmen, real artists working in the *cabinets* of the Fabrique as watchmakers, goldsmiths, engravers, and enamelers. Until the late nineteenth century, when they began to disappear, the *cabinotiers* of Geneva formed a community made unique by its intellectual and professional characteristics. The *cabinotier* was a master craftsman as well as an artist, a cultivated man with an open, curious mind, who jealously protected his freedom. He carefully managed his work to give himself plenty of time to meet friends, relax, and learn. He spent eight or ten hours at a time in the cabinet, didn't work on Mondays, and could negotiate a contract with his employer that gave him a large number of days off. He often used them to take part in political discussions. At that time, Geneva was suffering under an authoritarian government, which, in 1763, would ban Jean-Jacques Rousseau, who came from a long line of Genevan watchmakers: *cabinotiers* were the seeds of the Geneva revolution in December 1792 that finally proclaimed political equality among every class of population. Many *cabinotiers* used their free time to write and, particularly in the Age of Enlightenment, to read the works of scientists and philosophers. It was in 1755 that Rousseau described his watchmaker father, Isaac, in his *Discourse on the Origin and Basis of Inequality Among Men:* "I can still see him living from the work of his hands and feeding his soul with the most sublime truths. I see Tacitus, Plutarch, and Grotius appearing before him, among the instruments of his craft." In 1755, when the long history of Vacheron Constantin began, watchmaking in Geneva was expanding rapidly and its craftsmen, the aristocrats of the working world, were prospering. So it is not surprising that Ésaïe's father agreed to pay more than 1,000 florins – about 10,000 Euros today – for his son to be trained in the highest-paying craft in Geneva. It is estimated that the number of watches produced in Geneva's workshops became twenty times greater during the eighteenth century, from 5,000 to about 100,000 pieces per year. In 1800, close to half the active population in Geneva was employed in the Fabrique. Inevitably, not all the craftsmen benefited equally from this growth. By increasing the division of labor to meet the consistently rising demand, the Fabrique established a hierarchy between the various crafts. At the tip of the pyramid, of course, were the master

A GENEVE

watchmakers and their "finishers," whose job was to check, finish and assemble parts and movements made by others. In 1760 there were 600 master watchmakers in Geneva, an enormous number for a small town of 20,000 people. At the bottom of the ladder were those who made blanks or *ébauches*, the least complicated elements of the movement (plates, pillars, wheel bridges, fusées, etc.). These were generally poor peasants from Savoy, located outside of Geneva, who worked at home. In the middle were the various case makers and decorators, the dial and hand makers, and the tool makers. The amazing success of the Fabrique also owed much to the system of *établissage*, which enabled the production and sales of watches to be properly organized. The *établisseur* was often a respected master watchmaker. He decided which watch should be produced and specified all its details, recruited each of the different craftsmen, advanced their pay, distributed the materials required (particularly precious metals such as gold and silver), collected the finished pieces, distributed them among the assemblers, supervised the finishing of the watch and, lastly, took charge of selling it. Either he would sell it directly to the client, or he would entrust it to a merchant, who was able to offer it on more distant markets. This system made the division of labor more efficient and led to increased productivity.

These were the circumstances that shaped the world that the nervous young apprentice Ésaïe Hetier would discover the next day. High up in a building in the heart of Geneva was a *cabinet* flooded with light, where Jean-Marc Vacheron and five or six workers finished and assembled valuable watches for highly demanding clients. As the boy was shown several components laid out on a bench, he struggled to remember their strange names, barrel, fusée and escapement among them. But they would soon become very familiar to him. As would objects like files, lathes, bows, hammers, pins and polishing tools.

At that time, watchmakers only produced a few dozen unique pieces each year and there are few examples remaining from the hands of the first Vacheron watchmakers. Around 1985, a collector arrived at the Geneva office with his latest discovery: a watch with "J M Vacheron à Genève" engraved on the movement. It is the only known piece to include the first name of the founder (left-hand page), and it is now part of the Vacheron Constantin heritage collection. It is not radically different from the watches produced by the Fabrique from 1750 to 1760, but its refinement clearly shows the great care that was given to its appearance. It features an escape wheel and hands that are very finely carved in gold, as is the balance cock, which supports the balance. This is the most visible component when the case is opened and it is delicately finished with very elegant arabesque patterns. In 2015, Vacheron Constantin paid tribute to the virtuosity of Jean-Marc Vacheron by reproducing this particularly refined decoration on the calibers of the watches created to mark its 260th anniversary. The first known watch to carry the Vacheron name already demonstrated the double commitment to quality that would gradually build the identity of the brand: to use the most advanced technology and to create beauty. It seems that the first Vacheron was already working to produce watches that were beautiful in both body and soul.

Jean-Marc Vacheron's first watches were manufactured at a time when new developments arrived that would have a greater impact than he could ever have imagined. Around 1770, James Watt finally made the steam engine reliable and efficient while James Hargreaves and Richard Arkwright laid the groundwork for the mechanical spinning wheel between 1765 and 1767, marking the beginning of the first Industrial Revolution in England. This would lend the nation economic, financial, and industrial supremacy in Europe. A supremacy that also applied to watchmaking: it had grown into a real industry on the British side of the channel by the second half of the eighteenth century. An estimated 200,000 watches were produced there at the end of the century, many for export, in workshops where part of the process was mechanized. But the majority of these watches were simple, rugged models without the refinement or mechanical sophistication of French or Swiss timepieces.

It was this period, from 1751 to 1780, that saw the publication of the thirty-five volumes of a

LEFT-HAND AND FOLLOWING DOUBLE PAGE
The first known watch by the brand's founder, signed "J M Vacheron à Genève," 1755. The silver case houses an enamel dial with Roman numerals. The watch is wound with a key.
Inv. no. 10198

Vacheron
A GENEVE

monumental work, the outstanding symbol of the Age of Enlightenment: *Encyclopédie* by Diderot and Alembert. This *Systematic Dictionary of the Sciences, Arts and Crafts* included contributions from Voltaire, Buffon, Rousseau and Turgot among others. It was an inventory of the ideas, science and technologies of the time, intended to combat irrationality, superstition, and the deliberate obscurity used to resist the spread of knowledge. Several of its entries dealt with watchmaking – Escapement, Fusée, Clock, Watchmaker, Watchmaking, Watch, Movement, Pendulum, Repeater, Striking – accompanied by very detailed drawings.

From about 1765 until he retired twenty years later, Jean-Marc Vacheron seemed content to sign his creations "Vacheron à Genève." Perhaps he removed his first name so that the signature included his two sons, André (born in 1755) and Abraham (born in 1760), who he trained in his *cabinet* and who both became master watchmakers. Some of the watches the father and two sons worked together on have survived. The first is a simple hunter-encased timepiece fitted with a cover to protect the glass and a pendant attached to it at the 3 o'clock position. The "Vacheron à Genève" signature appears on the dial, a practice that began in the eighteenth century. The same signature is found on a watch made in 1775 that is also quite plain but even more robustly built, probably to please customers in central Europe, whose tastes were simpler and somewhat more minimalist. It is a clear example of the effort made to adapt production to meet foreign requirements – whatever they might be – that was key to the success of the Fabrique. Another Vacheron watch from the beginning of the nineteenth century also demonstrates this effort: its silver case back is engraved with a typical Ottoman motif. It is highly likely that the *établisseur* who ordered it from Jacques Barthélémi, the son of Abraham Vacheron, planned to sell it in Venice or Trieste, markets that traded with the Middle East.

The earliest known complicated movement from Vacheron dates from around 1790. A complication is an extra function added to the time display in a watch or clock. This movement was made for a small pendulum clock to be hung on a wall (left-hand page and 26-27). It includes a calendar: in addition to the subdial for hours and minutes at 6 o'clock, a subdial at 10 o'clock indicates the date , while a subdial at 2 o'clock shows the day of the week. While wall clocks were quite common at that time, those outfitted with calendars were quite rare.

In Geneva, the Fabrique was reaching the end of a golden age. At the start of the 1780s, some 20,000 craftsmen, workers, and their families lived in the town and its immediate surroundings. Some 100,000 watches a year were produced there. And this activity continued to grow despite the political struggle raging in the town with tradespeople and aristocrats extending their power, muzzling the press, and bringing in foreign mercenaries to impose order. In the Vacheron *cabinet*, as in most of the others, the foundations of a revolution were being laid. But it had nothing to do with politics. It was a revolution started by the inventions of a French watchmaker who had been working in Paris since 1744, but who was born in 1720 in Gex, just a few kilometers from Geneva: Jean Antoine Lépine. For the Vacherons, Lépine's influence only affected design at first. Around 1780, the first dials with Arabic hour numerals appeared. These seem to have been made for Protestant clients, as Catholics preferred Roman numerals. The first

1765

LEFT-HAND AND FOLLOWING DOUBLE PAGE
The first known pocket watch by Vacheron Constantin, 1790. Boasting a calendar with date and day of the week indications, the golden dial divided into three enamel subdials is hand-engraved in a floral pattern. Inv. no. 10870

BELOW
Jean-Marc Vacheron. A contemporary interpretation based on old documents.

Benard direxit.

1780

RIGHT-HAND PAGE
Pocket watch, 1780.
The guilloché and engraved yellow gold case houses a silver guilloché dial engraved in the center.
Inv. no. 10718

Vacheron timepiece with Arabic numerals, a silver watch with a finely carved hinge, was still signed "Vacheron à Genève." As on a slightly later watch, probably dating from 1785, its numerals followed the typical Lépine design with its elegant interplay of thick and thin lines. But in 1785, the Vacheron family adopted a Lépine invention that was much more important: the movement that the brilliant watchmaker had gradually perfected between 1760 and 1772, based on research carried out by his equally brilliant and much more famous brother-in-law, Pierre Beaumarchais. This movement, the Lépine caliber, complete with improvements from the great watchmaker Abraham Louis Breguet, would soon be fitted in all mechanical watches. The reason was simple: this movement made it possible to produce flat watches, which appealed to elegant French gentlemen because they did not create a bulge in the pocket. Around 1755, Lépine looked again at the principal features of the movement developed by Beaumarchais, who at that time was still known as Pierre-Augustin Caron. In a letter to the editor of *Le Mercure de France*, he explained that he had managed to eliminate "all the parts that required height in the movement, such as the fusée, the chain, the bracket, and the crown wheel…" When he gave up watchmaking to concentrate on business and literature, his brother-in-law Lépine took up the challenge. His chief contribution was to replace one of the two plates with bridges. And so the flat watch was born, an important step toward the watch we know today.

In Geneva at the end of the 1780s, Abraham Vacheron, the second son of Jean-Marc, made the earliest surviving Lépine-type watch signed by a Vacheron. But the signature was not "Vacheron à Genève": Jean-Marc had stopped working in 1785 after thirty years at the bench. This first flat, modern Vacheron watch, which was wound by key at the back instead of on the dial, was signed "Abraham Vacheron Girod"; Abraham was now working for himself. To avoid confusion with his brother André – also a master watchmaker and living in the same street – he added the surname of his wife, Anne Elisabeth Girod, whom he married in 1786. This was quite common practice at the time. Did the Vacheron clients really understand who he was? Each of the family members signed differently of course (André with a simple "André Vacheron"), but they appear to have worked together at times, for between 1790 and 1810 some watches were signed "Vacheron Frères," others "Vacheron à Genève" as before, and still others "Abraham Vacheron" without Girod – not to mention the "J P Vacheron " watches made by their cousin, Jean-Paul. However, this family proliferation would not last. André had a son, Pierre André, who looked as if he would become a master watchmaker, but apparently he had no children. Jean-Paul had a daughter.

It was therefore only the descendants of Abraham, second son of Jean-Marc, who kept the Vacheron name alive in the world of watchmaking. Until the early 1950s, Vacheron Constantin's archives reached only as far as him. Recently, they have been reopened and reorganized – as will be discussed in greater detail further on – and now, apart from documentation found in specialist museums, they constitute the largest documentary collection of watchmaking history in the world. From the early nineteenth century, the time of Jacques Barthélémi, the Vacherons began retaining all the documents relating to their work, including books of accounts, manufacturing and sales registers, and correspondence. However, it was not in these private records but in the archives of the State of Geneva that, around 1950, the apprenticeship contract signed by Jean-Marc in 1755 was discovered. This enabled the founding date of Vacheron Constantin to be fixed at thirty years before the previously known date of 1785, which was probably the year that Abraham Vacheron had established his own workshop.

It was just a few years after taking this step that Abraham, like all his colleagues, saw the Fabrique start its long decline. The revolutionary movements in Europe, particularly in France, followed by the Napoleonic Wars profoundly disturbed the commercial networks that Geneva had patiently built up, and its chief markets shrank to an extent that varied from year to year. At the same time, the remarkable organization of the Fabrique, especially its trade associations, began to break down, forcing it to develop new methods of work.

1810

From 1789, the annals of Vacheron Constantin show it navigating though alternating periods of storm and calm. Peace returned between the wars, and crises were followed by temporary recovery. What the record clearly shows is the remarkable ability of Vacheron Constantin to adapt to even the most difficult circumstances and find ways to overcome adversity.

Abraham Vacheron never seemed to lose his optimism – not when the French Revolution broke out, not when French troops were at the gates of Geneva threatening to annex it in 1792, and not even when this pressure drove the city to start its own revolution. As evidence, during these difficult years that marked its beginning, Vacheron Constantin produced its first true jewelry watches, such as this example preserved by Vacheron Constantin. It features a case in two types of gold and an off-center dial decorated with a very fine garland set with garnets (left-hand page). Abraham's only son, Jacques Barthélémi, who was born in 1787, was raised amid great political and economic turmoil. He was just five years of age at the time of the Geneva revolution and nine when the Directory (the name given to the French government during the last stage of the Geneva revolution) banned the import of watches from the Fabrique (on the pretext that they contained English steel). He was eleven when Directory troops attacked Geneva and quite simply annexed it to the "Great Nation" of France. So it was in "France" that Jacques Barthélémi served his apprenticeship as a watchmaker. In 1805, at age 18, he may have made – jointly with his father – the earliest known alarm watch by Vacheron Constantin. The signature was "Vacheron à Genève" as in the days when his father was being trained by his grandfather. Sadly, that grandfather, founder Jean-Marc, died in the same year at the age of 74.

In 1805 at dawn on December 2, the first anniversary of Napoleon's coronation, it is almost certain that some of the emperor's officers were woken by their alarm watches. The sun was rising over both Austerlitz and the new French empire that would soon cover more than half of Europe, created simply by the will of Napoleon. Militarily, the shadow of the eagle did not reach as far as Eastern Europe or Russia. But its cultural and, later, commercial influence came to extend all the way around the world. The Napoleonic aura soon captivated all European intellectuals, whether they considered him a brilliant strategist, a rational politician, or a megalomanic tyrant. Paradoxically, the success of the Napoleonic era was based on the spirit it created after the Enlightenment among the "sister republics" of the Directory, but in fact it devastated, impoverished, and spilled the blood of all the countries it reached. However, when the soldiers were dead and the blockades lifted, the poets and intellectuals, followed by the merchants, made something resembling Napoleon's dream of

LEFT-HAND PAGE
Pocket watch, 1815.
The yellow gold case is engraved and embellished with garnets. The floral decoration features two types of gold. Inv. no. 10128

BELOW
Manufacturing book, 1813–1821.

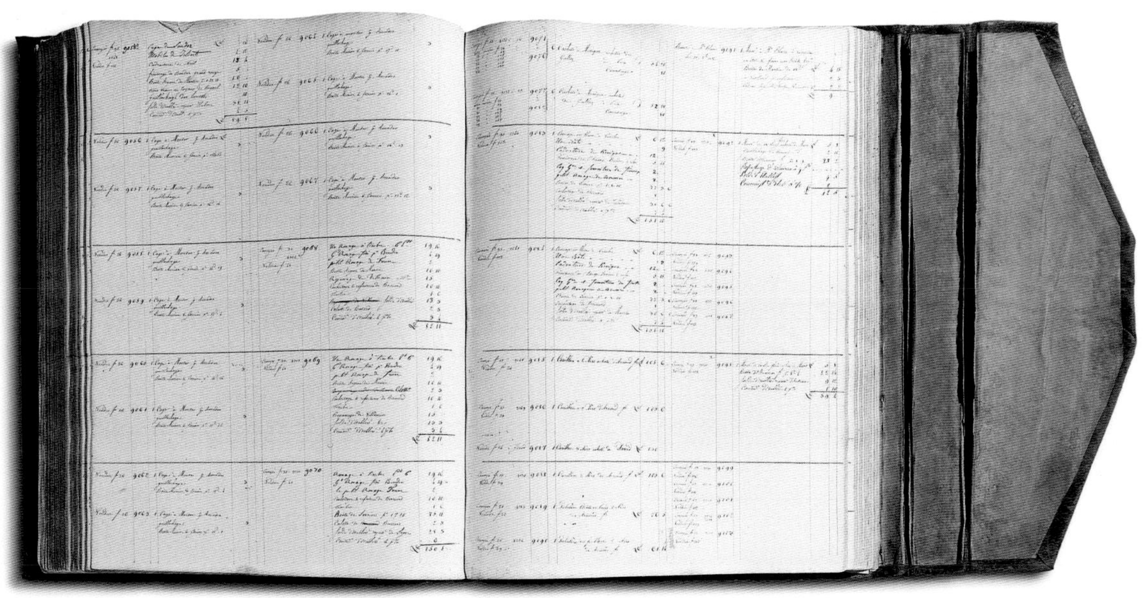

1816

BELOW
Company register, 1779-1814.

RIGHT-HAND PAGE
Pocket watch, quarter repeater, 1812. Made of 18K pink gold, the case features a guilloché back engraved with floral decorations. Blued steel serpentine hands hover over the enamel dial. Inv. no. 10302

Europe rise from the rubble. Despite the borders and their customs posts, a huge market would open up for bold men. Vacheron developed commercial links with Italy from 1816, with Russia from 1819 then with Austria in the years that followed.

Beginning in 1810, Jacques Barthélémi Vacheron took charge of the Vacheron-Girod company, which was officially registered under this name. His father Abraham continued to work there when his health permitted despite long absences: in 1827 at the age of 67, he was still repairing watches. But Jacques Barthélémi was more entrepreneurial than his father and more talented in a technical sense. He would lead Vacheron in such a way that it would take its place among the major watchmakers. At this time, the company began producing more complicated pieces, such as musical watches that could play two tunes on demand. It also took on new commercial activities. The Napoleonic Wars were ruining Europe, and the economic situation was disastrous. In 1812, to keep the company going, Vacheron started selling cloth as well as seven-year-old cherry brandy at 50 sous a bottle. During those hard times, it became critical to find new outlets. Right from the start, Jacques Barthélémi involved his uncle, Barthélemy Girod, who was ready to move to Paris to sell the company's products there. But the results were disappointing and the association only lasted a few years. However, Barthélemy Girod may have fostered the relationship between Jacques and Abraham Louis Breguet, a watchmaker born in Neuchâtel who moved to Paris and, in 1775, became the official supplier to the royal, then imperial, court. Breguet was an inventive genius who not only developed the shock-absorber (pare-chute) system but also the tourbillon (a complex type of escapement that enables the regulating organ to compensate for the influence of gravity). He also improved existing inventions, such as the Lépine caliber and the automatic watch of Abraham Louis Perrelet (1729–1826). The Vacheron archives show that,

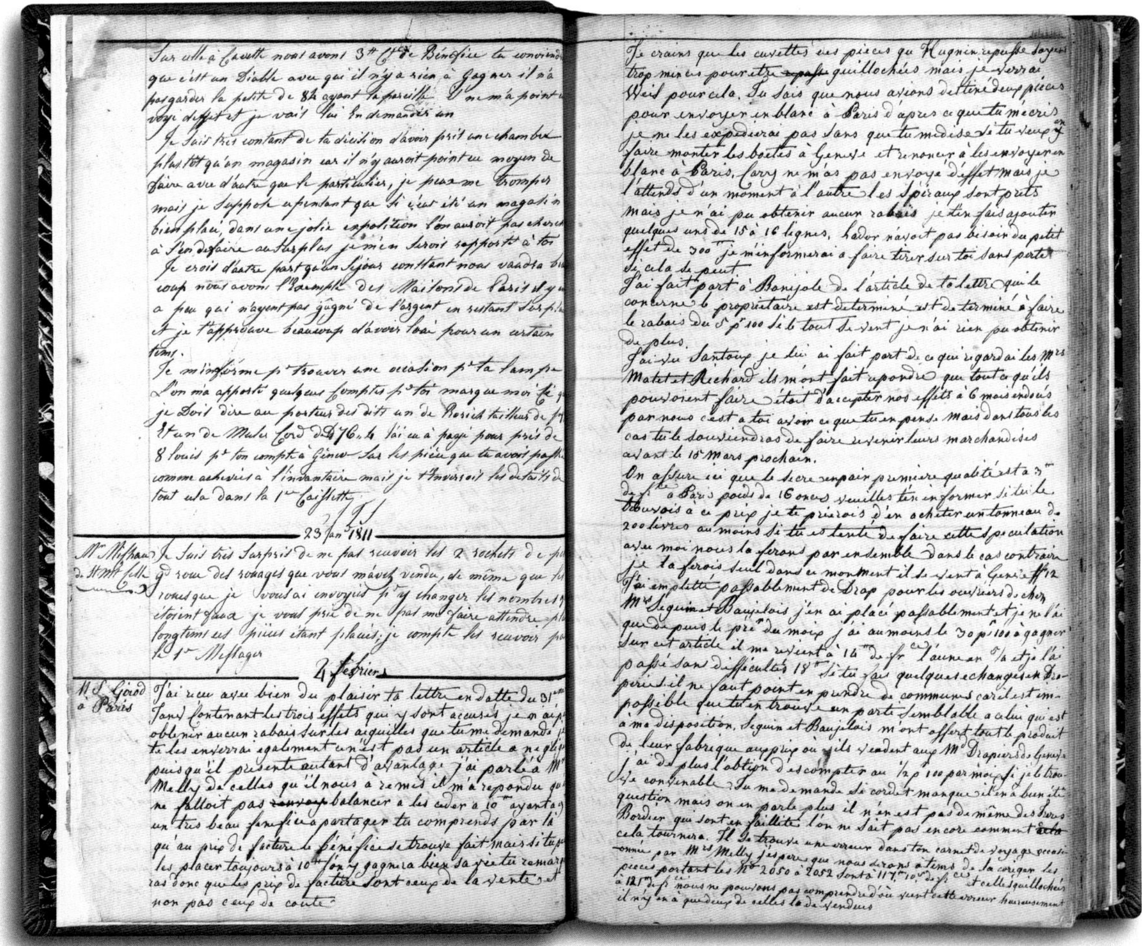

Vacheron Chossat & Comp.
A GENEVE

in the 1810s, Jacques Barthélémi made movements for this legendary Parisian watchmaker. At the same time, he replaced a failed colleague from Geneva as the supplier to Ventroux-Hersant, dealers in Caen, who regularly bought his beautiful complication watches, musical timepieces, repeaters and Lépine-style flat watches. This enterprise in Normandy was the first important foreign market won by Vacheron. And thanks to Jacques Barthélémi's hard work, many others would open up in the ensuing years. Using a traveling salesman or visiting the markets himself, he succeeded in placing his watches first in Milan, then Turin, Florence, Genoa, and Livorno.

In those years, he wrote regularly to his uncle Girod with news of his travels and of fluctuations in the business. In 1810, he married Catherine Chossat, the daughter of a wealthy iron merchant in Carouge, near Geneva. Six years later, he joined forces with her brother, Charles François Chossat, who brought Vacheron the funds he needed to further develop the business. A new company was set up for a period of four years, Vacheron-Chossat & Cie, which replaced Vacheron-Girod and altered the signature on the watches. One of these watches, now kept in Geneva, features a quarter repeater mechanism (strikes the hours and quarter hours on two gongs of different pitch) and decorative, serpentine-style hands (page 33 and left-hand page). It is signed "Vacheron Chossat et Comp. à Genève". When Jacques took on his new associate, he started sending his letters to him instead of his uncle when traveling. So it was Chossat who received a letter from Turin in 1816 that described his growing reputation among the watchmaking elite: "Since I have been here, Martina, the watchmaker to the king, never ceases visiting me to talk about watches. If we improve our offering, both in terms of quality and prices, we can be sure of supplying him merchandise for 20,000 francs a year. Martina is entirely reliable, he has bought two of our chiming clocks with two tunes..."

It was often an ordeal to travel in Italy where the roads were in such poor state that a horse-drawn carriage could tip over twice a day, and where it was advised to drink "orange lemonade" as protection against typhus. The states restored by the Congress of Vienna were barely able to keep control within the cities in those troubled times. In another letter, sent two years later as he arrived in Rome from Turin, he gave his associate striking insight into what it was like. He had traveled in the company of a certain Monsieur Degrange, a representative of Geneva watchmaker Jean-François Bautte: "Apart from the disturbing reports we had received as to the safety of this route, at regular intervals as we progressed we observed legs and arms nailed onto the signposts to indicate where brigands had been executed for murder. I admit that this disgusting spectacle would have persuaded me to turn back had I been alone; but being with Degrange, both of us armed and determined to fight to the end rather than give up our wares, we did not waver and continued ahead. [...] Had I been stopped and killed, the second being the inevitable result of the first, what would become of my family and my aged father, who have none but me to depend on? This thought alone is more than enough reason for me to renounce traveling entirely, and I assure you that such is my intention, even if it means taking up the file again..."

It was not long before he did just that. While he was traveling, his father Abraham had directed the *cabinet* in Geneva. It was he who received his son's recommendations and his constant insistence on quality as the key to commercial success. Concerning musical watches, for example, Jacques asked for "the sound to be richer and the tunes more lively." His high standards produced results: in 1816, Vacheron watch sales in Turin reached 16,000 francs. In November of that same year, he received good news from his associate in Milan: "It is not without pleasure that I inform you that we continue to sell more merchandise, and several clients have told me that they are without doubt the finest that they have ever bought. [...] We only need to offer a little more variety in the cases to please different tastes." The company's archives for the following year mention a prestigious client: Prince Charles Albert de Carignan, the future king of Sardinia, head of the House of Savoy and father of Victor Emmanuel, who would become the first King of Italy. This ambiguous hero

LEFT-HAND PAGE
Pocket watch, quarter repeater, 1812. Inv. no. 10302

OPPOSITE
Quarter repeating pocket watch, 1817. Positioned upon a period rose engine, it features a silver guilloché dial housed in a red gold guilloché case. Inv. no. 10436

of the Risorgimento (Italian unification) would be the first of a long list of major figures – including crowned heads – to wear a watch signed Vacheron.

The company, whose finances had recovered, occupied a floor of a building in Geneva for some time. On the last day of 1813, Austrian troops entered the city, thereby restoring the Republic of Geneva. Vacheron had only been a French company for fifteen years and now it became purely Genevan once again. As of September 13, 1814, it could proudly call itself Swiss as the Republic of Geneva entered the Swiss Confederation.

In the late 1810s it grew strongly and its future looked bright. But Jacques Barthélémi had grown tired of traveling, worrying about long, dangerous roads and problems with customs. He had a young son and likely felt it was time to look after his education. So he picked up the file again, creating the necessity for another to travel to the markets around Europe. In 1818, he dared dream of offering this task to one of his best friends, a commercial representative he had often met during his travels. Did he sense that this man, François Constantin, would substantially widen the scope of the company that three generations of Vacherons had built?

Vacheron & Constantin
A GENEVE

1819–1890
MEETINGS AND JOURNEYS

In the nineteenth century, Vacheron Constantin's prestige really began to grow when a highly talented watchmaker and an outstanding businessman came together. Always striving to "do better" in the Geneva workshops while traveling tirelessly in search of new markets and improving products by opening up to the world, the pair discovered the formula for extraordinary longevity and success.

1819

PREVIOUS LEFT-HAND PAGE
Pocket watch, 1827.
Made of silver, it boasts an alarm and an enamel dial.
Inv. no. 10713

RIGHT-HAND PAGE
Abraham (1785–1855) and François (1788–1854) Constantin. Vacheron Constantin archives.

Jacques Barthélémi Vacheron and François Constantin were both from Geneva. They were almost exactly the same age, traveled for the same reasons, and shared the same passion for refined and complicated watches. They had likely met in Italy, either on one of its long, dangerous roads or in a large city where people were always eager to see the latest watches from Geneva or London. Perhaps they had crossed paths with a great lover of the southern country, a certain Henri Beyle, soon to be better known as the writer Stendhal. It has been documented that in 1817 he was in Rome and went to the puppet theater in the Fiano Palace, where he was delighted by the character of Casandrino of whom he wrote in his travel journal *Rome, Naples, Florence,* "all the people of Rome love to follow his adventures," an elegant old bachelor who falls in love and tries to seduce "all the beautiful women he has the good fortune to meet". One evening, one of these women congratulates him on his elegant attire and healthy glow: "Compliments that delight the old boy. He takes the opportunity to talk about his clothes. The cloth came from France; Casandrino then talks about his trousers from England and his superb repeater watch (he takes it out and makes it ring), which cost him a hundred guineas at the best watchmaker in London."

Although they were competitors, Vacheron and Constantin became friends. François Constantin was the son of a grain merchant. His father sent him out on the roads through the Alps and the Jura, on foot, to buy what was needed from the age of 14. This tough adolescence, spent walking the steep roads, not only made him remarkably strong but also provided him with a keen sense of business. Around the age of 16, he became a traveling salesman for a company assembling watch cases. Word of his ability soon spread in Geneva and within a few years he was recruited by one of the most prestigious watchmakers of the period, Jean-François Bautte. Jacques Barthélémi Vacheron arrived at just the right time, with two important arguments to convince Constantin to start selling his watches. It was the right moment because Constantin had just left Bautte to set up on his own with an associate, but the two did not get on well. Jacques' first argument was his own worth and the reputation that he now enjoyed. The second was probably more convincing: his proposal to create a properly constituted association with legal safeguards. Constantin did not take long to make up his mind. On March 31, 1819, Vacheron-Chossat & Cie was dissolved. The next day, April 1, a new company called Vacheron & Constantin was formed for a period of six years. Happily, Charles François Chossat, who had clearly been a good manager, agreed to stay. Apart from a short period of eight years, the two names would be permanently linked, indicating the balance between creativity and business that formed the identity of the company. Just as a stable balance wheel represents both technical expertise and aesthetic perfection, Vacheron Constantin would grow by complementing horological creativity with commercial dynamism. This delicate, carefully maintained balance, perhaps unique in the history of watchmaking, would be the key to Vacheron Constantin's success and its amazing longevity.

François Constantin set to work immediately. First of all, he wanted to pursue the idea of selling jewelry as well as watches. He saw this as a way of attracting clients who did not find watches particularly interesting. In early May, he traveled to Paris and bought an assortment of jewelry for more than 60,000 francs from a jeweler named Watin. Watin also became the Vacheron Constantin agent in Paris and remained so until 1828. Just a few years later, seeing that this method of selling had proven highly effective, the company began creating its own jewelry, specifically designed for the clientele it frequented in Paris and the major cities of Italy. In taking this approach it was following the lead of certain watchmakers in Geneva, notably Jean-François Bautte, who had always been a jeweler as much as a watchmaker. The pieces Vacheron Constantin produced were in the "Geneva jewelry shop" tradition of necklaces, rings and earrings, usually in 18-karat gold. They were hollow, for lightness, and generally decorated with enamel motifs.

With all this treasure to carry, Constantin returned to Geneva and ordered a carriage to be made in Paris, one that could take him around Italy quickly and safely. He would travel on behalf of the company in this horse-drawn carriage for the

OPPOSITE
François Constantin's passport, 1821.

1820

next thirty years. His letters to Jacques Barthélémi provide us with vivid descriptions of his journeys, which laid the foundations of Vacheron Constantin's spectacular growth. The fact is that François had some extraordinary qualities, including a talent for trading. For example, he arranged for a dealer in Livorno to pay him with barrels of Cypriot wine, which he then bottled to sell at a higher price. He was a good psychologist and a sharp observer of people, equally at home in serious and social situations. His easy charm helped him build a prestigious clientele; just five years after the company was formed, he received orders from the highest ranks of Italian nobility, up to Prince Borghese and King Victor Emmanuel I. Before long, the great European families were vying for the outstanding watches and refined jewelry made by Vacheron Constantin's craftsmen. In 1822, for example, while some of the craftsmen were preparing a repeater watch with an enameled case and a replaceable silver dial for the Austrian ambassador, others were working on a high-precision piece intended for the Hungarian Count Esterhazy. It appears that some of these new clients, including Prince Borghese, were introduced to François by his brother Abraham. It seems the now-famous porcelain painter was friendly with princes, artists, and writers, including Stendhal, with whom he wrote a book, *Italian Ideas in Some Famous Pictures*. In 1827, he created some ornamental motifs for Vacheron Constantin, which its jewelers reproduced on elegant bracelets.

However, personal skills alone would not have been enough for François to make Vacheron Constantin one of Europe's most famous watchmakers in the early nineteenth century. In the best Geneva tradition, his most important quality was a deep understanding of the markets backed by extraordinary adaptability. He could sense trends, analyze requests and send Jacques precise descriptions of what his clients expected. An astute businessman, he would sometimes order "second quality" watches and jewelry from Geneva if they were good enough for him to get a foothold in a market. Then, later, he would help those customers learn to appreciate the best quality. But usually, to differentiate his company's wares from its competitors, he demanded higher and higher quality. Writing from Turin in July 1819 in one of his first letters to his business partner, he introduced an idea that would become his guiding principle, his "mantra": "If you support me well, I promise you that we will achieve as much in watchmaking as all the other travelers together. [...] I tell you we will be strong: our products are very highly regarded here and if we continue to do better if possible, which is always possible, we will gain control of the buyers. You know this is my vision, work to make it happen."

"Do better if possible, which is always possible..." It is easy to see how this message would motivate Jacques and his craftsmen. They turned their efforts to the repeater watches that were very much in fashion, and François kept insisting that they be made very carefully: "I cannot say this too often," he wrote from Florence in May 1821. "We have to make a big step forward in repeater watches and only if we persevere in perfecting this mechanism will we be able to compete with the other Swiss makers. [...] Do not be surprised if I always talk about these repeaters. They are essential for us and we must never lose sight of this for one moment. I am always afraid that you do not fully realize how important they are..."

Luckily, several of these watches have survived to show us the results of the effort. One example dating from the late 1820s is particularly elegant thanks to the simplicity of the Empire style that Breguet had made so desirable, as well as the fine guilloché on its dial – a silver dial as fashion dictated between 1815 and 1830. But this watch was certainly made even more valuable by the quality of its mechanism, produced with a technique that was very advanced for the time. Not only was the movement very thin, it was a quarter repeater with a grand strike on the hour. Another watch from the same date illustrates the company's capacity to respond rapidly to new client demands. It is a small hunter watch for ladies designed to be worn around the neck or in a side pocket, another fashion of the time. In fact, watches made specifically for women were an entirely new development in this period. Since they were smaller than men's watches, they required miniaturization. Swiss watchmakers

Genève le 9. Janvier 1813
Monsieur Michel Gay à Maglan
M.S Girod à Paris 20. Xbre 1812
L'unique but de la pr
de f 3692. 4 Centimes

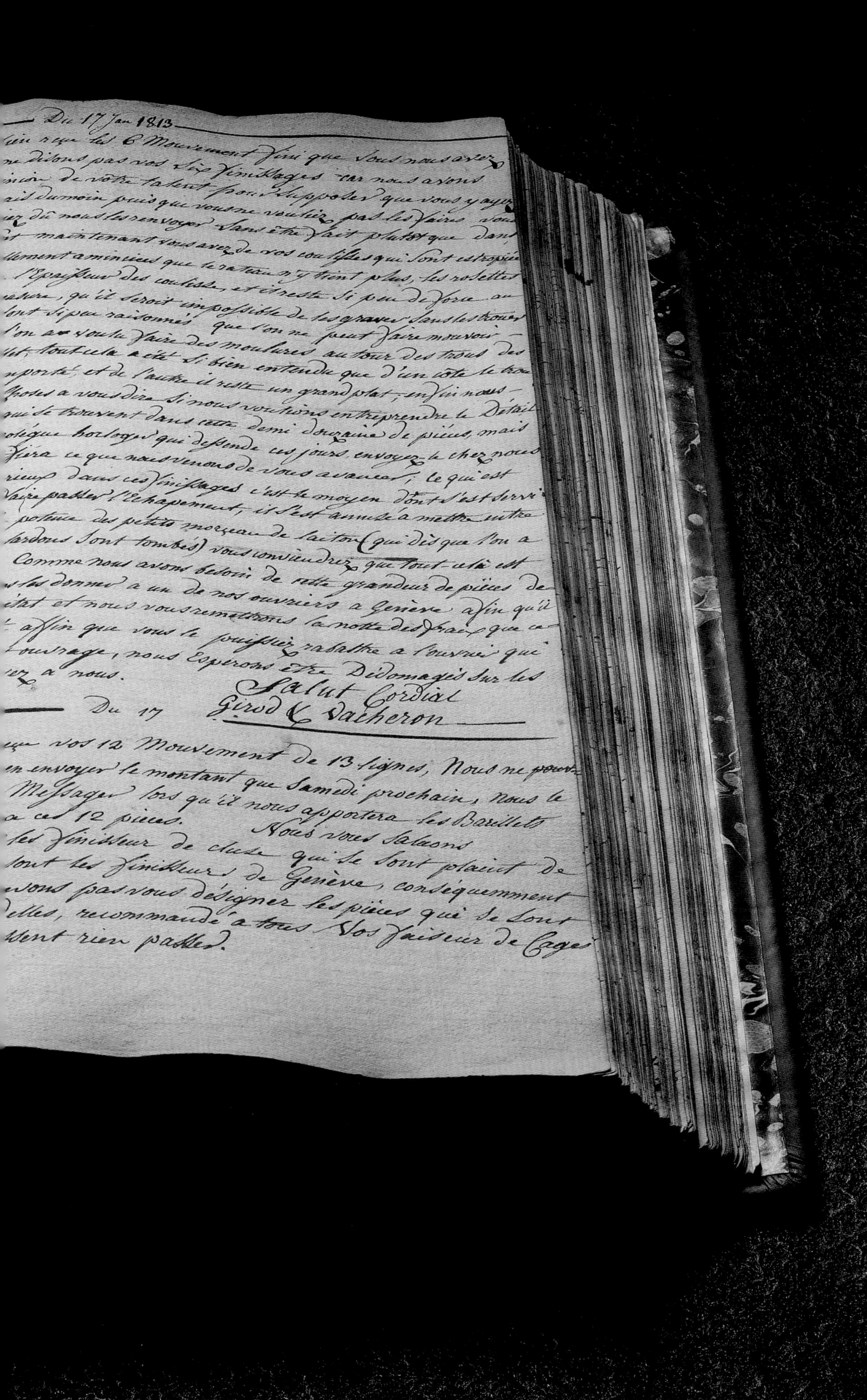

Du 17 Jan 1813

ein reçu les 6 Mouvement fini que vous nous avez
ne disons pas vos Sr Finissages car nous avons
inion de votre talent pour supposer que vous y ayez
ail du moin puisque vous ne vouliez pas les faire vous
ez dû nous les renvoyer sans être fait plutôt que dans
t maintenant vous avez de vos coulisses qui sont estropiées
ellement amincies que le rateau n'y tient plus, les rosettes
l'épaisseur des coulisses, et il reste si peu de force au
ature, qu'il seroit impossible de les graver sans les trouer
ont si peu raisonnés que l'on ne peut faire mouvoir
l'on a voulu faire des moulures au tour des trous des
tout cela a été si bien entendu que d'un côté le trou
nporté, et de l'autre il reste un grand plat; enfin nous
posés a vous dire si nous voulions entreprendre le Détail
ui se trouvent dans cette demi douzaine de pièces, mais
ologue horloger qui descende ces jours, envoyez le chez nous
fiera ce que nous venons de vous avancer; ce qui est
rieux dans ces finissages c'est le moyen dont s'est servi
faire passer l'échapement, il s'est amusé a mettre entre
potence des petits morceau de laiton (qui dis que l'on a
lardons sont tombés) vous conviendrez que tout cela est
Comme nous avons besoin de cette grandeur de pièces de
s les donner a un de nos ouvriers a Genève afin qu'il
état et nous vous remettrons la notte des frais que ce
t affin que vous le puissiez rabattre a l'ouvrier qui
ouvrage, nous Espérons être Dédomagés sur les
rez a nous.

Salut Cordial
Girod & Vacheron

Du 17

eu vos 12 Mouvement de 13 lignes, Nous ne pouv
n envoyer le montant que Samedi prochain, nous le
Messager lors qu'il nous apportera les Barillets
a ces 12 pieces. Nous vous Saluons
les finisseur de cluse qui se sont plaint de
ont les finisseurs de Genève, conséquemment
vons pas vous désigner les pièces qui se sont
elles, recommandé a tous vos faiseur de Cages
ssent rien passer.

OPPOSITE
Correspondence register, 1812.

RIGHT-HAND PAGE
Pocket watch, 1822. This unbelievably intricate piece of work sees the winding key and yellow gold case chiseled and set with precious stones, including amethysts of various shades. Expert craftsmanship extends to the dial in guilloché gold. Inv. no. 10469

were the first to realize the huge potential of this market – it had been neglected until then simply because it was thought that women had no need to know the time. The first women's watches were in finely engraved gold and decorated with enamel, like that example by Vacheron Constantin, and sometimes set with precious stones. They were worn around the neck or pinned to a gown using a brooch. Vacheron Constantin was one of the first to promote these delicate jewelry watches for women, who naturally took great care with their appearance. Another watch, dated 1827, is also a milestone in watchmaking history, specifically the history of watches fitted with an alarm: the hand indicating the time for the alarm to sound is set manually by lifting the bezel and the crystal. This large watch is distinguished by its wavy gold hands and by the mystical English text engraved for the client on the case back. A later watch, dating from 1840, was probably ordered by someone nostalgic for the Empire since it depicts the King of Rome sitting on the knee of his mother, Empress Marie-Louise. It demonstrates the quality of engraving and enameling that Vacheron Constantin was able to produce by then.

For François Constantin, this quality and success came at the cost of undertaking dangerous journeys and dealing with all kinds of difficulties in very stormy times. In addition to their valuable contribution to the history of watchmaking, his letters written over a span of twenty-five years provide a vivid description of Italy in the first half of the nineteenth century. The Italian peninsula was going through the early stages of the Risorgimento (Italian unification). From 1795 to 1815, the Napoleonic revolution was welcomed by liberal, middle-class supporters of the Enlightenment, and French troops had removed autocratic princes in the patchwork of states. Little by little, Napoleon constructed his kingdom, a new "Italy" of six million people – more than one-third of the population – comprising Piedmont, Liguria, Tuscany and Lazio with Milan as its capital. Its administration and laws were based on the French model. People could travel freely on new roads, and the green, white, and red flag flew everywhere. Despite being controlled from abroad, this new Italy managed to build a national identity, the first step toward true sovereignty. Then in 1815, the Congress of Vienna tore it all down and restored the previous monarchies under Austrian rule. The peninsula found itself divided into eight autonomous states, each with well-guarded borders and expensive customs. The middle-class elite and the enlightened aristocrats, who always championed the idea of unity and sovereignty, strongly opposed this restoration. For the next fifteen years, coordinated in secret societies such as the *carbonari* in Piedmont, they organized uprisings against loathsome Austria. Officers of the carbonari rebelled and proclaimed a constitution in Naples in 1820. The following year, liberal Piedmont aristocrats rallied the troops of the Turin garrison to their cause and forced the king, Victor Emmanuel I, to abdicate. François Constantin was present. His letters provide a vivid description of that March revolution as well as the advance of Austrian troops toward Genoa and Naples, called to the rescue by the successor of Victor Emmanuel, Prince Charles Albert de Carignan. Sadly, this royal client of Vacheron since 1817 had betrayed those who had brought him to power. In his letters, Constantin describes these historic events while recounting his innumerable problems at customs posts or his ordeals on the road: "I have arrived here after making the most difficult journey of my career," he wrote from Genoa in 1824. "Near Alessandria (between Turin and Genoa) the Bormida had swept away the bridge and I lost 24 hours before managing to cross the river in a small boat with my carriage. After terrible rain that lasted the entire night and continuously forced me to help the postilion move rocks that had fallen from the mountain onto the road, I found myself at 3 o'clock in the morning blocked by a landslide that prevented any further progress: the rain continued to pour down and it penetrated the carriage. [...] Finally I arrived at 3 o'clock [in the afternoon] and could think of nothing but going straight to bed."

The July Revolution dealt a serious blow to Vacheron Constantin's business in France in 1830. However, the company had been dealing with other countries such as England, Portugal, and even the United States since the 1810s. Previously,

BAVIERE
MUNICH
SALZBOURG
TIROL
SUISSE
ZURICH
BERNE
LAUSANNE
GENEVE
SAVOIE
TURIN
MILAN
MANTOUE
VERONE
TRENTE
BELLUNE
ETAT DE VENISE
TRIESTE
CROATIE
SEGNA
TURQUIE
MER ADRIATIQUE
RAVENNE
ANCONE
PLAISANCE
PARME
BOLOGNE
FLORENCE
PISE
TOSCANE
GENES
SAVONE
LIVOURNE
ROME
EGLISE
NAPLES
SALERNE
MER DE SIC

the Americans had only been supplied timepieces from England, but they were beginning to discover Swiss watchmaking. Vacheron Constantin even possessed its own ship, allowing it to import and export products directly. In 1832, a Geneva watchmaker established in New York, Jean (or John) Magnin, arranged to receive a selection of Vacheron Constantin watches with enamel motifs of landscapes and portraits through traders in Le Havre.

Politically and economically, the America of that time was precisely as Alexis de Tocqueville described it in a book that made a considerable impression in Europe when it was published in 1835: *Democracy in America*. During his stay in the United States, Tocqueville had observed the rising importance of "the common man." It was the prototype of a rapidly expanding social class of employees and workers who had moved into the cities as part of the still-young Industrial Revolution. Tocqueville understood that this social revolution was inevitable and that it would soon reach Europe and install a system of democracy there.

What happened in the United States? In the early years of the nineteenth century, all the country's energy was focused on developing the agricultural potential of conquered new territories and exploiting new resources, in particular in the South and West with cotton, grain, cattle, leather, and minerals. At the same time, immense effort was put into developing means of transportation – roads, canals, railways (and rivers when steamships arrived) – between these distant areas and the major cities of the East and North. It was in these cities that waves of immigrants transformed raw materials. With the influx of English, Irish and Germans, the population of America virtually doubled every twenty years: it grew from four million inhabitants in 1790 to thirteen million in 1830. This urban population employed in industry was the new look of America; it was much more interested in social organization and the improvement of working conditions than farmers, and it took an active role in political debate. It was this class who, in 1829, swept its preferred candidate, Andrew Jackson, into power as the seventh president of the United States and the first leader of the new Democratic Party. While these beginnings of the Industrial Revolution helped develop democratic life, they fell quite short of increasing social justice. A large part of American economic growth came from the cotton production of hundreds of thousands of black slaves, and the spread of industrial capitalism was setting up class barriers that were virtually insurmountable, despite what Tocqueville thought: in 1850, 50 percent of all industrial wealth was held by one percent of the urban population. And there were more millionaires in the United States than in the whole of Europe. Naturally, some of them were clients of John Magnin, importer of very precious, precise instruments: Vacheron Constantin's timepieces. For the new social elite, these watches were not only a way of displaying wealth and success, they also reliably indicated the time, of key importance when conducting business.

John Magnin remained Vacheron Constantin's representative in the United States until 1848, when he was replaced by Ferdinand Thieriot. In 1834, as Vacheron Constantin's timepieces were being sold not only in New York but also in Philadelphia and New Orleans, the company moved out of its premises on Rue du Rhône. Success had led to the hire of a number of additional workers and for several years space had been tight in the building that also doubled as the Vacheron family home. "I have decided to move several good workers into the bedroom at the back of our apartment," wrote Jacques Barthélémi in 1826. "It will be a nuisance to have them passing through our kitchen, but what else can I do?" However, eight years would pass between this declaration and the company moving to a new address. From 1829 onward, the new Bergues area began developing not far away, right next to the first modern hotel in Geneva. The famous Hôtel des Bergues was inaugurated in 1834, as was the bridge of the same name. Vacheron Constantin was located nearby. The *Baedeker* guide immediately named it "the finest hotel in the world" and it became a regular meeting place for Geneva watchmakers, their clients, and suppliers.

Jacques Barthélémi Vacheron and his wife Catherine had a son, César, born in 1812, and they naturally intended for him to become a

LEFT-HAND PAGE
Pocket watch, 1824.
Made of yellow gold, the back is engraved and enameled in the champlevé technique to represent a map of Italy.
Inv. no. 11324

1826

BELOW
Charles César Vacheron (1812–1868).

RIGHT-HAND PAGE
Pocket watch, 1836. Made of silver, it is decorated with a pattern of Moorish inspiration using the intaglio engraving technique.
Inv. no. 10311

watchmaker. In 1825, it was decided he should enter the watchmaking school that had just opened in Geneva (called École de Blanc at that time). There he learned the basics of the craft. It was a rigorous experience for students as they had to work from 5:00 am to 6:00 pm. Jacques requested that the school director lighten up this schedule for his son so that he might study some complementary subjects. The boy was given private lessons in mathematics, English, and drawing. Before long, it was decided that he needed extra instruction in watchmaking and a watchmaker named Dechoudens was engaged for the task. "You can see that his time is fully occupied," his father wrote to François Constantin. "However, the boy copes well with all his work and is looking forward to his future career." It seems that young César took to the world of watchmaking right from the start and developed wonderfully, much to the delight of his parents. Two years into his studies, his father described his progress to François: "César has finished a beautiful Breguet-style movement. He will have good hands. They are very happy with him

at the school." A few months later, it was decreed that he was ready to stop making blanks and move on to finishing. A watchmaker, Thomeguex, taught him to make the Lépine caliber as well as enough watchmaking theory to master the technology of his craft.

At this time, between the 1820s and the 1830s, the Industrial Revolution was gathering pace and the need for a solid understanding of the new technologies became evident in watchmaking. Its manufacturing processes were still quite archaic with even the simplest parts of the blanks produced by hand. Even worse, watchmakers were supplied by different blank makers – part-time farmers, part-time artisans – who delivered components that were often inconsistent and mismatched. At that time, no movement was identical to another so it was not possible to produce a small series of calibers in a more economical way. It also prevented the easy repair of a defective movement by substituting a spare part kept in reserve. Vacheron Constantin was a pioneer in developing a more rational system, one that could produce watches that were as beautiful and as complicated as those made by hand, but at a more affordable price. The company began standardizing part of its production in 1826, as a letter from Jacques from January 1827 attests: "At present we are 'systematizing' all our Lépine watches on the same calibers arranged by size. We will have elegant pieces of the same height whereas, until now, they were all irregular. It is a difficult task, but we have already made good progress." However, three years later, the work was still not finished, as Jacques indicated in another letter to his associate: "We continue to work relentlessly on improving our quality in general; we have dealt with the calibers for each size of the pieces that are made for us. The blank makers are obliged to rigorously conform if they wish their work to be received: we are now organized to ensure that the verification can be done promptly and efficiently. It will be most advantageous for us to have all our watches produced according to a uniform plan; the task of our suppliers and finishers will be made easier and our pieces will be infinitely more reliable."

1839

The fact that after three years of work Jacques was still writing about the future suggests that the results thus far had been disappointing. But could the rigorous standards that Vacheron Constantin was imposing on its blank makers ensure that all of them would produce parts to within one tenth of a millimeter, the precision required for the most complicated watches? Of course not. Even if some progress had been made, the company's finishers still had to examine each part individually and take the time to rectify it. In fact, it took another fifteen years and the development of machine tools adapted to watchmaking to achieve efficient standardization at Vacheron Constantin. This decisive stage was reached thanks to a brilliant watchmaker whom Jacques employed in 1839: Georges Auguste Leschot.

His task was to perfect a range of exclusive tools and machines making it possible to produce movements with an anchor or cylinder escapement that could be easily adapted to fit into cases of all shapes and sizes. It was not just a matter of producing interchangeable parts in small series at lower cost, but also of creating machines with the capacity to produce them in different sizes. A contract signed by Leschot and Vacheron Constantin saw the company financing all his work and paying him an annual salary of 4,000 francs until he had finished. At that point, Leschot was to become a full associate entitled to one-fifth of Vacheron Constantin's profits instead of a salary.

This agreement was respected to the letter, and it produced all the desired results. After two years, Leschot presented his employers with a series of entirely new, fully perfected machines, and they immediately launched the production of watches at a lower price. Together with the machines, Leschot provided all the tools required to maintain and produce them. They were kept secret until 1844, giving Vacheron Constantin a healthy lead over its competitors, both technically and commercially. One of the machines produced barrels (a component that contains the mainspring) at the rate of 150 pieces per hour. Another polished particular pieces on a grinding wheel, and a third made the principal components of the anchor escapement. However, Leschot's most famous invention was the pantograph, which enabled the standardized production of calibers and their parts in many sizes. His work was recognized in 1844 when he received the prestigious Prix de Rive.

That same year, when his agreement with Vacheron Constantin was renewed, he employed a watchmaker with a similar name, Antoine Léchaud, a specialist in the anchor escapement. This young man became directly involved with the production of high-precision watches at Vacheron Constantin. In order to make the company even more independent, Leschot worked on a series of eight right-angle lever movements, produced entirely mechanically, that became famous as "Vacheron Calibers." A few decades later, its lead in technology enabled the company to fare better than its rivals in resisting competition from America. In the New World, machine tools were considerably more advanced and watches were being produced industrially on a large scale.

Between 1843 and 1844, another major event for Vacheron Constantin took place: it moved to the Tour de l'Île, a famous Geneva landmark comprising the last vestige of a thirteenth-century castle built by bishop Aymon de Grandson, which once controlled this natural bridge, an important crossing point on the Rhône. The opportunity to move into the tower arose the previous year when the *gendarmerie* vacated the premises. The tower certainly offered more space: Vacheron Constantin was able to rent the first-floor living quarters as well as three floors of workshops. No doubt there were other reasons for the move, too: pride in occupying a historic monument (which later became a motif adorning several watches, see pages 12-13), the prestige it lent the brand, and the fact that the tower was a conspicuous symbol of watchmaking: since the seventeenth century it had been crowned by a large clock. At great expense, Vacheron Constantin installed central heating (set to keep the workshops at just 12°C on winter mornings). This remained in place until 1875.

In 1844, a second important event took place in the company: the arrival of César Vacheron and the departure of his father Jacques Barthélémi, only 57 years of age. With the challenge of American

LEFT-HAND PAGE AND PAGES 54–57
Pantograph, 1839. Designed by Georges Auguste Leschot, the company's technical director, this pantograph revolutionized the production of movements, now called "calibers," making for a considerable breakthrough in terms of the reliability, precision, and quality of watchmaking at Vacheron Constantin in Geneva.

3

1843

industry growing stronger, the father probably thought it was time to pass the baton to a talented young man full of energy and ambition. That year, the association with François Constantin was renewed in the name of César. Vacheron Constantin was rapidly expanding. It devoted the first half of the nineteenth century mainly to prospecting and studying the Chinese market, among others. In 1835, it found a representative in Brazil and planned to set up in Cuba (and would succeed ten years later). It regularly supplied the imperial court of Russia – in 1845 for example, it delivered a repeating watch to Prince Nicolas Alexeievitch Dolgorouky. In 1846, the Austrian and Belgian markets were opened, followed by the Dutch East Indies, Germany, and India in 1847.

In Europe, the railways played a major factor in this growth. The first railway intended for passengers used steam locomotives and was inaugurated in England in 1825. It extended 40 kilometers, linking the towns of Stockton-on-Tees and Darlington in the county of Durham. On the continent, the steam railways took over from rivers and canals in transporting merchandise. Despite initial reluctance, it won the confidence of travelers. Nearly 10,000 kilometers' worth of railway was laid in Europe in the second quarter of the nineteenth century, half of it in England. In 1858, the Geneva-Lyon railway was opened by the Paris–Lyon–Mediterranean railway company (PLM). On top of the Tour de l'Île, the large clock had been replaced by three smaller clocks: one indicated the time in Geneva, another the time in Bern (which was 5 minutes and 6 seconds ahead for rail traffic and Swiss internal telegraphic communications), while the third showed the time in Paris (a reference for the PLM network, which was 15 minutes and 16 seconds behind Geneva). This was the nightmare that rail travelers faced at the time, juggling some thirty official times. This situation did not change until 1886.

Europe was entering a period of political crisis that would seriously undermine this progress. Already in 1846, in an ominous sign of things to come, a bullet fired by government troops at rioting Saint-Gervais workers had accidentally landed on a table in Vacheron Constantin's office in the tower. The people of Geneva were protesting against the conservative government's implicit support for the Sonderbund, a separatist league of seven Catholic cantons. The riots lasted three days and brought down the government. Two years later, revolutions were blossoming all over Europe – "the people's springtime" – which seriously hampered business. The 1848 revolution in France that led to the abdication of King Louis-Philippe, as well as the general insurrection in Italy and all the German states, had a direct impact on Vacheron Constantin. Sales collapsed, and some employees spontaneously offered to take a 40 percent cut in salary.

It seems there is a rule that Vacheron Constantin has never forgotten: always profit from a crisis. In fact, a crisis can be an opportunity to reorganize, explore distant markets, develop a new technology, or even perfect a new movement. The 1848 crisis was an excellent example. François Constantin was in Italy when the whole peninsula rose up to demand unity and independence. The letters he sent to César at this time represent some of the final examples of his passionate correspondence since he stopped traveling the following year. He describes the fervor of the Piedmont troops, the revolution in Naples, and the capture of Peschiera. In a letter from Turin in December 1848, reporting a conversation with a client, he fortuitously mentions an important event: "He asked me if we were doing anything new. I told him about the elevated spring escapement." It seems that during the troubles that halted production, Leschot had remained at his workbench and invented the mechanism that would evolve into the highly reliable Swiss lever escapement.

Happily, business quickly returned to normal, starting in the Netherlands where César went in the autumn of 1848, having no work to tend to in Geneva. The journey proved fruitful. A year and half later, in April 1850, the new representative of Vacheron Constantin in that country, F.-A. Decoster, wrote to the head office from Amsterdam: "Next month, the Prince of the Netherlands, uncle of our king [he was referring to Prince Willem-Frederik, uncle of King William III of the Netherlands], a very rich man, is celebrating

OPPOSITE
The Tour de l'Île in Geneva, circa 1870. Established in the Tour de l'Île in 1843, Vacheron Constantin occupied these prenises until 1875 when it moved to the building bearing its name.

1850

25 years of marriage, so there will be many gifts to make, both in jewelry and watches. It would be good to be well prepared for the orders we may receive from the suppliers to the court here and in The Hague. Please, therefore, send me all kinds of popular pieces and add some beautiful, expensive watches that have a good chance of selling on such an occasion."

In 1853, César Vacheron made several journeys around Europe to visit his agents and explore new markets. During his time in Paris he wrote a letter that speaks in detail about the reputation that Vacheron Constantin had acquired by then (a reputation that had attracted counterfeiters since the 1850s): "I get nothing but favorable opinions and encouragement, and I congratulate myself for starting with Paris... We have a real reputation here. I have seen some of our watches in private hands; there are nothing but compliments and recommendations for our company." The order books were full, and Vacheron Constantin was taking on new workers. One year before, it had significantly enlarged its premises by setting up new workshops in the north part of the tower. A few watches retained by Vacheron Constantin show the impressive refinement and technical perfection it achieved in the 1840s and 1850s.

In 1853, Vacheron Constantin also supplied Count Salino of Turin with a gold chronometer intended for astronomical observations. The company had clearly acquired real expertise in the highly technical area of chronometers. From 1855, it incorporated pendant winding, the modern system that replaced the winding key. A version had just been invented by watchmaker Antoine LeCoultre. Vacheron Constantin improved it by inventing the more reliable jointed winding stem.

François Constantin, who had made such an important contribution to the international reputation of his eponymous company, died in 1854. Since he had no children, he was replaced by his nephew, Jean-François Constantin, who took charge of the accounts for several years before leaving the company altogether in 1867. As for Jacques Barthélémi Vacheron, he passed away in 1864, ten years after his close friend and associate, François Constantin.

The principal commercial development at that time was Vacheron Constantin's move into several new countries, such as Egypt and Uruguay, and timepieces could even be found in Martinique. In around 1865, the best craftsmen in the Tour de l'Île were working on a few truly exceptional pieces, including a spectacular large watch in blue enamel set with fine pearls and diamonds that was intended for the Emperor of China.

BELOW AND FOLLOWING DOUBLE PAGE
François Constantin's travel trunk, circa 1840.

OPPOSITE
Charles Vacheron (1846–1870), grandson of Jacques Barthélémi, took charge of the company in 1869.

The transaction had been arranged through agents in Italy. At that time, China was suffering the humiliation of the "unjust treaties" imposed on it by Great Britain and France after the two Opium Wars. The brutal imperialism of the Western powers had never been so arrogant. Purely to protect profits from smuggling opium, they blatantly violated Chinese sovereignty by introducing "Concessions": enclaves of foreigners that were entirely freed from Chinese law and administration. Other exorbitant rights included the systematic bleeding of customs revenue and free use of the rivers to enable them to exercise "gunboat diplomacy." In 1860, they pillaged the imperial capital and even ransacked the Summer Palace, an infamous event that scandalized many Europeans, including Victor Hugo. All the treasures of the court, including some beautiful pieces of horology, were carried off by French and English troops. The scene was described by a witness, Count d'Hérisson, in his *Diary of an Interpreter in China*: "Soldiers were stuffing rubies, sapphires, pearls and pieces of rock crystal into their pockets, inside their shirts and caps, and some wound necklaces of large pearls around their chest. Others left with clocks and wall clocks under their arms. Combat engineers had brought their axes and they smashed pieces of furniture to get hold of the precious stones that were set in them. Appallingly, one of them broke open a beautiful Louis XV clock to tear out the dial set with crystals that he mistook for diamonds. […] It was like the dream of a hashish eater." Several of the most beautiful stolen objects found their way into European palaces and some can still be seen in the Chinese Salon of Empress Eugenie in the Fontainebleau chateau. Since the quality of Chinese watchmaking was very poor, the emperor quickly put together a collection of clocks and watches from the best European craftsmen. It could be that the Vacheron Constantin watch made for the Emperor of China was one of the few positive consequences of the Summer Palace's ransack. What is certain is that fifteen years later, some 3,400 clocks and watches were cataloged in the palace of Emperor Guangxu. A link was made between the past and present when the last descendant of the Chinese imperial family was presented with a contemporary watch during the Richemont exhibition in Beijing's Forbidden City.

Vacheron Constantin went through some important changes at the end of the 1860s. In 1867, as mentioned, Jean-François Constantin retired. César Vacheron then decided to change the company name to César Vacheron & Cie (Ancienne Maison Vacheron & Constantin). In the same year, his son Charles, born in 1846, joined the company. Poor health prevented him from attending the school of watchmaking, but he learned enough about the craft in the company workshops. Since he loved Germany, a country in which he had lived when he was eighteen years old, his first task was to build up the company's presence there. A few months later, in October 1868, his father succumbed to a virulent disease. Charles found himself alone at the head of the company at 22 years of age. On July 1, 1869, its name was changed once more, to Charles Vacheron & Cie. The young owner decided to recruit a man with experience to help him manage the company: Philippe Auguste Weiss, who was a senior bank

V & C

THE GROWTH OF VACHERON CONSTANTIN'S

INTERNATIONAL BUSINESS

FROM 1755 TO 1955

1755
Switzerland

1810
France

1811
England

1812
Italy

1817
United States
Turkey

1819
Russia

1820
Poland

1829
Austria

1835
Brazil

1838
Sweden

1842
Hong Kong

1845
Portugal
China
Mexico

1846
Spain
Belgium

1847
Germany

1849
Holland
and Dutch
East Indies
India
Cuba

1858
Peru

ROUGHLY 1860
Uruguay

1863
Martinique

1864
Egypt
Panama

1869
Denmark

1880
Argentina

1885
Norway

1887
Canada

1888
Chile

1890
Venezuela

1898
Romania

1900
Syria
Australia

1904
Serbia

1907
Finland

1917
Japan

1928
Tunisia

1933
Bulgaria

1939
Morocco

1950
Saudi Arabia
Iraq
Iran

1951
Thailand

1952
Jordan

1955
Ethiopia

LEFT-HAND PAGE
Detail of François Constantin's travel trunk.

FOLLOWING DOUBLE PAGE
Map depicting Vacheron Constantin's international business development from 1755 to 1955.

THE GROWTH OF VACHERON CONSTANTIN'S INTERNATIONAL BUSINESS FROM 1755 TO 1955

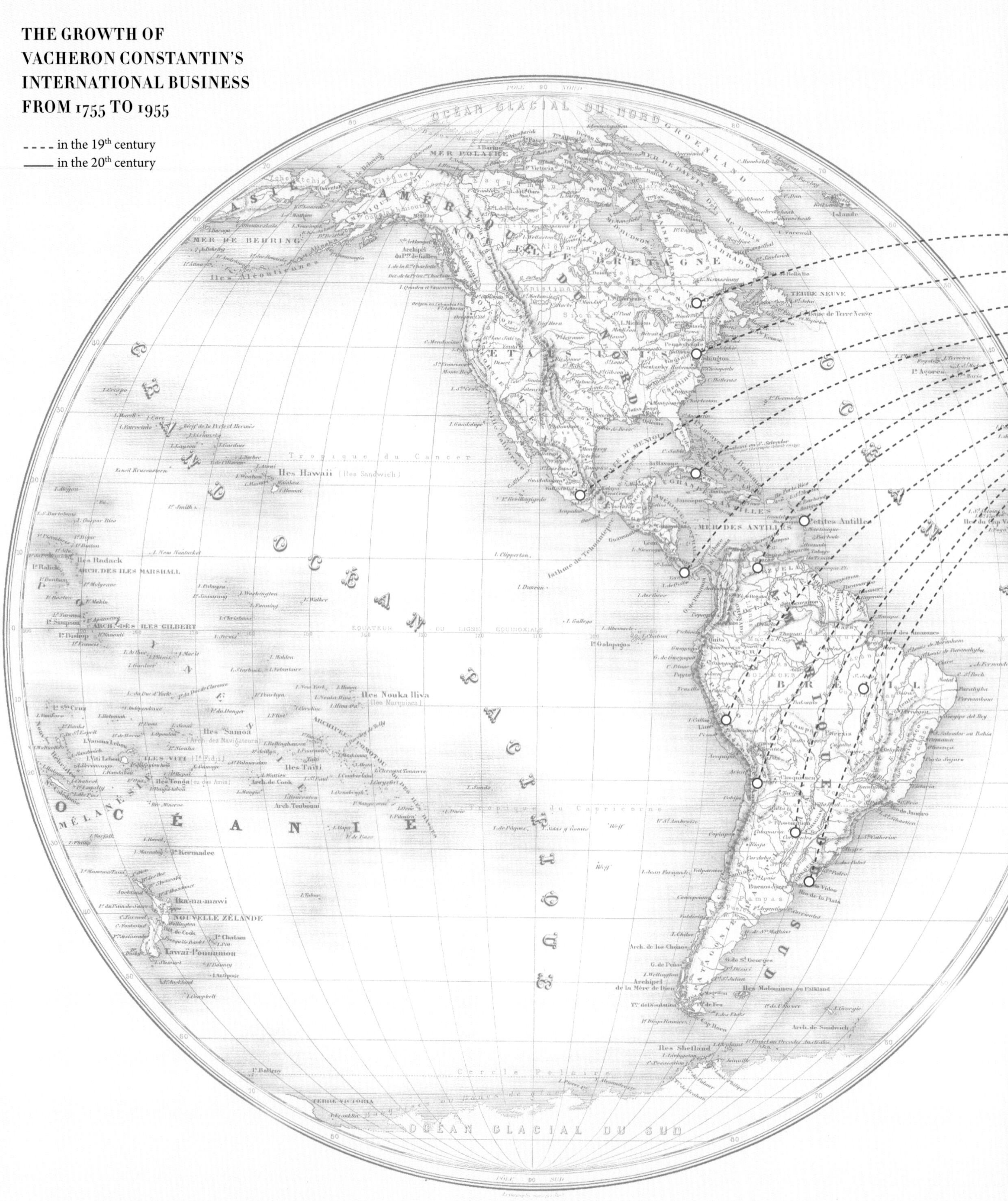

OPPOSITE
Pocket watch, 1855. This double case consisting of seven wholly engraved parts in 18K yellow gold boasts an enamel dial with Roman numerals and Breguet hands. Inv. no. 10329

OPPOSITE
Joseph Mallord William Turner, *Bonneville, Savoy,* 1803. Oil on canvas illustrating the road to Italy, 92 cm x 123 cm. Dallas, Dallas Museum of Art.

executive at the time. Weiss would end up directing the company alone for the next 30 years, inducing important growth for the brand, for in April 1870, young Charles Vacheron died from an attack of albuminuria. On his deathbed, he was presented with a sumptuous miniature calendar watch that had just been completed. Ordered by Tsar Alexander II and his wife, it was intended for their son, Grand Duke Vladimir Alexandrovitch of Russia. The ownership of Vacheron Constantin now passed to Catherine, grandmother of Charles Vacheron and widow of Jacques Barthélémi, her daughter-in-law Louise (née Pernessin), the widow of César, as well as Jean-François Constantin. It was Louise who changed the name for the third time in three years, to Vve César Vacheron & Cie. The company was essentially managed by Philippe Auguste Weiss with Georges Auguste Leschot remaining in charge of production. From 1874, however, he was assisted by Jules Weiss, brother of Philippe Auguste. Until this point in time, Vacheron Constantin's international reputation had been based on the decoration of its watches, but now their high degree of precision became more important. From 1846, the company had been interested in ways of protecting the mechanisms from magnetic fields and had even fitted a watch with an experimental balance spring and balance in bronze. When the company became a member of the Association for Research into Non-Magnetic Materials in 1862, its workshops created the first watches to include a balance spring in palladium. This was followed in 1885 by a mechanism containing a balance, balance spring, pallet lever, and balance wheel machined in palladium, while the pallets themselves were in bronze and the escape wheel in gold. In 1872, the Geneva observatory organized its first precision competition, and the watches submitted by Vacheron Constantin received the highest awards. Subsequently, Leschot and his team collected many records. Toward the end of the century, the company even started to offer "waterproof" pocket watches. This was a generous description by today's standards, relying on felt and cork seals around the case back, bezel, and crown.

Thanks to these improvements, and despite all the family events, Vacheron Constantin prospered and once again found itself short of space, even in the enlarged premises in the Tour de l'Île. Finally, in 1875 it moved into a new building designed by Jacques Élisée Goss, the

1875

LEFT-HAND PAGE
The Vacheron Constantin workshops, on the Quai des Moulins in Geneva, early 20th century.

BELOW
Vacheron Constantin building en l'Île, at number 1 Quai des Moulins in Geneva. This building was designed in 1875 by architect Jacques-Élisée Goss, commissioned by Jean-François Constantin, and is still owned by Vacheron Constantin today.

1880

architect behind Geneva's Grand Théâtre, which had been ordered by Jean-François Constantin a few years earlier. Constantin had also contributed to its design, and his initials JFC can still be seen above the main entrance. The building stands just a few meters away from the tower at no. 1 Quai des Moulins. Today it is home to the Vacheron Constantin boutique and the company's Heritage Department (which will be discussed further on). Also in 1875, following a break of eight years, Louise Vacheron and Jean-François Constantin agreed to restore the name that had made the company famous: Vacheron & Constantin.

Starting in that year, competition from the American watch industry was starting to have an impact in Geneva. In a country where a watchmaker's annual output was around 150 watches (in Switzerland it barely reached 40), people were quite ready to do without Swiss quality. In 1876, Swiss watch sales in the USA amounted to around five million Swiss francs. But four years earlier, they had been more than eighteen million. So Swiss watchmakers collectively decided to send one of their number, Edouard Favre-Perret, a watchmaker in Le Locle, to study the reasons for this decline. The timing was ideal: Americans were celebrating the centennial of the Declaration of Independence and had organized a great Centennial Exhibition in Philadelphia where the document was signed. This vast exhibition covered 150 hectares and brought together more than 30,000 exhibitors. It was the first major international exhibition ever held on American soil and almost sixty countries were present and accounted for. As at the International Exhibitions in Lyon (1872) and Vienna (1873), Vacheron Constantin presented several pieces at the stand of the Swiss Watchmaking Federation. From May to November, the exhibition attracted ten million visitors. It was a giant celebration of mechanization and industry, and a demonstration of the enormous strength of the United States, a new industrial power that had now overtaken old Europe. Alexander Graham Bell presented the new communication apparatus he had just patented, the electric telephone, and demonstrated it in front of Pedro II, Emperor of Brazil. The telephone would go on sale the following year. Favre-Perret was naturally most interested in the stands of the leading American watchmakers, particularly the two most powerful, Elgin and Waltham. Established in 1850, the Waltham Watch Company had already become the biggest watchmaker in the world. Its founders, Aaron Lufkin Dennison, Edward Howard, and David Davis, had followed a simple recipe: apply the principles of industrial standardization. They had maximized the number of interchangeable parts, mechanized most of the production, created their own machines to achieve the extreme precision required in watchmaking, and rationalized the tasks that had to be performed manually. During the Civil War, Waltham had supplied Union soldiers with his famous Ellery watch, and this had lent his company a whole new dimension. By 1876, the year of the exhibition, Waltham was producing 100,000 watches annually. In the same year, despite its centuries of tradition – or perhaps because of them – the biggest Swiss watchmakers only produced one-tenth as many timepieces. And while the One-Dollar Watch would not arrive until the next century, American-made timepieces were already affordable for a large part of the population. These price and quantity criteria would not have affected Switzerland if the average quality of Swiss watches had been higher than the American models. Unfortunately, it wasn't.

OPPOSITE
The stand of the American watch company Waltham from Massachussetts at the Philadelphia International Exhibition, 1872. Centennial Photographic Co., 21 cm x 26 cm. The Free Library of Philadelphia.

It would take two generations for the Swiss watchmaking industry to meet the challenge of the United States of America. Only the best watchmakers, offering a quality that far exceeded that of industrial watches, could feel secure. Naturally, Vacheron Constantin was among them. It resisted better than most of its competitors, thanks to processes perfected by Leschot and the loyalty of a European clientele that appreciated its incomparable watches. Proof of its optimism came in 1880 at the height of the crisis when Vacheron Constantin introduced its famous Maltese cross logo, recognizable by its four arms and eight points. From that point on, the brand was identified by the very graphic symbol that appeared on the dial of all its watches. In 1880, the drawing of the cross was registered at the Federal Office for Industrial Property in Bern, then Italy, and finally the United States in 1882. Inspired by a component of precision watches that increases the reliability of the spring, it makes for a powerful quality label. The fact that one of the company's Paris agents was installed for a time in the Rue de Malte may have helped.

This symbol impresses above all with its nobility, its age, and what it represents in history. While it is unknown if it possessed a symbolic meaning, it appeared in Susa (in today's Iran) on beautiful ceramic dating back to the foundation of the city in around 4000 BCE. The Department of Oriental Antiquities at the Louvre has some magnificent cups from that area decorated with one or more Maltese crosses. In the seventh century, it appeared as a Christian cross, decorating the beautiful belt fittings of bronze and inlaid iron in the Kingdom of Burgundy's art. But it was the foundation of the Order of the Knights of Saint John, one of the chief Christian military orders, that gave the cross its real historical dimension. Around the year 1000 CE, the merchants of the Republic of Amalfi built a hospital for pilgrims to Jerusalem and gave it to Benedictine monks. The monks took the symbol of the Amalfi republic as their emblem, the Maltese cross that was still known as the "Amalfi cross." At the end of the eleventh century, the community of monks was reorganized as the Order of Hospitallers, based on the teachings of the Augustines. From that time onward, the monks wore a sleeveless habit decorated with a large Amalfi cross. They purchased the old monastery of St. John the Baptist and adopted him as their patron. Some time later, their superior, Raymond du Puy created a military branch of the Order. It soon became a powerful force in battling the Saracens. Driven out of the Holy Land by Saladin, the Order recaptured Acre at the end of the Second Crusade. It built a new hospital that became so highly regarded that the town was renamed St. John of Acre. Again expelled by the Saracens, the Order set up in Cyprus then conquered Rhodes. The Order of the Knights of Saint John became a veritable sovereign power, housed in the greatest fortress in the world at that time and headed by a grand master. In 1522, after a long siege, Suleiman the Magnificent drove the knights of the Order out of Rhodes. Seven years later, Charles V gave them Malta where they were based for 250 years. The "Amalfi cross" became the "Maltese cross." In 1798, Malta was captured by Napoleon on his way to Egypt. All knights under 60 years of age were expelled from the island and a French style of administration was introduced.

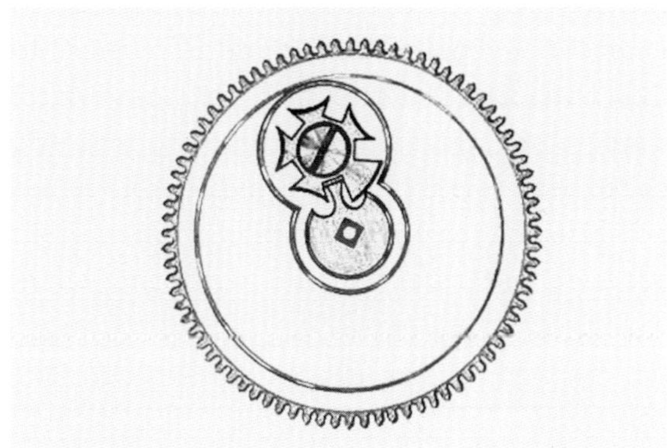

BELOW, LEFT
Sketch of the Maltese cross stopwork with a five-branch cross – the most common variety. This old component attached to the barrel lid allowed the movement to use the most consistent part of the spring and therefore it ensured greater precision in the watch.

BELOW, RIGHT
The Maltese cross logo was filed with the Federal Office of Industrial Property in Berne in 1880.

FOLLOWING DOUBLE PAGE
Evolution of Vacheron Constantin signatures and logos over 260 years.

Jean-Marc Vacheron

1775

Abraham Vacheron

1785

A. Vacheron Girod
A GENÈVE

1786

*Vacheron Chossat & Comp^e^*

1816

Vacheron & Constantin

1819

*Vacheron & Comp^nie^*

1850

César Vacheron & Cie
GENÈVE
ANC^NE^ M^SON^ VACHERON & CONSTANTIN

1867

Charles Vacheron & Cie

1869

Vacheron & Constantin
GENÈVE
VACHERON & CONSTANTIN

1870

VACHERON
&
CONSTANTIN

1880

VACHERON
VACHERON & CONSTANTIN

1880

VACHERON
GENÈVE
VACHERON & CONSTANTIN

1880

VACHERON &
CONSTANTIN
VACHERON & CONSTANTIN

1880

VACHERON & CONSTANTIN
fabricants
GENÈVE

1880

VACHERON & CONSTANTIN
fabricants
GENÈVE

1881

VACHERON & CONSTANTIN
GENEVA

1883

VACHERON & CONSTANTIN
fabricants
GENÈVE

1883

VACHERON & CONSTANTIN

1883

VACHERON & CONSTANTIN
fabricants
GENÈVE

1883

VACHERON & CONSTANTIN

1883

VACHERON & CONSTANTIN
fabricants
GENÈVE

1883

VACHERON & CONSTANTIN
fabricants
GENÈVE
Mouvements de montres, boites de montres et accessoires de mouvements de montres.

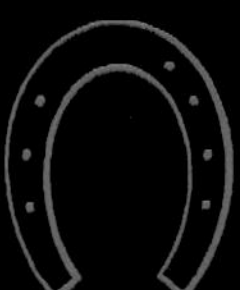

1883

VACHERON & CONSTANTIN
fabricants
GENÈVE

1883

VACHERON & CONSTANTIN

1883

VACHERON & CONSTANTIN

1884

VACHERON & CONSTANTIN

1884

Ancienne fabrique
VACHERON & CONSTANTIN

1888

V & C

Ancienne Fabrique
VACHERON & CONSTANTIN

1889

V & C

1903

CHRONOMÈTRE ROYAL
VACHERON & CONSTANTIN
GENÈVE.

1907

CHRONOMETRE ROYAL

ROYAL CHRONOMETER

1908

1939

1970

1988

VACHERON CONSTANTIN
Manufacture Horlogère. Genève, depuis 1755.

2000

2015

RIGHT-HAND PAGE
Ladies' pendant watch, 1887. A hunter-style watch in red gold and green enamel, it is decorated with a monogram set with diamonds. The chain is in red gold and green enamel. Inv. no. 10554

The treasure of the Order was seized to finance a part of the Egyptian expedition. Nevertheless, a number of knights joined the cause and some of them, such as Chanaleilles and Lascaris, would play an important role in the administration of Egypt. What remained of the Order was established permanently in Rome in 1834.

For the knights of the Order of Saint John, the Maltese cross had precise significance. Its branches each represented one of the four virtues: prudence, temperance, justice, and strength. The eight points referred to the eight beatitudes: humility, courtesy, mercy, peace, compassion, devotion, purity, and endurance. Was Vacheron Constantin inspired by all these virtues and qualities when it chose the Maltese cross as a distinctive shape? Perhaps not. But even if it has no religious significance for the company, its long history makes it a fine emblem of nobility, courage, and pride. The nobility of an artistic craft, the courage to confront difficulties and take risks, the pride in creating beauty and in doing hard work well.

In 1882, Vacheron Constantin received a prestigious order for a naval officer's watch from Prince Thomas of Savoy, Duke of Genoa. In the following year, the company welcomed a new leader, Ernest Roux. He was a grandchild of Jacques Barthélémi Vacheron and the son of his daughter Louise Abrahime. Catherine, Jacques Barthélémi's widow, was still alive at that time. She died the following year at the age of 102. So when her grandson Ernest Roux, the only surviving adult male in the Vacheron line, became head of the company, the requisite power of attorney was signed by someone more than a century old. By that time, it seemed as if the company had always been led by the Weiss brothers, as it would be for another fifteen years. In 1884, Georges Auguste Leschot passed away at the age of 84, after spending forty-five years in the company. He had made great contributions to the success of Vacheron Constantin, particularly to its high technical standards. One year after his death, the company delivered a complicated watch that has meanwhile reappeared. It indicates moon phases and is equipped with a perpetual calendar – a calendar that automatically adjusts the display to the length of each month, regardless whether it contains 28, 29, 30, or 31 days. It was very technically advanced for the time.

Leschot died in the very year that the International Meridian Conference in Washington DC brought together 25 countries to adopt the principle of dividing the globe into 24 equal time zones of 15° each. After much debate, the reference meridian or "prime meridian" was established at the Royal Observatory, Greenwich, London. As the countries gradually adopted this system, a unified world time was recognized. In the 1930s, the time zone principle would enable Vacheron Constantin to demonstrate its capacity for innovation with the first "world time" watches, which incorporated a system that would become a milestone.

In 1885, Vacheron Constantin employed 70 people including seventeen women, all in the building on Quai de Moulins. Attached to the building, a hydraulic turbine in the Rhône had already been driving the blank-making machines for several years. Famous around the world, in good financial health, and on the cutting edge of technical innovation, Vacheron Constantin was well prepared to meet the great challenges of the twentieth century.

VACHERON & CONSTANTIN
GENEVE

LEFT-HAND PAGE AND OPPOSITE
Double-sided pocket watch, 1884. On one side of this 18K yellow gold chronometer is an enamel dial sporting Roman numerals and small seconds at 6 o'clock; on the other side is an enamel dial with a 48-month perpetual calendar and moon phases.
Inv. no. 10155

OPPOSITE
Edouard Kaiser, *Atelier des monteurs de boîtes,* 1893.
Oil on canvas,
141 cm x 187 cm.
Musée des beaux-arts,
La Chaux-de-Fonds.

Grand Hôtel

CAUX

MANUFACTURE D'HORLOGERIE

VACHERON &

Feine Taschenuhren

Fine Watches

1890–1938
DARING TO BE MODERN

Despite the ups and downs provided by history, Vacheron Constantin continued its quest for perfection: technological mastery proven through numerous patents, record-setting precision, and the creation of watches with grand complications combined with aesthetics comprising daring modern cases in tonneau, rectangular, and cushion shapes.

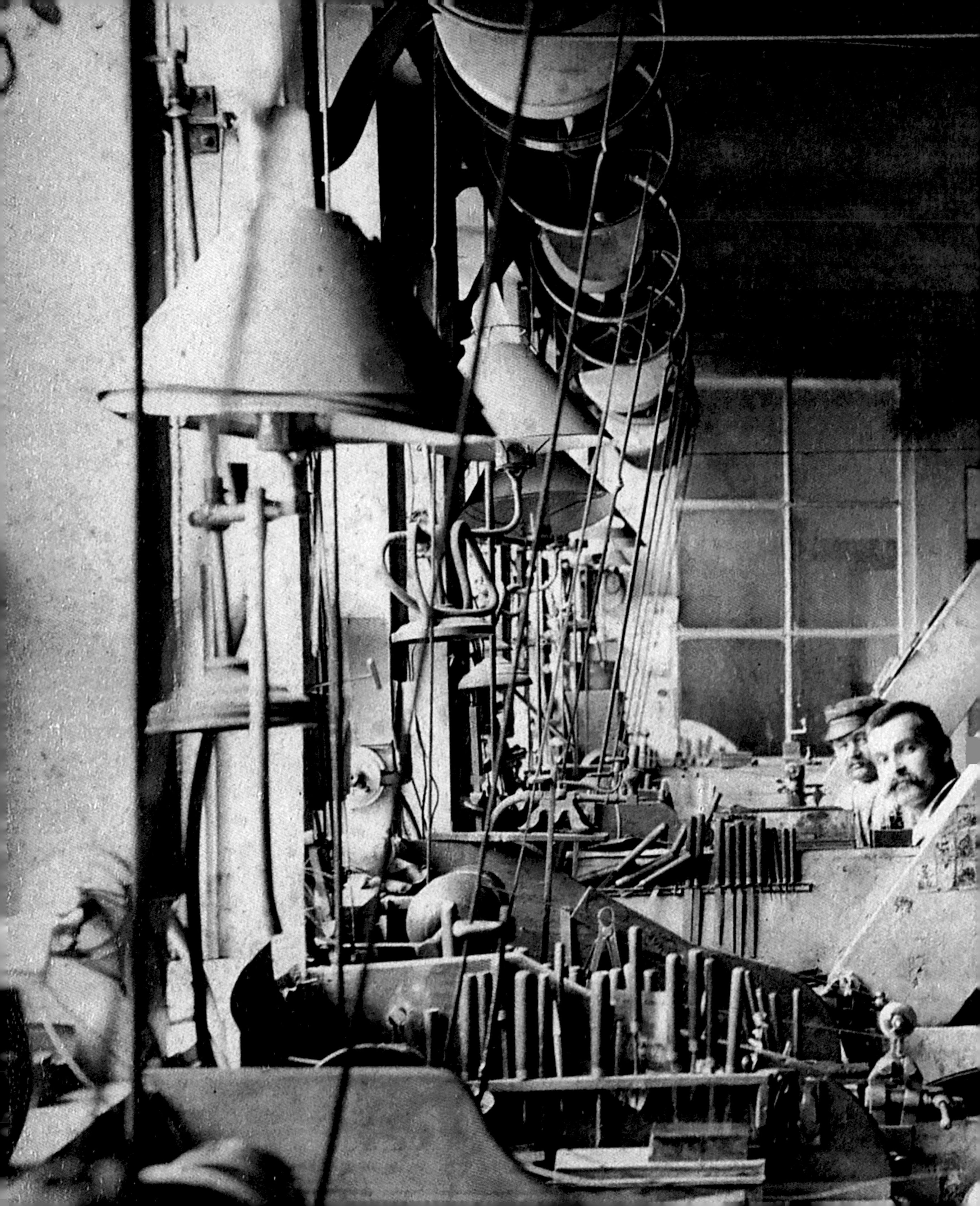

1889

PAGE 84
Pocket watch, 1899. Hunter in Louis XV style, it is entirely engraved in 14K red gold. The "ES" monogram is engraved on the lid. Inv. no. 10926

PREVIOUS DOUBLE PAGE
The Vacheron Constantin workshops on Quai des Moulins in Geneva, early 20th century.

BELOW
Elaine Augusta Villiers (née Guest, then Mrs. Hunter) wore her watch on a châtelaine. Photograph by Alexander Bassano. Negative on glass plate, 1898, 16 cm x 11 cm. London, National Portrait Gallery.

RIGHT-HAND PAGE
The watchmaking pavilion at the 1889 Universal Exhibition in Paris. Vacheron Constantin was represented among a community of watchmakers brought together by the Geneva committee.

In this period, modernity triumphed, particularly at the Paris Universal Exposition of 1889. France, celebrating the centennial of its revolution, welcomed 60,000 exhibitors from around the world to a site of almost one hundred hectares overlooking the River Seine. It was an anthem to international friendship and, more importantly, to industry, machines, and metal. Thirty million visitors flocked through the gates. Buildings with impressive metal architecture had been specially constructed, including the great Machinery Hall. But, of course, what immediately caught the eye was Gustave Eiffel's astounding cast-iron tower. At 300 meters, it was the tallest construction in the world and remained so until the Empire State Building went up in 1930. And, yet, it was not the most fascinating attraction in the exhibition. No, what everyone was talking about was the "electricity fairy" used on a large scale for the very first time. Just after dark, bridges decorated with twinkling bulbs reflected in the Seine, the gardens and pavilions were illuminated, and the Eiffel Tower was wrapped in garlands of light with a powerful beam shining from the top. The Universal Exhibition gave amazed visitors a glimpse of the city of the future where millions of tiny suns would abolish the dark.

Vacheron Constantin's contribution was a movement for a ladies' wristwatch. The company participated as part of a watchmaking group assembled this time by the Geneva Committee, and would do the same at many subsequent international events. At the Milan International Exhibition in 1906, it was awarded the Grand Prix for watchmaking. There, alongside its latest creations, Vacheron Constantin proudly displayed a watch from 1825. In addition to international events held in Switzerland, it successfully took part in the Brussels International Exposition in 1910 and the International Exposition of Decorative Arts in Paris in 1925.

Paradoxically, the company entered the brand-new century under a rather old-fashioned corporate title: in 1887, following the death of Louise Vacheron – the widow of César – it became the Ancienne Fabrique Vacheron & Constantin SA. It kept this official title until 1946, although its dials and movements were always signed with the name that was famous around the world: Vacheron Constantin. In any event, its modernity was clearly established by the advanced technology and aesthetic design of its watches, the dual identity that lies at the heart of all its creations. Since the late 1880s, it had continually registered brands and patents in Switzerland and the United States. Some of these new brands were for a series of watches, such as the Horse Shoe brand in the USA; the logo of two linked horseshoes identified them as watches intended for lovers of equestrian sports. Above all, it patented important technical innovations, such as "a new system for setting the time" and "a new system for attaching the pendant ring to watches." At the same time, its continued development in the area of chronographics and chronometry was recognized in 1895 when it received the only first prize to be awarded that year in the Chronometer Competition of the Geneva observatory; Vacheron Constantin had taken part for the first time. One year later, it won a gold medal at the Swiss National Exhibition in Geneva, particularly for its ultra-thin movements. The same year, it also won first prize in the international timing competition of the Geneva Observatory. Distinctions rained down year after year until competitions of this kind came to an end in Switzerland, as well as in the USA, Italy, and England.

Horlogerie
CLASSE
HORLOGERIE FRANCAISE (Collective)
SAUNIER

From 1888 on, the company also helped finance the Swiss syndicate's research into the use of non-magnetic metals in hopes of producing watch movements that ran with more precision.

Yet the major innovation of this period was not within the watch movement. In 1887, Vacheron Constantin produced a set of more than thirty round movements, an unusually large number at that time. It was a milestone event, as these movements were made to equip one of the first wristwatches ever produced identically in series. The fact is that until the start of the twentieth century, the pocket watch reigned supreme. It had to be protected from shock, dust, and variations in temperature. Of course, the watch worn on the wrist had existed since the sixteenth century. It was quite rare and valuable, always a unique piece, and worn by women as jewelry: it was simply a bracelet that also indicated the time. Very occasionally, at the end of the nineteenth century, certain watchmakers received orders from military organizations for wristwatches for their officers. In contrast, the watch outfitted with the Vacheron Constantin movement was a serially produced model for ladies, worn on a bracelet. Its fine gold case was delicately decorated and engraved, while the dial was encircled by a ring set with diamonds. The need for a winding crown was abolished by a technical innovation: the watch was wound and set by turning the bezel. Vacheron Constantin has kept an example of this historic watch, which won a prize at the Paris Universal Exposition of 1889 (below). The regular production of wristwatches began later, in the early 1910s. In 1912 the company introduced the first tonneau-shaped wristwatch, a design that would become a Vacheron Constantin classic.

Philippe Auguste Weiss died in 1899, and was replaced as head of the company by Georges Grandjean, one of the managers responsible for production. His brother, Jules Weiss, remained managing director. Jean-François Constantin died in 1900. The company was constantly being asked to present a retrospective of its watches at national and international exhibitions. This often meant it had to borrow them back from clients, as in the case of the Milan exhibition of 1906. To avoid this, and because he was aware of their growing value, George Grandjean began to acquire some of Vacheron Constantin's older pieces. This collection has been continually expanded since then and today is maintained by Vacheron Constantin in Geneva. But in those years of great prosperity for the company, which continued up to World War I with new

LEFT-HAND PAGE
Pocket watch, 1906. Made of yellow gold, it is the result of incredible enamel work using the cloisonné technique to depict a thistle motif. This watch was presented at the Milan Universal Exhibition of 1906. Inv. no. 10655

BELOW
Ladies' wristwatch, 1889. Made of yellow gold set with diamonds, this watch, a prize-winner at the 1889 Universal Exhibition in Paris, is one of the first serially made watches in the world. A technical feat allows the wearer to wind it and set the time by turning the bezel. Two winged goddesses form the bracelet. Inv. no. 10531

1901

BELOW
Hand-engraved scrolls.

RIGHT-HAND PAGE
Pocket watch, 1900.
This hunter-style watch with bull's eye, in chiseled 18K yellow gold, belonged to Prince Louis Napoléon.
It features a minute repeater and chronograph with 30-minute counter. Its back is hand-engraved to feature an N with an eagle's head.
Inv. no. 10803

FOLLOWING LEFT-HAND PAGE
Extract of the sales catalog, 1900.

FOLLOWING RIGHT-HAND PAGE
Drawings, 1890–1900.

markets opening up, particularly in Latin America, Grandjean was not thinking so much about the past but rather the present and the future. The present was good, with full order books and an increasingly prestigious list of clients. Painter Claude Monet was one of them, buying several watches when he stayed in Switzerland in 1899. Henry James, author of *The Bostonians* and *The Aspern Papers*, and his brother, psychologist William James, were also regular clients. In 1901, Marie of Romania, Queen Consort , granddaughter of Queen Victoria on her father's side and Tsar Alexander II on her mother's side, ordered a very valuable chronometer. The same year, Prince Napoleon, grandson of Jérôme Bonaparte, took delivery of a chronograph watch with a minute counter and a minute repeater, decorated with the initial N and the imperial eagle. In 1904, Ambassador Soueng of the Chinese Empire ordered two hunter-encased watches with enamel decoration that included a portrait of Marie-Antoinette. Later that year, an even more promising market opened up for Vacheron Constantin when King Peter I of Serbia commissioned twelve chronometers and twelve watches with engravings. At the same time, he appointed Vacheron Constantin as watchmaker to the royal court and awarded it the Royal Order of Saint-Sava. The commission was produced in rather unusual circumstances: while he was in exile in Geneva, Prince Peter Karađorđević was proclaimed King of Serbia following the revolution that brutally ended the Obrenović dynasty. He placed his order just before returning to his country. In Geneva, his young son Alexander – the future Alexander I – was a fellow student and friend of Charles Constantin, grandson of Jean-François, born in 1887.

On a different note entirely, in 1901 Vacheron Constantin received an order for 300 gold watches to be awarded as prizes by the Swiss Federal Shooting Committee. Then in 1905, the railway company of Northwest Greece placed a large order for its staff. At the same time, the company began to receive many orders for its "Very High Complication" (THC) watches and even "Very Very High Complication" (TTHC) watches. These models incorporated a series of functions that very few watchmakers were capable of producing. This was the case in 1901 with a watch ordered by Louis du Bouchet, a client in Paris, and again four years later when a surgeon in Lyon requested a very rare combination of functions: an alarm, a chronograph, and a full calendar (one indicating the day of the week, the date, the month, and the moon phases). Its large silver dial was marked in fifths of a second.

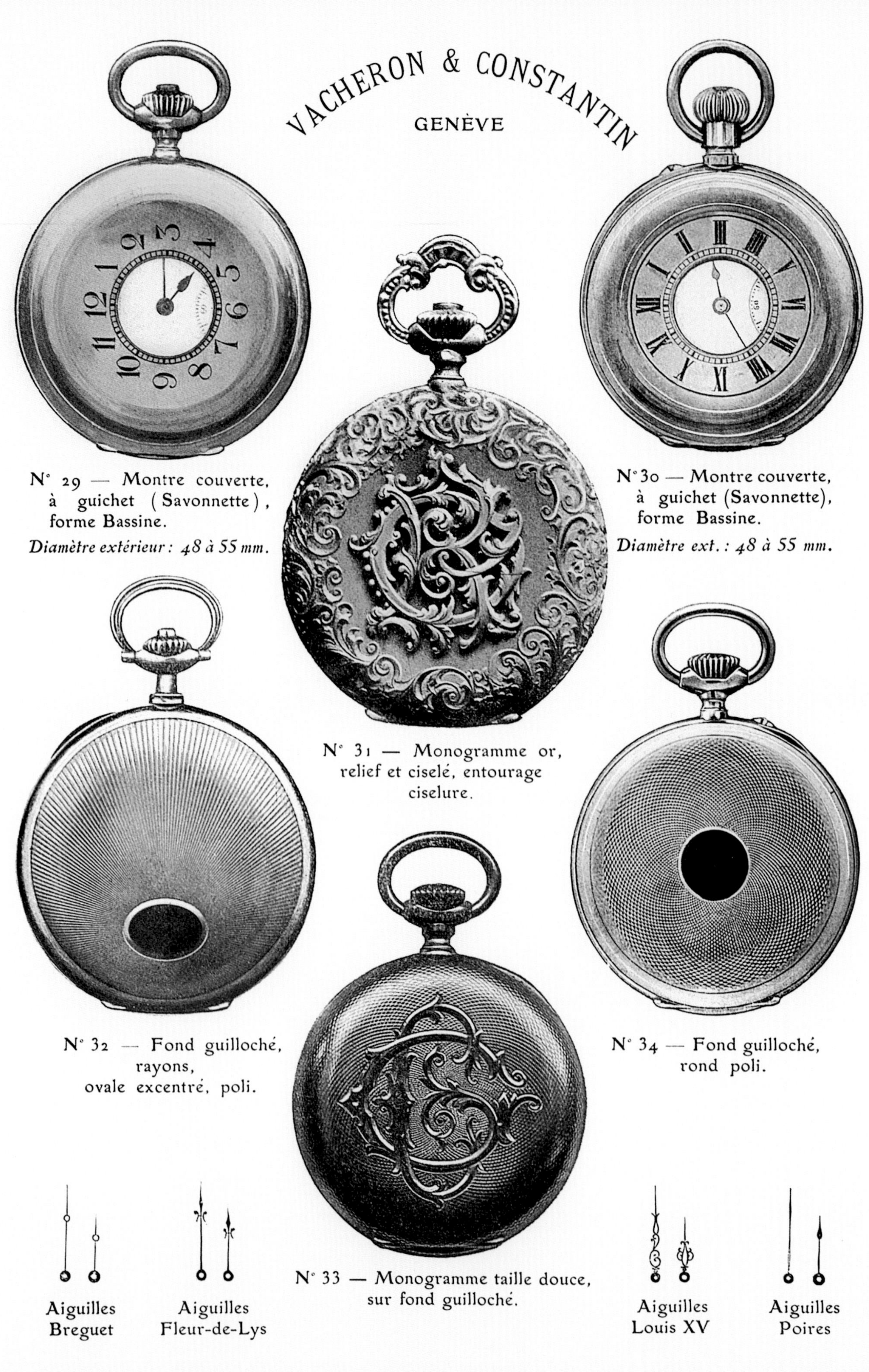

VACHERON & CONSTANTIN

GENÈVE

Nº 29 — Montre couverte, à guichet (Savonnette), forme Bassine.

Diamètre extérieur : 48 à 55 mm.

Nº 30 — Montre couverte, à guichet (Savonnette), forme Bassine.

Diamètre ext. : 48 à 55 mm.

Nº 31 — Monogramme or, relief et ciselé, entourage ciselure.

Nº 32 — Fond guilloché, rayons, ovale excentré, poli.

Nº 34 — Fond guilloché, rond poli.

Nº 33 — Monogramme taille douce, sur fond guilloché.

Aiguilles Breguet

Aiguilles Fleur-de-Lys

Aiguilles Louis XV

Aiguilles Poires

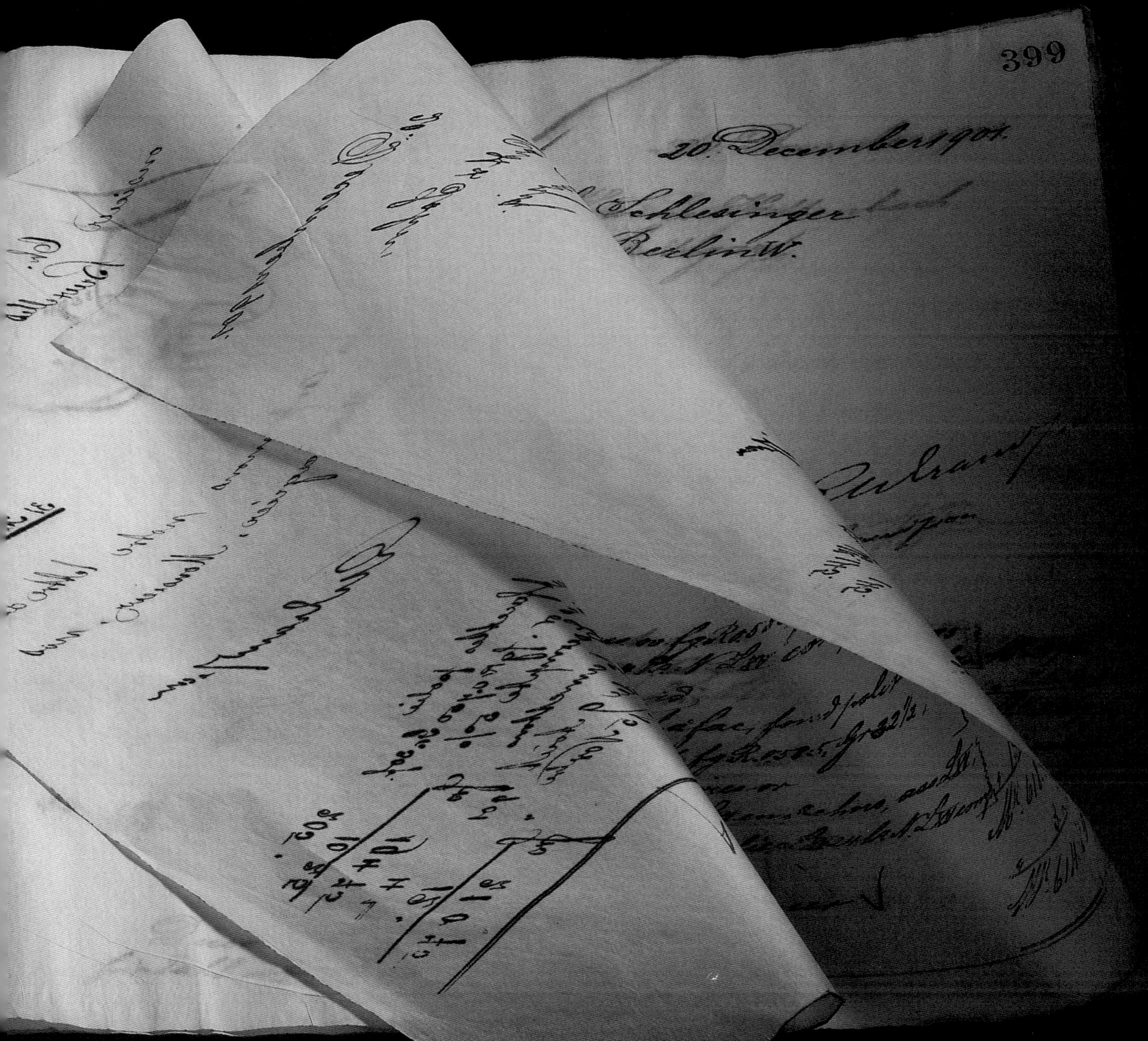

399

20. December 1904.

Schlesinger

Berlin W.

PREVIOUS DOUBLE PAGE.
Left: pocket watch, 1901. This hunter-style watch in 18K red gold is a grand complication: minute repeater, monopusher chronograph and tachometer, astronomic perpetual calendar. Inv. no. 10536
Right: pocket watch, 1901. Made of 18K yellow gold, this minute repeater comes with a split-seconds chronograph, a perpetual calendar, and a moon phase and age of moon indicator. Inv. no. 10158

LEFT-HAND PAGE
Ladies' pendant watch, 1910. This platinum, gold, and diamond jewelry piece features a guilloché and enameled back with floral decoration. The matching necklace is in enamel. Inv. no. 10184

OPPOSITE
Advertisement, 1900.

1904

OPPOSITE
Louis Charles Joseph Blériot (1872–1936), September 15, 1898. Photograph by Sir John Benjamin Stone. Platinum print, 20 cm x 15 cm. London, National Portrait Gallery.

RIGHT-HAND PAGE
Aviator watch, 1904. Designed by the brothers Orville and Wilbur Wright, this steel watch is fitted with a Vacheron Constantin chronometer movement. It was worn strapped to the thigh. Inv. no. 10756

Meanwhile, Georges Grandjean was also thinking about the future and continued to press for innovation. In 1904, he filed three important patents to improve certain parts of a movement. With his enthusiasm for progress and new technologies, he happily accepted a request from Orville and Wilbur Wright, the American pioneers of aviation. That year, in their first biplane, the *Wright Flyer*, they had progressed from covering just 40 meters to a distance of one kilometer, and now needed a chronometer watch they could wear in the air. It was a wristwatch, if it can be called that, since it was actually strapped around the thigh, just above the knee. This positioning made it easy to see when seated at the aircraft controls. It was the first of its kind in the world. Conceived and designed by the brothers themselves, it was fitted with a rugged, yet precise, movement that Vacheron Constantin had developed in 1890 (right-hand page).

It was a purely functional watch that offered robustness rather than elegance in complete contrast to the charming jewelry watches Vacheron Constantin made at that time. In truth, the company was still devoted to the Geneva tradition of refined, decorated, ornamental watches. For example, ladies' brooch watches remained one of its specialties, only two examples of which dating from the beginning of the twentieth century have been found with the pin used to attach them. One is decorated with gold *fleurs de lys* encrusted with diamonds against a background of blue enamel. Its matching pin in the form of wings is also decorated with enamel, gold, and diamonds. The second is even more interesting as it shows a concern for modernity among the traditional Genevan company's decorators: it is in pure Art Nouveau style with a floral motif in blue, mauve, and green enamel against a gold background with diamonds set along the swirling lines derived from nature. It received an award at the Milan International Exhibition of 1906.

To display all these marvels in a suitably splendid setting, Vacheron Constantin commissioned an architect called Bettinger to create a shop on the ground floor at Rue des Moulins. Previously, all sales had been conducted on the first floor. The shop opened on August 1,1906; from then on, Geneva's residents and tourists were able to see Vacheron Constantin creations beautifully displayed in the window.

Among them, in the following year, was a pocket watch that would be particularly important: the Chronomètre Royal. The name was registered as a brand on May 28, 1907. Its precision, reliability, and robust construction made it an immediate success around the world, particularly in South America where its resistance to high humidity and variation in temperature was fully appreciated. Even the dial, produced in grand feu enamel, was specially designed to be rustproof. Over the years, the Chronomètre Royal brand came to signify robust reliability and grew to include some twenty models, including its first wristwatch introduced in 1953. In 2007, the centennial of the brand was marked by a reissue of the precious 1907 Chronomètre Royal, in a limited series of 100 pieces with the 12 o'clock numeral in red enamel. Its self-winding Vacheron Constantin mechanical movement was granted both the Hallmark of Geneva and C.O.S.C. (*Contrôle Officiel Suisse des Chronomètres*) certification in addition to passing Vacheron Constantin's own thirty-day test to confirm the superb quality of the Chronomètre Royal brand. Just like the original model, its dial was produced in *grand feu* enamel.

PREVIOUS DOUBLE PAGE
Henri Farman making the first air flight in the world between Bouy and Reims, October 30, 1908.

OPPOSITE
Advertising card, 1914.

RIGHT-HAND PAGE
Pendant watch, 1915. Made of 18K yellow and white gold, ivory, onyx, and diamonds, this watch highlights the glyptic art with its black and white onyx cameo featuring a cherub while the ivory dial has Arabic numerals.
Inv. no. 11696

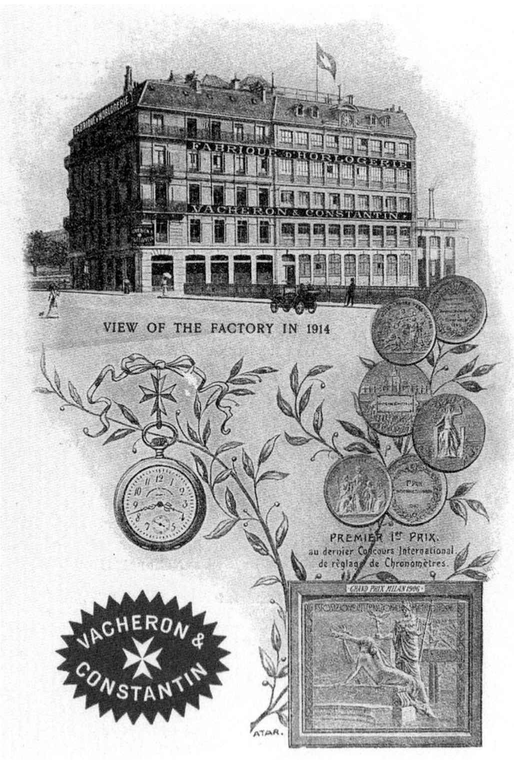

The death of Jules Weiss in 1910 meant that the statutes of *Ancienne Fabrique Vacheron & Constantin SA* had to be changed. At that time, Marc Eugène Constantin, the son of Jean-François, was only a shareholder in the company, not directly involved in its management. But his son Charles, born in 1887, was being prepped to take on an important role. He first studied law at university, then took a course at the La Chaux-de-Fonds' school of mechanical engineering before attending the Geneva Watchmaking School. Charles Constantin joined Vacheron Constantin on June 1, 1914, after visiting its representatives in Germany, England, and the United States. On June 27, he married Pauline Chaix, daughter of the famous Swiss professor, Émile Chaix. The next day, the heir to the Hapsburg throne, Archduke Franz Ferdinand, was assassinated in Sarajevo by a Serbian nationalist. On July 28, Austria-Hungary declared war on Serbia, then a rapid escalation among alliances began: on August 1, Germany mobilized its army and declared war, first on Russia then two days later on France and Belgium; on August 4, Great Britain declared war on Germany. Three days previous, Charles Constantin had been called up and sent to the northern front.

On the main front, the French and German armies were face to face, with one and a half million men on each side. The German high command was sure of the superiority of its heavy artillery, and its objective was to defeat France quickly before turning against Russia; it would be disillusioned. Hostilities broke out on August 2 and continued for four years. Between the western and eastern fronts, with all the offensives and counteroffensives, stalemates, and trench warfare, the result was an appalling bloodbath: more than 37 million dead, 22 million among the allies and 15 million on the side of Germany and Austria-Hungary. The United States, which entered the war in 1917, lost 350,000 men out of almost two million. In France, Louis-Ferdinand Céline's *Journey to the End of the Night* and in Germany Ernst Jünger's *Storms of Steel*, would describe the horror and absurdity of the conflict. The war not only had a devastating impact demographically, it was equally disastrous on economic, social, moral, and political levels. The consequences were particularly dramatic in Russia where it cost more than nine million lives and threw the country into revolutionary turmoil, followed by 70 years of a totalitarian regime. As for the Treaty of Versailles, it brought an end to the conflict but planted the seeds of World War II.

The war also had a scientific and technical impact, and not only in military terms with the arrival of tanks and chemical weapons. Aerial reconnaissance and accurate bombardment were made possible by the first aircraft and fostered the development of aviation. The Blériot and Fokker monoplanes at the start of the war gave way to the Handley Page bombers of the newly formed Royal Air Force by its end. These were powered by 360-horsepower Rolls-Royce engines – a huge improvement in power and technology. In parallel, some modest improvements were made in instruments for measurement and navigation. Such progress made during the war enabled the rapid growth of civil aviation. On June 14, 1919, English pilots John Alcock and Arthur Brown made the first nonstop flight across the Atlantic, from Newfoundland to Ireland, in 16 hours and 27 minutes. Their aircraft was a bomber from the war, a Vickers Vimy. Carried on a wave of popular enthusiasm, civil aviation would develop enormously in the 1920s and 1930s, transporting mail, freight, and passengers, and stimulating trade between continents.

PREVIOUS DOUBLE PAGE
Ladies' watch, 1912. Set with diamonds in platinum and 18K gold, this jewelry watch is an example of the highly creative Art Deco period. It features a guilloché dial in the center and blued steel hands. Inv. no. 10668

LEFT-HAND PAGE
Ladies' jewelry wristwatch, 1916. Commissioned by Sir Bhupindra Singh, Maharajah of Patiala, this surprisingly designed and remarkably manufactured watch is made of platinum set with diamonds. It offers a side view of the time with its inwardly directed dial. The chiseled bangle bracelet is openworked. The silver dial pivots on a hinge and offers easy access to the movement, which is one of the first "baguette" calibers, here equipped with a curved plate to perfectly fit into the case. Inv. no. 10939

OPPOSITE
Sir Bhupindra Singh, Maharajah of Patiala, surrounded by the ladies of his court.

1917

BELOW
Topographic engineer of the American expeditionary force drawing a map during World War I.

RIGHT-HAND PAGE
"Corps of Engineers USA" chronograph, pocket watch, 1918. Specially designed for the engineer corps and engraved with the words "Corps of Engineers, U.S.A", these watches were designed to satisfy the following requirements: they had to be made of silver, resist temperature differences, and possess luminescent numerals and hands. Inv. no. 11093

However, by setting the whole of Europe ablaze, World War I had seriously hampered activity at Vacheron Constantin. It was practically paralyzed in 1914 as a large number of employees signed up for military service, but it slowly began to recover the following year. The company was forced to adapt to the situation by creating a series of silver pocket watches at a modest price named "19 lignes ART" (ART stands for "*Ancre Remontoir Tirage*," a technical reference to the movement, while "*19 lignes*" refers to the caliber's size). In 1915, as the low volume of business left watchmakers with time to experiment, one of them made a small movement in the shape of an extended rectangle, measuring 6.5 mm wide and 26 mm long. He named it the *tuyau*. His intention was that it could be mounted into a pen or fountain pen. While this excellent idea would never be implemented, the tuyau movement would go on to have a meaningful future described a bit further on.

Although business was slow, Switzerland's neutral status had positive consequences for all its watchmakers and jewelers. Vacheron Constantin, like others, received orders that only a neutral country could execute: Russian and Scandinavian clients deprived of French jewelry turned to Switzerland. Vacheron Constantin was able to restart its jewelry activities and supply new clients such as the house of Bolin, jeweler to the Russian imperial court. The war also provided the opportunity to renew the company's links to the American market. When it entered the war in 1917, the United States opened an equipment purchasing office in Geneva for its expeditionary force. It ordered 3,289 Vacheron Constantin chronograph pocket watches with cases in oxidized silver and hands in fluorescent radium. They were engraved with "Corps of Engineers" (right-hand page). The contract was renewed several times up to 1920. In 1917, the company became a shareholder in the American Watch Case Company and supplied it with watches under the registered brand name Merlimont.

While the workshops adapted to new client requests, they continued to innovate by outfitting watches with different external parts and creating new mechanisms. The war had also led to the popularity of tonneau-shaped watches. This barrel shape that made its debut between 1900 and 1905 was intended for new wristwatches: by making a deliberate break with the tradition of round watches, it announced that the wristwatch was not just an adaptation of the pocket watch but a totally new object. Beginning in 1912, Vacheron Constantin produced this shape with a great deal of freedom and fantasy playing with the design of the numerals, giving the case a "Genevan" Greek border, even reforming the shape for a ladies' watch with a very sophisticated design, the traditional tonneau (page 114). Versions of this shaped watch appear today in the Malte collection. In a more technical area, the company's watchmakers developed their chronograph movements: for one of its very first sports watches they invented a start mechanism on the winding stem. From 1914 to 1918, they won several awards at various chronometer competitions, particularly those organized by the observatories of Geneva and Teddington in England. They also developed an extraordinary watch for American carmaker James Ward Packard, which was delivered in 1919. The two great watchmaking arts – complications and decoration – were combined in this pocket watch: it was fitted with a chronograph, a minute repeater, and a petite and grande sonnerie with a half-quarter repeater. It was also notable for some surprising details ordered by Packard; these

CORPS OF ENGINEERS
U.S.A.
No. 2341

CORPS OF ENGINEERS U.S.A.
VACHERON & CONSTANTIN
GENÈVE

Telephone 6252 Berne

Vacheron & Constantin,
Geneva.

I hereby purchase from you, by order of
American E.F. the materials

DESCRIPTION : 2,000 watches,
and hands, as per sample No.
Paris. On the back of each
U.S.A. 10,351 " up to 12,350.

ANCIENNE FABRIQUE
VACHERON & CONSTANTIN
SOCIÉTÉ ANONYME
FONDÉE EN 1785

Schweiz. Telegraphen- und Telephonverwaltung. — Administration des télégraphes et des téléphones suisses. —
Telegramm — Télégramme —
SS URGENT PARIS 44/75
PARIS BD1
BUREAU DES TELEGRAPHES GENÈVE 23 V 18
Genève
Erhalten von — Reçu de
Ricevuto da
Consegnato il

OPPOSITE
Packard advertisement, 1918.

RIGHT-HAND PAGE
Pocket watch, 1918.
A special commission for James Ward Packard, the famous American car manufacturer, who loved fine watches. This timepiece conceals a complex mechanism beneath apparent simplicity. Delivered in 1919, it offers the following complications: chronograph, minute repeater, small alarm with chimes at half and quarter hours. Expressly requested by its owner, this model boasts features rarely seen in timepieces. It is a tribute to Vacheron Constantin's artistic crafts with a 20K gold engraved case customized with the owner's monogram on a blue enameled back. Inv. no. 11527

VACHERON &
GENEVE
CONSTANTIN
SUISSE

CHERON & CONSTANTIN
GENÈVE-SUISSE
VACHERON & CONSTANTIN
GENÈVE

included a rock crystal glass and a Guillaume balance. The latter was named for its Swiss inventor, Charles Édouard Guillaume, a Nobel laureate for physics in 1920, who developed an iron-nickel alloy for the balance that improved the precision of the watch. The watch case, in 20-karat gold with very fine engraving and guilloché work, carried the initials J.W.P. in blue enamel. In June 2011, this magnificent example of Vacheron Constantin watchmaking was sold at auction in New York for 1.8 million dollars.

In Switzerland, the post-war period was marked by two social and political events. The first was the introduction of the 48-hour work week in 1920 with offices and workshops forced to close on Saturday afternoon. This meant the 58.5-hour week was abandoned in a return to something like the more humane conditions once enjoyed by the cabinotiers. The second was the creation of the League of Nations, the forerunner of the United Nations, which was established in Geneva in January of 1920. It made the city an international meeting place for diplomats and heads of state. Vacheron Constantin certainly made the most of the city's new status, welcoming a good number of them to the Rue des Moulins location. Among the first was Punjab's ruler Sir Bhupindra Singh, Maharajah of Patiala, who attended the General Assembly of the League of Nations in the autumn of 1921. Accompanied by his two wives, bodyguards, and secretaries, this great collector of sumptuous jewelry chose from among dozens of pendants, bracelets and watches, spending a total of 150,000 francs (around 800,000 euros today).

What the staff presented to the prodigal maharajah probably included watches with finely finished guilloché dials – a decoration that was starting to become one of the distinctive signs of Vacheron Constantin. Between 1920 and 1930, it became a majestic illustration of "1925 Style," a modern aesthetic that came to be called Art Deco. Its simple, often geometric shapes were a radical departure from the natural, sinuous lines of Art Nouveau. The story of how Vacheron Constantin became involved in this excitingly modern style began in 1880. That year, following the death of Vacheron Constantin's representative in Paris, the agency was taken over by an ex-employee of the Paris manufacture Ferdinand Verger, who was a young watchmaker with very good taste located on Place des Victoires. He proved a dynamic representative and a friendly relationship of mutual esteem gradually developed as he contributed to the success of the company. His agency's location put Vacheron Constantin right at the heart of the world's fashion capital, firmly in touch with changing tastes and trends. In 1888, he moved to Rue Sainte Anne, close to the Paris opera. In 1896, while remaining Vacheron Constantin's representative, buying its watches and movements, Verger set up on his own as a maker of watch cases. His business carried his name, and his creations – often manufactured for jeweler Cartier – were marked with his initials, "FV." The two letters were arranged on a fruit tree, symbolizing his name, Verger (French for "orchard"). In 1901, he took over the Lépine company. He was both a technician and a designer who, throughout his career, invented beautiful, ingenious instruments: one was a watch case with a hinged frame that enabled it to stand on a piece of furniture like a small clock. He retired in 1920, passing the baton to his two sons, Georges and Henri. They changed the company name to Verger Frères and began to sign their work with their father's initials inversed: "VF." They remained Vacheron Constantin's exclusive representatives in Paris while still creating superb, modernly styled watch cases for several jewelers.

Their very close relationship with Vacheron Constantin resulted in numerous joint creations introduced between 1910 and 1930. Around 1920, the brothers asked to see new movements the company had recently created. Georges Grandjean showed them the little "tuyau" movement from 1915 that had been fitted one year later into a watch sold to Sir Bhupindra Singh, Maharajah of Patiala (page 108). The brothers examined it carefully and made an initial order for a dozen examples. It enabled them to design a watch for Vacheron Constantin, the ultra-thin *baguette* for ladies, which would become very successful and a symbol of modern watchmaking. The shape of the movement, and therefore the watch, was perfectly suited to the very simple,

1920

LEFT-HAND PAGE
Wristwatches, early 1910s. These 18K yellow gold watches boasting a tonneau shape, demonstrate, if ever there were a need, Vacheron Constantin's creativity in the shapes of its watch cases. Inv. no. 10144 and 10594

FOURNITURES
DE BUREAUX

PAPETERIE

FABRIQUE
DE REGISTRES

NEW YORK
B

BEL-AIR, 4
GENÈVE

ROBERT FRÈRES
SUCCESSEURS DE CH. GEISENDORF

Horlogerie New-York.

PREVIOUS DOUBLE PAGE
Wristwatch, 1921. As with the Driver watches, this 18K yellow gold cushion-shaped timepiece illustrates Vacheron Constantin's freedom in design and the bold style of the Roaring Twenties. The winding crown is positioned at 11 o'clock, extending the 12-6 o'clock axis of the enamel dial, pivoted 45° counterclockwise. Produced by Vacheron Constantin specifically for the American market, this watch was re-issued in 2009 and is still a great success. Inv. no. 11677

BELOW
Skeleton pocket watch, 1926. Made of 18K white gold, this piece features a rock crystal case and twelve black enamel Arabic numerals on its bezel. Its crown is adorned with an onyx cabochon. Inv. no. 11131

RIGHT-HAND PAGE
"Surprise" pocket watch, 1928. This rectangular 18K white gold watch with shutters boasts a silvered dial with Arabic numerals. Inv. no. 10252

straight-line taste of the era. A style that was dubbed "cubist" within Vacheron Constantin infused the shape of the cases, the hands, and the numerals. Every curve was banished. Between 1922 and the end of the 1930s, the Verger brothers created several models of this kind for Vacheron Constantin, most of which were jewelry watches set with diamonds.

Verger Frères also developed joint designs with Vacheron Constantin that were very typical of the "1925 Style": watches with shutters known in French as *à volets* (pages 120–121). The dial, or a part of the dial, was hidden behind blinds that were activated by a button or a crown. One of the most successful of these models was a rectangular pocket watch created in 1928 for men or ladies called a "surprise watch" (right-hand page). One of them was sold to Infanta Beatrice of Spain in 1931. The collaboration between the Verger brothers and Vacheron Constantin was finally marked by some sumptuous pieces, still in the spirit of Art Deco: small clocks, jewelry watches for ladies with richly decorated bracelets, pocket watches in rock crystal and platinum, and *montres d'habit* in platinum and set with sapphires. Beautifully presented and always fitted with a Vacheron Constantin movement, these pieces were sometimes produced for the world's most famous jewelers including Cartier, Van Cleef & Arpels, Boucheron, Chaumet, Bulgari, Mauboussin, Gübelin, and Tiffany, for renowned watchmakers like Breguet, Baume & Mercier, and Jaeger-LeCoultre, and even for leading brands of luxury accessories such as Hermès and Dunhill. Some of these watches simply carried the name of the client's brand on the dial. Others, much rarer and highly sought-after by collectors, are labeled *Vacheron & Constantin pour Cartier* or *Vacheron & Constantin pour Van Cleef & Arpels*, etc. The cases of these jewelry watches were usually produced by Verger Frères, but sometimes by Vacheron Constantin itself according to drawings sent from the Paris company. This production of watches for other companies was a very important part of the business in the 1920s and continued until World War II.

The Roaring Twenties and Art Deco encouraged the creation of jewelry watches as much as watches with surprising, innovative, offbeat designs. Vacheron Constantin had great success in the United States with a 1921 cushion-shaped wristwatch made unusual by the position of the crown at 1 o'clock. The watch repeated its successful run as part of Vacheron Constantin's Historiques collection in 2009 as the l'Historiques American 1921. It retained most of its daring external parts, now considered classic and highly elegant, but was equipped with a brand new, hand-wound mechanical caliber developed and produced by Vacheron Constantin and stamped with the Hallmark of Geneva. The cushion shape, which made its debut at Vacheron Constantin in 1917, was at its most popular in the 1920s but was never dropped from the portfolio. Today, it has been splendidly revived in the Harmony collection.

However, Vacheron Constantin never forgets the spirit that has always been its strength: the balance between technical expertise, the authentic craft of watchmaking, and the sense of style that makes it art. While many clients, both men and women, are attracted by the design of watches, others, including some of the most prestigious, are fascinated by the complexity of watch movements. To satisfy this second group, the company created some exceptional, very highly complicated watches during the interwar period. These were

OPPOSITE AND LEFT-HAND PAGE
Wristwatch with shutters, 1929. This 18K yellow and white gold rectangular watch hides its dial behind blinds that are activated by the crown. Inv. no. 10405

FOLLOWING DOUBLE PAGE
Art Deco-style clock, 1926. Exhibiting exceptional artfulness and skill, this black lacquered clock set with rose-cut diamond hour markers stands on an agate base. Its dial is decorated with lapis lazuli, jade, turquoise, nephrite, opals, and pearls above which serpentine hands make their rounds. Inv. no. 10547

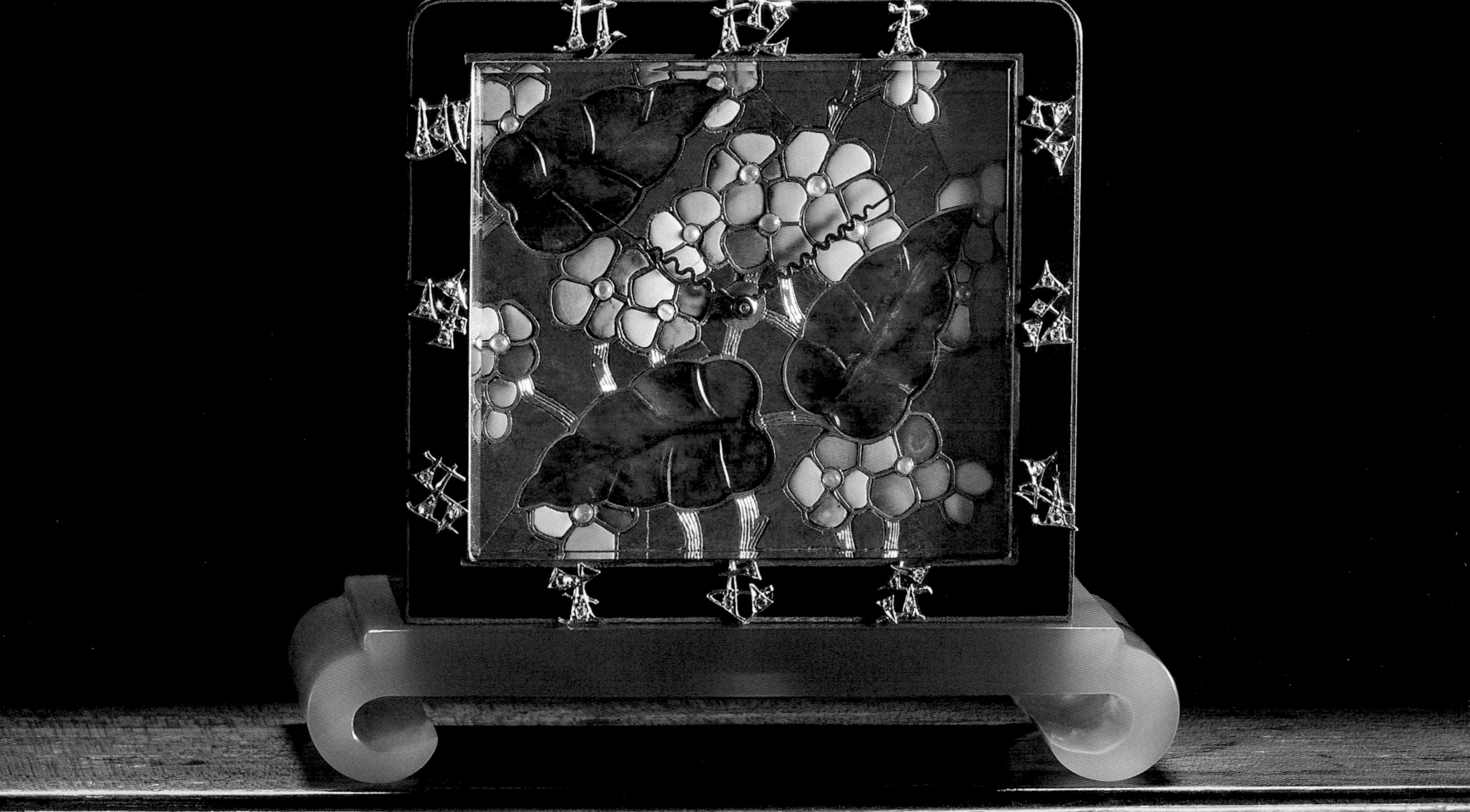

HOTEL SUISSE

produced to order in collaboration with craftsmen who specialized in this kind of movement. Clients had to wait several months, if not years, for delivery. In 1927, a Mr. Francis Peter visited the Rue des Moulins location. A Swiss citizen living in Egypt, he was president of the Joint Tribunal of Cairo. He had been delegated by the Swiss colony in Egypt to choose a watch to be offered to King Fouad I. The king was a keen watch collector, a passion he would pass on to his son, Farouk. From the many complicated watches shown to him, Peter chose a chronograph in yellow gold that represented the very peak of the watchmaker's art. A Geneva enameler was needed to decorate the case: the back had to display the royal coat of arms surrounded by diamonds. The watch was finally delivered in November of 1929 in a rosewood box inlaid with the royal crown and the king's Arabic symbol in gold. Inside, the date 1929 was inlaid in gold and flanked by the Swiss shield and the royal coat of arms painted on enamel (pages 126–127).

Rather less complicated, but outstandingly innovative, was the first "world time" watch launched by Vacheron Constantin in 1932 with a mechanism developed by Louis Cottier, a brilliant watchmaker from Carouge. Watches indicating the time in the 24 time zones already existed. But it was only in 1930–1931 that Cottier perfected this special complication: once the owner had chosen a reference city for the principal time display, it immediately indicated the time in the other cities marked around the dial by means of a disc divided into 24 parts and making a complete revolution once a day. Called the "Cottier system", and later including a day/night indicator, it was adopted across the world of watchmaking with Vacheron Constantin at the forefront.

The company was already present on all continents. With intercontinental travel and transport growing rapidly, it developed the complication further and in 1936 presented two new versions of the watch: one displayed the time in 30 cities and the other in 31 cities. The company continued to create world time watches and small clocks covering as many as 67 cities, some of which would go on to be acquired by a wide range of personalities such as Suzanna Agnelli, King Farouk of Egypt, and American Secretary of State John Foster Dulles.

At that same time between the two wars, the most avid collector of complicated watches, in addition to art, was probably American banker Henry Graves, Jr., who bought two Vacheron Constantin watches. The first, purchased in 1928, was a hunter-encased watch fitted with a tourbillon. The second, also equipped with a tourbillon, was offered in 1932 by correspondence that described it in full detail. It was a chronograph with a perpetual calendar, moon phases, and a power reserve indicator. It later won first prize at the Geneva Observatory competition of 1934. By that time, the great illusion of the Roaring Twenties had totally evaporated, and dark clouds were again gathering over Europe. Did people still remember the euphoria of the 1920s, the *joie de vivre* and the passion for sport and speed that captured the headlines? In 1927, two years before the start of one of the darkest chapters in human history, Charles Lindbergh flew alone from New York to Paris in 33 hours and 27 minutes in his *Spirit of St. Louis*. When he arrived at Le Bourget airport, 20,000 people were waiting to give him a rapturous welcome. His achievement was tremendously popular and had an impact all round the world. That same year, a young typist named Mercedes Gleitze became the first woman to swim the English Channel. This was an achievement for both sports and women, and symbolized the entire era. It also marked a date in the history of watchmaking and modern communications: a large advertising campaign showed photographs of Gleitze wearing a Rolex Oyster watch while she swam. Meanwhile, Vacheron Constantin continued undistracted through this period of change. Its expertise and style did not alter, and its image and energy were recognized by the greatest watch lovers and collectors of the time. Their attitude showed that, regardless of fashion trends and innovation in technology and manufacturing, what always mattered most was the quality of design.

In early October of 1929, Charles Constantin traveled to Belgrade to be received

1929

LEFT-HAND PAGE
King Fouad with Swiss President Robert Haab in Berne, during his official visit on July 3, 1929.

FOLLOWING DOUBLE PAGE
Pocket watch, 1929.
In 1927, Francis Peter, then president of the Combined Court of Cairo and a Swiss citizen, visited the workshop of Vacheron Constantin on the Quai d'Île in Geneva. He was commissioned by the Swiss community in Egypt, who wanted to offer a gift to King Fouad I, a well-known collector of fine watches. He passed on his passion and his unique collection to his son, King Farouk. At the time of his visit, Vacheron Constantin's watchmakers were working on an exceptional timepiece consisting of a sophisticated set of complications, which caught Francis Peter's eye. The watch was delivered in 1929, engraved with the words "À sa Majesté Fouad 1er Hommage de la Colonie Suisse d'Égypte." (The mechanism of this exceptional piece can be seen in from a fourth angle on page 250.)

SAM 3
VACHERON & CONSTANTIN
GENEVE - SWISS

VACHERON & CONSTANTIN
GENÈVE
A SA MAJESTÉ
Fouad 1er
HOMMAGE
de la Colonie Suisse
d'Egypte
1929

BELOW
World time pocket watch, 1932. In 18K yellow gold, it features a silver dial divided into three sections. The central part boasts applied gold hour markers; the 24 hours in Arabic numerals revolve with the movement; the outer part indicates 31 major cities and locations worldwide. Model 3372

RIGHT-HAND PAGE
Ultra-thin pocket watch, 1931. Behind the apparent simplicity of this piece in 950 platinum, confirmed by an understated silver dial and its Arabic numerals, hides all the complexity of an ultra-thin watch. The caliber measures 0.94 mm thick. Inv. no. 10726

by his childhood friend King Alexander, who bought some of his most beautiful watches. One of them featured a square platinum case set with baguette-cut diamonds. Another was a skeletonized watch with an engraved movement in pink gold and a black-enameled gold case. At the end of that month, the New York stock market crash signaled the start of a terrible economic crisis around the world. It would shake the entire planet, ruin hundreds of thousands of people financially, and leave millions unemployed. Vacheron Constantin was not immune; from 1930, it was sucked into the storm. To avoid being laid off, its 75 employees took on jobs that were normally contracted out, such as making blanks. Some of them were even given the tasks of cleaning and repainting the workshops. The following year, the company was forced to reduce salaries, cut the working week to eighteen hours, and take on various mechanical jobs for a Geneva company that produced scientific instruments. Nevertheless, it gave all its personnel nine paid days off. Charles Constantin started to develop movements that could be sold at a lower price. In 1932, the workers were all moved into two workshops in order to save on heating bills. It is likely that one of their jobs was to assemble a

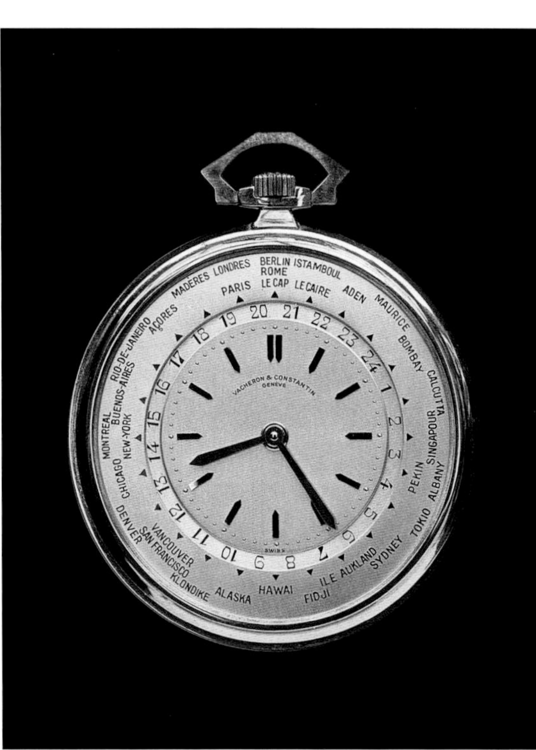

completely new watch with an extremely modern geometric design (a round bezel with a ten-sided flange on an octagonal case). They could not have known that this design, together with its screw-down case back, made it the first authentic sports watch at Vacheron Constantin, a forerunner of the Overseas. It was introduced the following year. Meanwhile, Charles Constantin traveled around Europe with his *marmotte*, a presentation box full of watches, trying to sell his stock and rustle up some new orders. Nothing worked, not even a general reduction in prices since all Swiss watchmakers were doing the same. The next two years saw the crisis reach its peak. Beginning in early 1933, all the workers were laid off. Some of them would be called in as required to meet the occasional order. To avoid total collapse, the management tried very hard to diversify its activities. Aside from the work it carried out for the Geneva manufacturer of scientific instruments, it developed some mechanisms for the Geneva gas works and even went as far as to produce silver trimmings for a shoe company. In the autumn, some female workers were employed to pick grapes on Charles Constantin's property.

However, as always in difficult times, Vacheron Constantin took advantage of the crisis to invent and create. Of course, its imagination was active at other times, too: in the 1920s, two important innovations emerged from the workshops. In 1922, Georges Grandjean asked one of the best young mechanics to develop a microphone that, like a stethoscope, would enable watchmakers to check the rate of small movements. This invention helped pave the way for the vibrograph timing machine that is commonly used by all watch manufacturers today. In another area, less technical but still essential for the correct functioning of a movement, a high-quality lubricating oil was developed in 1926. It was soon being ordered by all of Vacheron Constantin's watchmaker clients. In the 1920s, the company also filed a number of patents. Among them was an index (used to adjust the precision of a movement) invented by Georges Grandjean and a barrel developed by another in-house mechanic named

VACHERON & CONSTANTIN
GENEVE
SWISS

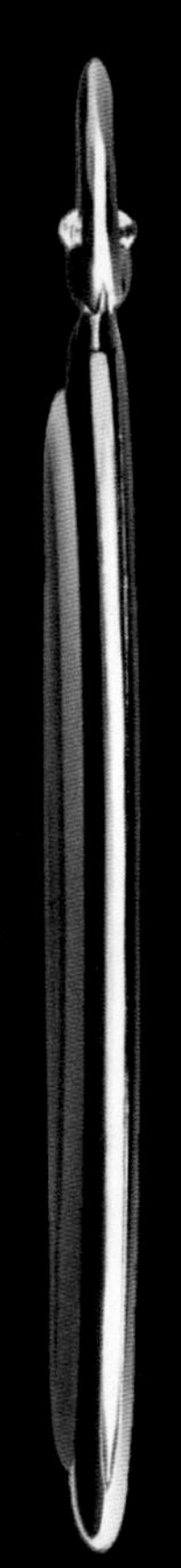

VACHERON & CONSTANTIN
GENEVE

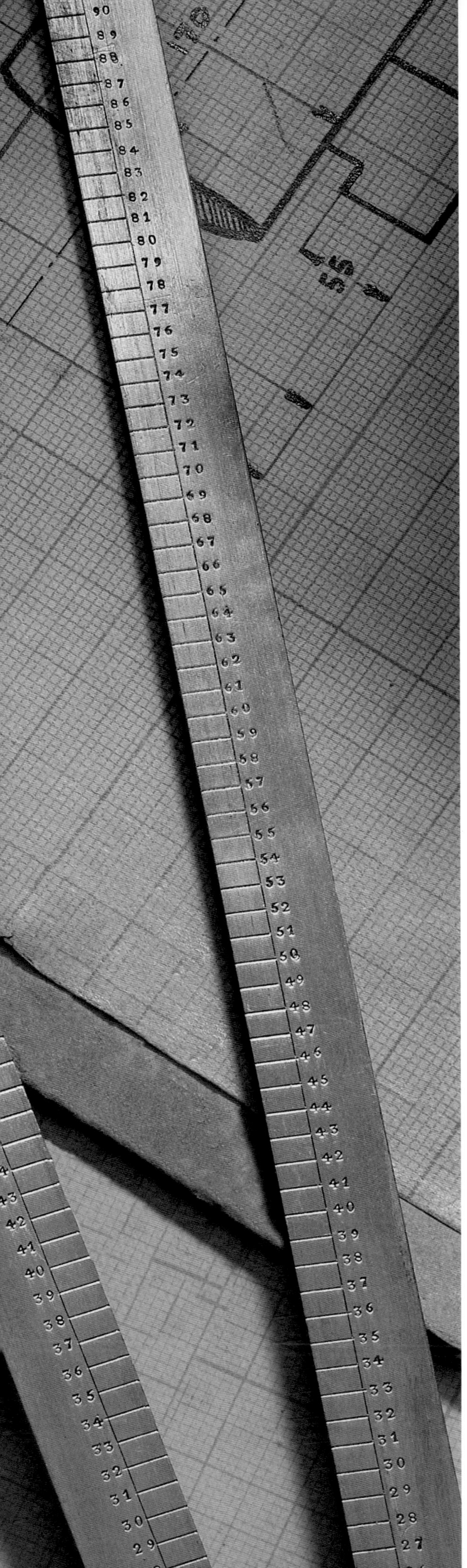

Köchli. Other highly innovative movements were also introduced, including one for the ART series of watches. A chronograph watch, Medicus, was intended specifically for use by doctors; its pulsometer scale enabled them to precisely check a patient's pulse rate. Vacheron Constantin, which had made pulsometers at the end of the nineteenth century, brought the tradition back for this modernized new model (it was reintroduced in a skeletonized version in the 1990s).

The economic crisis of the 1930s did not hinder innovative efforts – quite the contrary. The first evidence of this was the integration and rationalization of tasks in the workshops, led by Charles Constantin. Then came the crowning achievement, a brilliant invention by Albert Pellaton, who had joined the company in 1919. He became its senior technician and, in the dark years of 1933 and 1934, developed a portable timing instrument intended for sports events that could measure times to within one-tenth of a second. Its lightness, accuracy, and capacity to store timings on a metal strip would revolutionize top-level sports competitions. Its success began in motor racing when in 1935 it was the only official chronometer of the Swiss Grand Prix in Bern. Then, in 1937, it won first prize in the Colladon competition organized by the Geneva Society of Arts. But, more importantly for the company, it was an immediate commercial success. The management was greatly relieved when four examples were ordered in the first year: two by the Swiss Automobile Club and two by the Swiss Aero Club.

Time began to smile on Vacheron Constantin, and on precisely measured time in particular, in 1935 – which everyone thought would be the last of the dark years. The company, still under the impression it had been born in 1785 at the time of Abraham Vacheron, celebrated its 150th anniversary. But with the economic outlook still gloomy, the celebration was quite discreet. It was agreed to simply mark the occasion with two variations on a round anniversary wristwatch for men. Vacheron Constantin again proved its ability to adapt elegantly to difficulties: it based both models on one excellent pocket watch movement

OPPOSITE
Wristwatch, 1930. This 18K white and rose gold cushion-shaped watch with minute repeater highlights its functions by playing with contrasts. Inv. no. 11243

OPPOSITE AND FOLLOWING DOUBLE PAGE
Portable timing instrument and its automatic timekeeping system. Patented in 1935 and invented by Albert Pellaton for Vacheron Constantin, this timing instrument for sporting events is capable of measuring times to within 5/100th of a second.

0
500
1000
1500
2000

75
35

1935

FOLLOWING DOUBLE PAGE
The only man to have held the land and water speed records at the same time, Sir Malcolm Campbell (1885–1948), was the first to drive faster than 300 mph (485 kph), achieved at Bonneville Salt Flats (Utah, USA) in 1935 in his "Bluebird." Vacheron Constantin timed the record holder's performance on water in September 1938 on Hallwyl Lake when he broke his own record by reaching 210.68 kph.

ACE SUPER DISCS

RIGHT-HAND PAGE
Men's watch, 1935. Created for the 150th anniversary of Vacheron Constantin, which is believed to have been established in 1785, this 18K yellow gold timepiece is fitted with an antique pocket watch movement: the winding mechanism and the second subdial are on the same axis.
Inv. no. 10794

created thirty years prior. This explains why, in one model, the crown is positioned at 12 o'clock with the subdial for seconds at 6 o'clock. This arrangement was highly original in a wristwatch and since it enjoyed some success, was occasionally reproduced in the following years and redesigned in the 1990s. On the other model, the movement was turned to position the crown at the usual 3 o'clock location. This, of course, moved the seconds subdial to 9 o'clock. September 1935 gave the company more reason to believe its star was rising: the Prince of Wales – the future Edward VIII, then Duke of Windsor – paid a visit and bought three magnificent small clocks each with the crystal in blue, his favorite color. He signed the "Golden Book" created by Vacheron Constantin for its anniversary, in which all distinguished future visitors could add their signatures.

In 1936, another book appeared, but this time it was a piece of literature: *Sparkenbroke*, a novel with reflections on the act of writing, by a very famous English author at the time, Charles Morgan. At Lucques in Italy where he has a palace, the principal character, Lord Sparkenbroke takes the woman he loves to a jewelry shop. "The sound of a bell came from the inside room and when they entered the workshop, behind the counter she noticed the clock on a table with the names of Vacheron and Constantin engraved on the dial. "'What a delightful clock!' she said. 'And the interior is just as beautiful as the outside,' the jeweler told her, smiling and lifting the clock so gently that it might have been a child. This could not be said for all the clocks. [...] Piers mentioned that the escapement was outstanding for the period. 'But you know about clocks!' exclaimed the jeweler..."

The romantic fictional world of *Sparkenbroke* was apparently much sweeter than the grim reality of 1936. Yet business recovered, albeit slowly, stimulated by the devaluation of the Swiss franc. Employees were brought back and the reorganization started to bear fruit. However, the production infrastructure had deteriorated during the crisis and in 1937 the company was unable to meet the sudden increase in orders. The optimistic mood was tempered with anxiety. A position was found for Léon, the young nephew of Charles Constantin, born in 1919. The same year, Vacheron Constantin helped its employees set up a savings fund. But the anxiety increased, driven by the unstable political situation across Europe and by the aggression of neighboring Germany where Adolph Hitler, in power for four years, was threatening to seize back the territories lost in 1918. That was not a situation likely to improve the company's financial situation. It did not have the capital to invest in research, to modernize production equipment, or to support some of its agents in financial difficulty. Charles Constantin had just finished writing Vacheron Constantin's *"Annales de la Maison d'Horlogerie Vacheron et Constantin,"* a magnificent historical work covering the development of the company from 1785. He summarized the situation in a single phrase: "Despite my faith in the future, the financial question needed an immediate solution... and we could not find it." Yet the solution did appear in 1938 with a bold association between two of the most prestigious watchmakers in the world.

VACHERON CONSTANTIN
GENEVE
SWISS

V&C
GENEVE

1938–1999 EVOLUTION AND NEW HORIZONS

In the second half of the twentieth century, Vacheron Constantin continued to innovate and enchant with extra-thin watches, sporty and luxury styles, and exquisite jewelry watches: royalty, heads of state, and film stars alike flocked to the boutique on the island in the heart of Geneva. The company then became the Richemont group's icing on the cake.

1938

PREVIOUS LEFT-HAND PAGE
Wristwatches from the Driver line, 1939. Typical of these models, the 18K pink gold case takes the original form of a horizontal rectangle. Depending on the model, the winding crown is at 3 o'clock or 12 o'clock.
Inv. no. 11155 and 11164

RIGHT-HAND PAGE
Wristwatch, 1940. This curved rectangular piece is named Air Flow.
Inv. no. 11198

FOLLOWING DOUBLE PAGE
The master jeweler and engraver workshops of Vacheron Constantin, Quai de L'Île in Geneva, 1930s.

In April 1938, a company employee, Carlo Sarzano, announced that he wanted to set up in Turin to represent watchmaker Jaeger-LeCoultre along with Vacheron Constantin, if the management agreed. It did agree, and on April 16 he was asked to tell Jaeger-LeCoultre about his idea of an association between the two companies. The next day, Sarzano telephoned Georges Ketterer, the commercial director of Jaeger-LeCoultre, to explain his project and received a positive reaction. On April 25, two managers from Vacheron Constantin, Charles Constantin and Henri Wallner (who joined the company in 1908) met with Georges Ketterer in Lausanne to outline a possible association. The discussions continued in total secrecy until August 4, when a definitive agreement was signed, which came into force on September 1. SAPIC (*Société Anonyme de Produits Industriels et Commerciaux*), a joint company, was formed, comprising Vacheron Constantin, Jaeger-LeCoultre, and the latter's various subsidiaries. Jaeger-LeCoultre would leave Lausanne and move its headquarters into the refurbished premises of Vacheron Constantin in Geneva. Vacheron Constantin would remain independently managed but a majority of the board of directors would be from Jaeger-LeCoultre, including its president, Jacques David LeCoultre, its chief executive, Paul Lebet, and its commercial director, Georges Ketterer.

As Charles Constantin privately admitted, the agreement was signed "not without sadness," but it did present some obvious advantages for Vacheron Constantin: Jaeger-LeCoultre provided the means to continue technical and commercial development; in other words, it secured the company's future. Critically, it also guaranteed total freedom to grow and preserve its own technical expertise. Vacheron Constantin's identity, based on its long history, would be protected, and the company would remain distinct from Jaeger-LeCoultre. One of the main constraints was that the development of movements would be shared, under the leadership of Vacheron Constantin's partner, but this would not affect the quality of the watches. More painfully, the agreement meant giving up the long and cordial relationship with Verger Frères, its agent in Paris. In practice, however, this would do no harm since it was replaced by Établissements Jaeger with its many prestigious clients. For Jaeger-LeCoultre, the agreement was just as beneficial: Vacheron Constantin was a brand boasting worldwide prestige, excellent technical expertise, efficient staff, extensive and valuable stock, a network of agencies abroad, and a magnificent shop in the center of Geneva.

Jaeger-LeCoultre was a flourishing business in healthy financial condition. It was created through the merger of the manufacture *LeCoultre et Compagnie* in Le Sentier and the *Société Anonyme des Établissements Edmond Jaeger* in Paris in 1937.

The Jura manufacture was founded in 1833 by Antoine LeCoultre in Le Sentier in the Vallée de Joux. One of its many inventions was the crown winding system developed between 1846 and 1847, which became widely adopted both in Swiss watchmaking and abroad. The company specialized in producing high-quality movements that were promptly purchased by the leading watchmakers of the time. *La Société Anonyme des Établissements Edmond Jaeger* was set up in 1919; it continued the approach of the watchmaking workshop opened by Edmond Jaeger in Paris in 1880.

As soon as the agreement was signed, the two companies set out to combine their strengths and skills. In 1939, they exhibited their products together at the Basel Fair and the Universal Exhibition in New York. As an aside, in those days when people were still fascinated by automobiles, trains, and airplanes, their new products included two shaped watches, one intended for drivers, aptly named Driver, and the other with an aerodynamic profile named Air Flow. At Vacheron Constantin, the agreement led to an important reorganization of the management team. Paul Lebet took over the workshops and supervised the case-making operations. Georges Ketterer was the new commercial director, assisted by Léon Constantin. Henri Wallner, the driving force behind the agreement, took charge of day-to-day management, while Charles Constantin was responsible for the shop. Albert Pellaton, however, left the company, since the movements were chiefly produced in the Le Sentier

VACHERON CONSTANTIN
GENÈVE
SWISS

VACHERON & CONSTANTIN
GENÈVE
SWISS

workshops. Fundamentally reorganized, but stronger, Vacheron Constantin prepared to face the dramatic years ahead.

On September 1, 1939, the invasion of Poland by Nazi Germany marked the start of World War II. Two days later, France and Britain declared war on Germany and proclaimed a general mobilization. The tragic events that ensued over the next six years would be an appalling catastrophe. Sixty million people would die in the greatest cataclysm in human history, one-third of them in the Soviet Union, which was attacked by Germany in June of 1941. At the end of the war, half of Europe would be considered severely damaged. Yet beyond the measurable cost in lives and materials (two trillion dollars' worth of damage), the toll was very heavy in moral terms: international treaties torn up, human rights violated, entire peoples humiliated, massive deportations, bombardment and massacre of civilians, forced labor and torture of prisoners, meticulously planned mass murder of Jews and, at the end, the fear of total annihilation by nuclear weapons. World War II revealed the full extent of mankind's inhumanity. Yet, out of this horror, this weakness of the human spirit, and the hesitation when faced with such a cruel but well organized beast, a few rare artists emerged who were able to reflect on it without hatred, but with dignity. Some were survivors of the holocaust, such as the writers Primo Levi (*If This Is a Man*) and Imre Kertész (*Fatelessness*).

At the start of the war, many foreigners living in Geneva and nearby cities left Switzerland to return home. Switzerland itself called upon all men, including the technical staff, office workers, and managers of Vacheron Constantin. Even Georges Ketterer spent several months in the army. Business stopped almost entirely until the end of the year, then gradually recovered slightly in 1940. However, Swiss watchmaking again benefited to some extent from the country's neutrality, and Vacheron Constantin again managed to find ways around difficulties and adapt to dramatic circumstances. In the war years, when Switzerland was a haven of peace at the heart of a blazing continent, it restarted jewelry work that was badly damaged everywhere else, published its own magazine, *Heure*, and successfully took part in the annual watch and jewelry exhibitions in Geneva. People looking for a safe investment in a time of crisis were buying heavy gold objects as well as cigarette boxes, bracelets, clip watches, and brooch watches set with precious stones. At the same time, the company launched larger sized wristwatches with dials measuring 42 mm in diameter. Switzerland's special status meant it could also produce items ordered from abroad. Although the country was surrounded by Axis forces, Vacheron Constantin could still send watches to the United States and to Great Britain. It was constantly searching for solutions to new problems that arose every day. When, in 1941, the Italian government banned all trading in gold objects, the company acted to avoid losing one of its most important markets, adapting its tooling to produce cases and bracelets in steel.

It was important to keep spirits up despite the grim events and thus in the summer of 1942, the city of Geneva celebrated its 2,000th anniversary (dating from the first written record of its existence): Julius Caesar mentioned it in *The Gallic Wars* when he described crossing the Rhône in 58 BCE. Was it so silly to celebrate this event when the German army was launching its grand offensive toward the Volga and oil wells of the

LEFT-HAND PAGE AND BELOW
Aluminum pocket watch, 1945. The dial, hands, and most of the mechanism of this watch are in aluminum, weighing a total 19.61 grams. Inv. no. 10167

1948

RIGHT-HAND PAGE
Ladies' jewelry watch, 1948. The 18K yellow gold case is set with 26 carved emeralds and 38 diamonds that frame a red gold dial. Inv. no. 10353

Caucasus? When Rommel was just 100 kilometers from Alexandria and train cars pulling sinister, sealed wagons were moving all across continental Europe? Perhaps. But at least the children of Geneva could enjoy the beautiful picture book they received, a grand parade displaying historical costumes, and a wonderful window-dressing competition. Vacheron Constantin received first prize for the old Cabinotier workshop it recreated in one of its windows on Quai de Moulins, including the very bench that Georges Leschot had used for decades.

But the festivities were only a brief distraction from grim reality. To deal with food shortages caused by the ban on imports, in 1942 the federal government obliged every company to cultivate a garden proportional in size to its number of employees. Vacheron Constantin bought some land in Cointrin and divided it into plots of 100 m^2 that were allocated free to employees, provided fertilizer, and installed a cabin with all the tools required. When it wanted to sell the land after the war, some employees who had grown fond of horticulture bought a few plots and built their own cabin.

In 1944, Vacheron Constantin and Jaeger-LeCoultre set up a joint provident fund for the staff. At that time, Charles Constantin was still in charge of the shop, a Swiss haven of peace where most of the company's retail sales would continue to be made. He recorded that an average of fifty clients came to the Rue des Moulins location every day. The temperature was more agreeable in the luxuriously furnished shop than in the offices and workshops where staff shivered under the stringent heating restrictions. However, the company had a more pressing concern: the supply of certain metals. Gold and silver were still available, although precious metals were subject to quotas. Platinum was much harder to find since it was a war material like tin and copper. The situation was no better for precious stones: all stocks had been exhausted since the start of the war. At the same time, the company lacked the finances to launch any new designs and was finding it difficult to keep some models in stock such as calendar watches and certain chronographs. Nevertheless, it did everything possible to continue producing new marvels that would excite its clients. For example, it created a large number of watches with dials decorated in cloisonné or champlevé enamel.

Nazi Germany finally collapsed. It surrendered on May 7 and 8, 1945, followed by Japan on September 2. On October 24, the birth of the United Nations was a tremendous sign of hope for the whole world, with its charter proclaiming human rights, equality among peoples, the principle of non-intervention, and the preservation of peace. Its headquarters were set up in New York, but Geneva retained much of its international role by hosting a satellite UN office together with numerous UN organizations such as the World Health Organization (WHO) and the International Labor Office (ILO).

For Vacheron Constantin, peace meant that everything was possible once again. Georges Ketterer replaced Paul Lebet, who had died in July, on the board of directors and his influence was growing. He seized every opportunity for Vacheron Constantin and constantly encouraged the creativity of its watchmakers. The postwar years were marked by a series of daring watches that seemed to celebrate the return of freedom. An aluminum watch, for example, was an extraordinary tribute to a new era. Yet it was really a response to the biggest aluminum company's search for new, peaceful, and prestigious applications for this metal now that wartime demand had come to an end. Vacheron Constantin was the only watchmaker to accept the challenge. It created one of the lightest pocket watches ever produced: at 19.61 grams, it weighed less than half of an equivalent watch in gold or silver. The case, the dial, and almost all of the movement were crafted in aluminum (pages 146–147).

At that time, some of the most enthusiastic clients in the Geneva shop were American soldiers on leave from their bases in Germany and Italy. It was thanks to them that watches were soon selling better than the jewelry that had represented half of the company's turnover during the war. American officers would even come into the shop with backpacks full of valuable items such as cameras and ask which watches they could have in

LEFT-HAND PAGE AND OPPOSITE
Butterfly wristwatch, 1952. The curved shaped rectangular case in 18K yellow gold perfectly hugs the wrist. The gilt dial features Arabic numerals. Inv. no. 10974

OPPOSITE
Advertisement, late 1940s.

RIGHT-HAND PAGE
Wristwatch ref. 6087, 1954. This 18K yellow gold chronograph with 30-minute counter and tachometer is water-resistant and features so-called "cow horn" handles. Inv. no. 11056

OPPOSITE
Advertisement, 1950s.

exchange. In 1946, the Bern office of the American army of occupation in Germany became one of the company's most important clients, ordering all kinds of watches and small clocks. That year, the new era even affected the official articles of Vacheron Constantin: it removed the *Ancienne Maison* that had rather weakened its name. From then on, all watch dials, as well as invoices, documents and correspondence, would simply carry the name Vacheron Constantin. In another sign of modernity, 1945 saw the workshops become equipped with new milling machines, drills, and lathes, each powered by its own electric motor.

Vacheron Constantin had never enjoyed such prestige. In 1946, Bulent Raouf, husband of Princess Fawzia, sister of King Farouk of Egypt, bought an extraordinary watch on behalf of his king. No fewer than thirteen hands were displayed on its dial. It was one of the most complicated pieces in the history of Vacheron Constantin, manufactured in 1931 then adjusted in 1934 by Edmond Olivier, the company's precision timer. In 1994 in Geneva, the Farouk watch sold for more than one million Swiss francs in the very first themed auction devoted to Vacheron Constantin. For other royals there were other fabulous gifts: in 1947, to mark the marriage of Queen Elizabeth II to Lieutenant Philip Mountbatten, the Swiss Federation presented her with a platinum wristwatch set with brilliant-cut diamonds signed Vacheron Constantin. In 1951, King Bhumibol Adulyadej of Thailand bought 176 very beautiful objects including 48 watches and approximately 100 small clocks. Also in 1951, Belgium's Leopold III chose two gold watches. Two years later, his son, King Baudoin, chose two watches, one in gold and the other in steel. Meanwhile, Crown Prince Akihito of Japan asked to visit the workshops on Quai des Moulins and marveled at the meticulous skill of the watchmakers. The signatures in the Golden Book of the Geneva shop included orchestra conductor Ernest Ansermet; film stars Mary Pickford, Tyrone Power, and Pierre Fresnay; and the mysterious Lana Marconi, who claimed to be the natural daughter of King Carol II of Romania and who had just married Sacha Guitry. Very often, the clients, whether famous or not, did not simply buy a beautiful piece of jewelry or a watch. Many of them were just passing through Geneva and, not having much to do, liked to linger an hour or two in the luxurious, welcoming ambiance of the shop, admiring pieces and chatting with the sales staff.

A watchmaker's reputation is all the greater if his movements are shown to be the most precise on the market. So in 1947, Vacheron Constantin entered nineteen pieces in the Geneva Observatory competition, winning thirteen first prizes and setting three precision records. The following year, it entered eight pieces in the Neuchâtel International Competition, taking home the first prize for each in its category. In 1949, Edmond Olivier set several records at the Geneva Observatory, including the record for individual pieces with 922 points out of 1,000.

The man whose company had supplied the blanks for these highly precise movements, Jacques David LeCoultre, a great watchmaker in the outstanding Jura tradition, passed away in May 1948. Georges Ketterer became president of the board of directors of Vacheron Constantin. The following year, Charles Constantin retired. This left his nephew Léon as the last representative of the famous line. Like his grandfather François, he enjoyed traveling. He went as far south as Africa to open new markets. After leading the company for more than forty years, Henri Wallner died in 1951 followed by Charles Constantin in 1954. They were the last surviving members of the team that had managed the company through its most difficult years, the 1930s. But most people simply wanted to forget that period; it was new men who prepared to celebrate the Vacheron Constantin bicentennial, which had been moved up to 1955 upon discovery of the famous Ésaïe Hetier apprenticeship contract.

Despite these events marking the end of an era, the company recovered well thanks to its creative heart that beat strongly. In response to an order in 1951, it introduced a new watch in 1952 with a curved square case that was a great success. It was immediately nicknamed Cioccolatone since it was shaped like a Swiss chocolate treat sold in Italy. In 1998, it inspired a watch named Toledo, which in 2003 first integrated a complete calendar display.

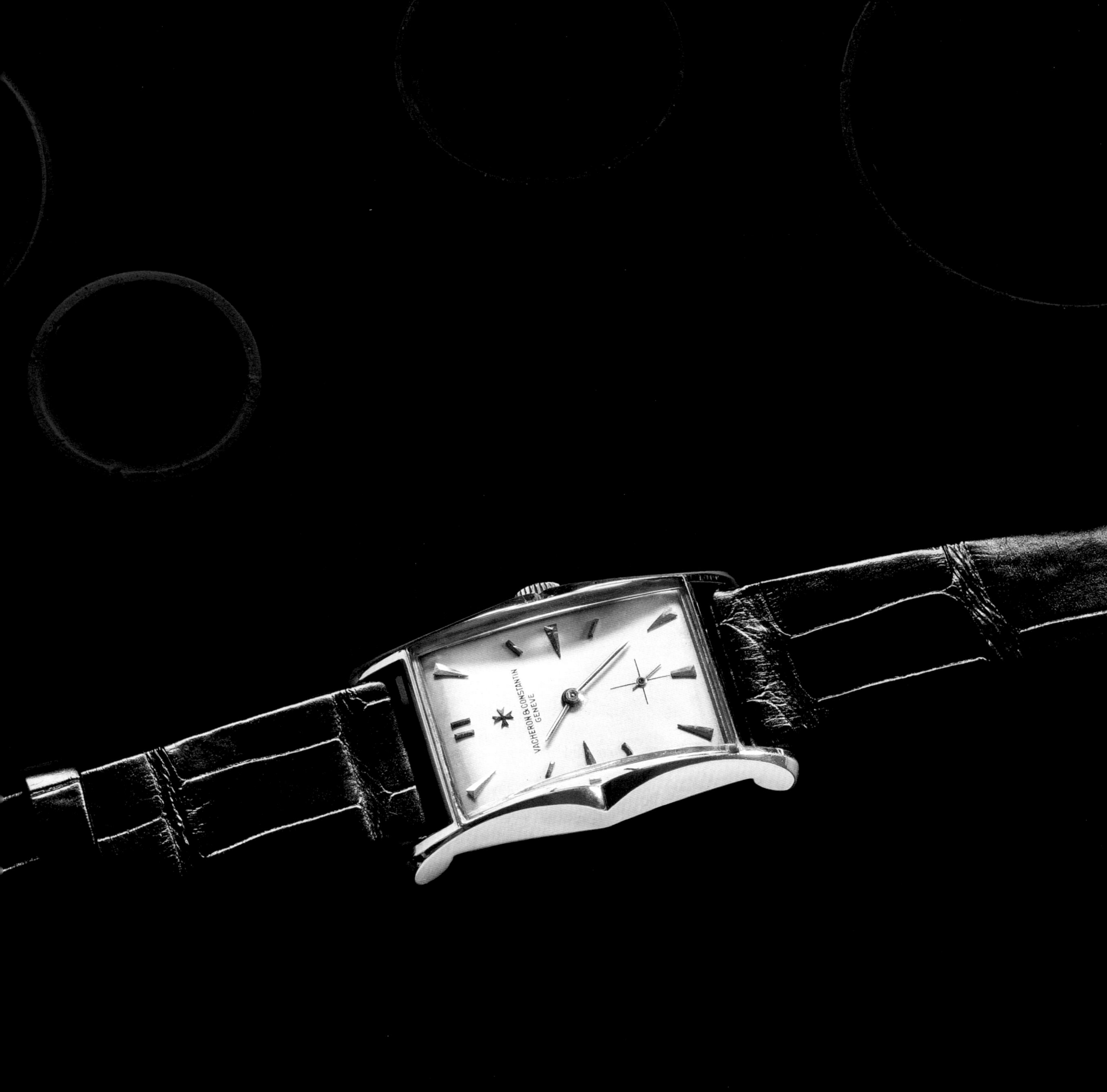
VACHERON & CONSTANTIN
GENEVE

OPPOSITE
So-called Aronde wristwatch, curved rectangular shape, 1955. Inv. no. 10416

OPPOSITE
AND RIGHT-HAND PAGE
Advertisement presenting the ultra-thin models created to celebrate the bicentennial of Vacheron Constantin, 1955.

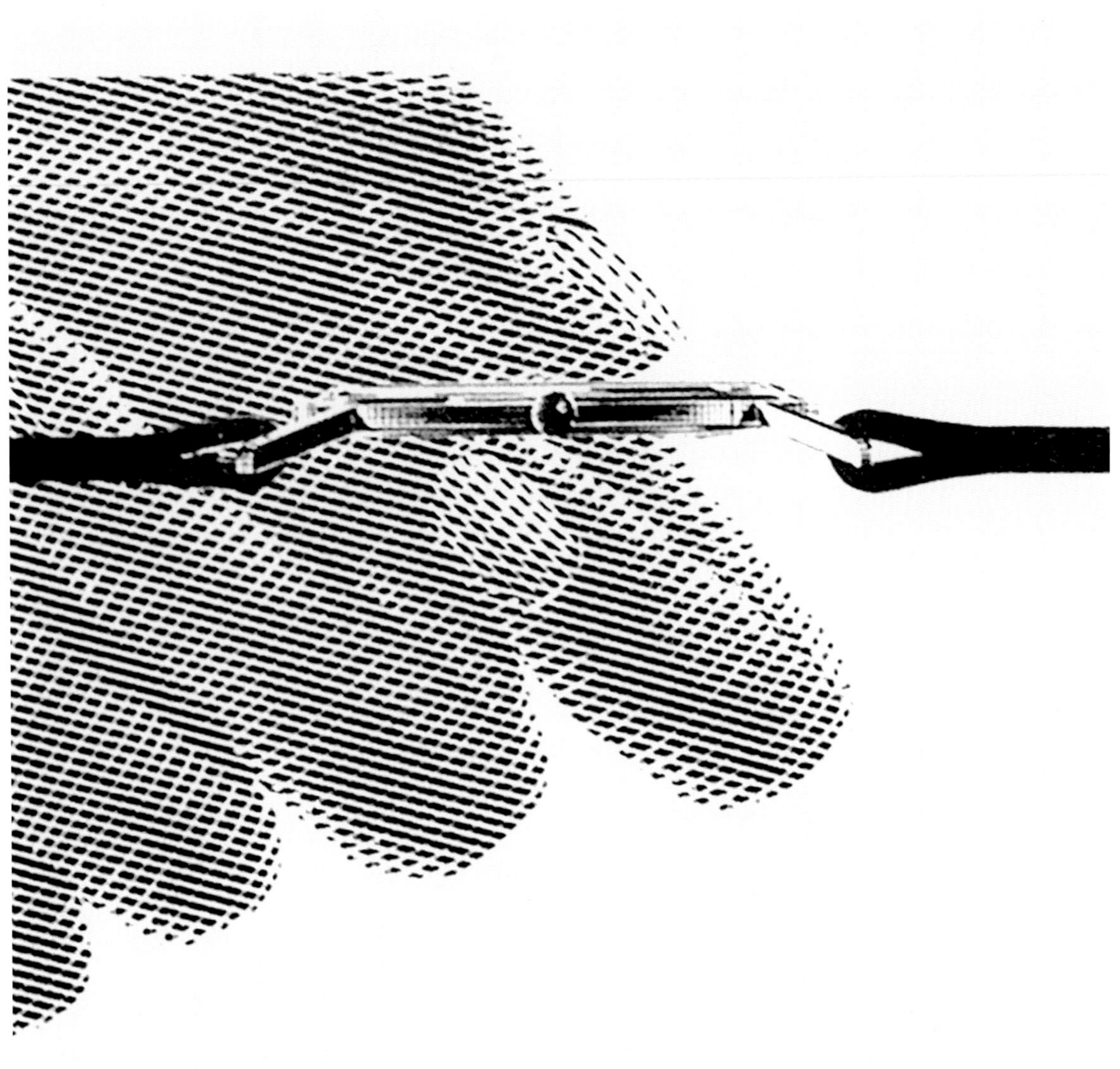

La montre
la plus plate
*du monde**

Elle représente le brillant aboutissement de deux siècles de maîtrise horlogère.

Abritant quelque 120 pièces dans l'épaisseur d'un écu, la montre Vacheron & Constantin «extra-plate» est non seulement un véritable miracle de la technique, mais aussi un chef-d'œuvre d'élégance.

Vacheron & Constantin sont fiers d'avoir présenté à l'occasion de leur Bicentenaire ce témoignage magistral de leur fidélité à la tradition dont ils assument la continuité.

* *la seule avec mouvement de 1,64 mm d'épaisseur*

Chaque modèle extra-plat est présenté dans un portefeuille en cuir de luxe.

A GENÈVE DEPUIS 1755

1955

RIGHT-HAND PAGE
Wristwatch, 1955. This 18K pink gold ultra-thin watch, launched to celebrate the brand's bicentennial, has a silvered dial with fine baton-shaped hour markers. Inv. no. 11607

The day of the week and the month appeared in two apertures while a red arrow hand indicated the date on a dial that was marked from 1 to 31. The phases of the moon were also displayed on a small subdial at 6 o'clock (page 241). The watch reappeared in 2003, and again in 2013, as the Historiques Toledo 1951, part of the Historiques collection. The 2013 model in pink gold maintained the simplicity of the original watch but enhanced it with a new graphic treatment, playing expertly with its curved-and-square form. The dial center was decorated with hand-crafted guilloché work and its self-winding caliber was stamped with the Hallmark of Geneva.

In 1954, three years after the Cioccolatone, another watch with an original design appeared, this time rectangular with double rounded corners on the sides of the case as well as a curved crystal. It, too, was reintroduced in the Historiques collection in 2011, as the Historiques Aronde 1954. The name, which means "swallow's wing" in old French, refers to the original shape of the case. Other technical and design features of the watch made it a success: a dial with fine hand-crafted guilloché work (inspired by one version of the original watch), and a hand-wound caliber stamped with the Hallmark of Geneva and boasting a power reserve of forty hours.

In the bicentennial year 1955, one of the world's most prestigious watch brands could finally announce that it was also the oldest watch manufacturer to have operated without interruption for 200 years. Georges Ketterer wrote the foreword to an elegant brochure, *Les Maîtres des Heures*, which told the story of these two centuries of excellence. While the men and women of Vacheron Constantin were certainly proud of its technical and design prestige, its purely horological achievements probably made them even happier. To celebrate the bicentennial appropriately, Vacheron Constantin produced three wristwatches in an anniversary series fitted with a new development that caused a sensation: at 1.64 mm, the nine-ligne, round movement was the thinnest ever made for a standard-sized watch to that point. Caliber 1003 crowned thirty years of development by the company's technicians. Since the 1920s, they had ingeniously inserted ultra-thin movements into precious cases and, sometimes, into valuable coins. The watch housing the movement, with a very simple round dial presenting only hour markers and two hands, illustrated the timeless, uncompromising classicism that was always admired in Vacheron Constantin, particularly in those years of the 1950s. This elegant simplicity was repeated from 1957 onward in a round, ultra-thin watch with circular graining between the hour markers and a fine cross at 6 o'clock where a delicate hand indicated the seconds. In 2004, the Patrimony collection was inspired to revisit this theme of supreme refinement and ultimate elegance. The movement created in 1955 would equip several watch models over the following decades, and was considered one of the masterpieces of twentieth-century watchmaking. In 2010, it was rebuilt in gold to meet the norms of the Hallmark of Geneva, and it comprised the heart of the ultra-thin Historiques 1955. This watch was the ultimate expression of ultra-thin expertise: at 4.13 mm, it was the thinnest hand-wound mechanical watch in the world at that time.

In July 1955, during the "Big Four" summit conference in Geneva, where the Americans, British, French, and Russians met for the first time since Yalta, leading figures in Geneva presented seven Vacheron Constantin watches to the heads of state and their ministers: American President Dwight D. Eisenhower; Russian ministers Nikolai Bulganin and Vyacheslav Molotov; British representatives Anthony Eden and Harold MacMillan; and French ministers Edgar Faure and Antoine Pinay. When in Geneva, a growing number of world leaders visited the shop, as their signatures in the Golden Books showed. In the months and years that followed, Vacheron Constantin welcomed Emperor Haïlé Selassie of Ethiopia, King Ibn Saud of Saudi Arabia, Queen Frederika of Greece, the Shah of Iran, and King Talal of Jordan to mention only the crowned heads.

In 1957, Vacheron Constantin again demonstrated its talent for innovation with the first world time wristwatch: Reference 6213 was powered by a self-winding movement that indicated the time in the world's major cities by

VACHERON & CONSTANTIN
GENÈVE

VACHERON & CONSTANTIN
GENEVE

means of a revolving dial. The development of this movement, derived from the "Cottier system," had initially begun in 1937 but had been disrupted by World War II. The company's expertise in precise chronometry was never in doubt, either; it was recognized in 1960 by the Cantonal Observatory of Neuchâtel with a series prize for the four best pocket chronometers presented in competition. Many other distinctions followed in the 1960s.

In 1965, the history of Vacheron Constantin took an important turn: Its president, Georges Ketterer, who had also become the majority shareholder, separated it from Jaeger-LeCoultre and from their joint holding entity SAPIC. The two companies had been together for almost thirty years, and had produced some wonderful advances in the world of watchmaking. But Ketterer wanted total freedom to create and manufacture. This meant that the company was on its own to face the great evolution just around the corner: the arrival of quartz, which would threaten Switzerland's overwhelming domination of the horological world.

In fact, this domination had been shaken once already by Timex, an American watchmaker of industrial scale. It had launched an eponymous low-cost watch in the 1950s. In 1962, one in every three watches sold in the United States was a Timex. It soon set up in France and Germany under the name of Kelton. Of course, this watch with its basic case and not-very-reliable movement was no competition for high-quality Swiss models. But Timex also produced more sophisticated watches, which began to gain market share thanks to significantly lower prices than the Swiss equivalents offered. The new challenge, however, came from the Japanese and was much more difficult to overcome. Quartz technology first appeared in the United States at the end of the 1920s. By replacing the vibrations of a mechanical watch with the very high oscillating frequencies of quartz, precision to two-thousandths of a second per day was guaranteed. This shattered all the records set by mechanical movements, but applied only to clocks that were isolated in cabinets three meters high. Some thirty years of miniaturization work was needed to produce a quartz watch that could be worn on the wrist. This arrived in 1968.

The Japanese watchmaking industry took a considerable lead in the quartz market and maintained it until the 1980s when Switzerland finally caught up with the Swatch. Its unique blend of electronics and imagination made the Swatch a perfect fit for the times with the brilliant engineering and sophisticated design of Swiss watchmaking.

The Swiss watchmakers' slow reaction to quartz can be largely explained by the great success of their traditional products: from 1963; the Swiss economy was booming and exports were significantly rising. A record was set in 1974 when 84.4 million watches and movements were exported. From that time onward, the industry was fully occupied in meeting the ever-growing demand for its mechanical watches and paid limited attention to the new technology.

However, there was another reason why most prestigious Swiss watchmakers avoided confronting the Japanese in their sector of the market: it was focused on very low-priced, virtually disposable watches. For watch lovers, quartz was always associated with the bottom range. The few big Swiss watchmakers who decided to invest in quartz movements fitted them into the kind of valuable cases that had made them famous for centuries. They soon found they were flirting with

1957

LEFT-HAND PAGE
Wristwatch, 1957.
The ancestor of the Patrimony, this 18K yellow gold watch features a manual-winding mechanical movement.
Inv. no. 11818

OPPOSITE
First wristwatch with World Time automatic movement, 1957. The silvered dial boasts a central zone with applied gold hour markers, 24 hours in Arabic numerals revolving with the movement with day/night indication, and an outer part indicating 42 major cities and locations worldwide. Ref. 6213

1972

RIGHT-HAND PAGE
Wristwatch 1972, presented at the Prix Prestige de la France. On June 23, 1972, in the ceremonial lounges of the prestigious Hotel Ritz, the Comité de France awarded Vacheron Constantin the rare and coveted *Diplôme du Prestige de la France* to pay tribute to the brand's distinctive expertise, supported by its determination to provide authenticity, technical perfection, and elegance. Vacheron Constantin was the first watch manufacture to receive this award. Made of 18K yellow gold, the watches christened 1972 are characterized by their asymmetrical shape. The watch in the center boasts two time zones. Inv. no. 10766, 11671, and 11689

disaster and returned to mechanical movements. Vacheron Constantin preferred to stick to traditional watchmaking by working with specialists in complications, continually improving the quality of its mechanical movements, and creating wonderful pieces that highlighted the prestige of fine watchmaking. The company believed it was not enough for its watches to be superb instruments produced by expert craftsmen; they also had to be beautiful examples of design.

During those years, Vacheron Constantin also started looking carefully at a promising niche that had not yet been fully explored: the jewelry watch, mainly intended for women. Georges Ketterer, the man who had understood the need to stay with traditional watchmaking, passed away in 1969. His son Jacques, born in 1931, succeeded him as president of Vacheron Constantin. His first important honor came in 1972 when the company was awarded the *Prestige de la France* prize, a major distinction at that time. To celebrate this event, the company created a wristwatch with a most unusual design: a trapezium-shaped case. It also featured a very elegant dial (right-hand page). The watch was widely admired and was even reissued almost thirty years later. In 1977, for its 222nd anniversary, Vacheron Constantin created another watch that was destined to have an unusual future. It was named the 222 and produced in steel, gold, and two-tone steel and gold. Loyal clients of the brand were astonished by its defiantly masculine design: it included a notched bezel like part of a mechanism, a Maltese cross emblem engraved directly on the case, and an integrated metal bracelet. It was the company's first luxury watch that was also a sports watch, and is considered the chief inspiration for the Overseas, which was introduced about twenty years later.

In 1979, the Kallista watch, the most dazzling piece of Geneva watchmaking ever produced, opened the way to very exclusive jewelry watches combining the three most valuable features: precious metal, cut gemstones, and a mechanical movement (page 169). This forerunner of the Kalla line, which lasted for many years, was made as a special order for a client who had the company swear an oath that his name would

VACHERON CONSTANTIN
GENÈVE
VACHERON CONSTANTIN
VACHERON CONSTANTIN
GENÈVE

VACHERON CONSTANTIN
GENEVE
AUTOMATIC
SWISS

222
de VACHERON CONSTANTIN

LEFT-HAND PAGE
The wristwatch named 222, 1977. In water-resistant stainless steel, this watch with self-winding mechanical movement celebrates the 222nd anniversary of Vacheron Constantin. Its distinctive design met with immediate public acclaim. Notched bezel, integrated bracelet, anthracite blue dial, and luminescent baton-shaped markers establish it firmly in the luxury sports watch segment. It is the ancestor of the Overseas. Inv. no. 11524

OPPOSITE
Advertisement, 1977.

BELOW
Lithograph inspired by Kallista, 1979, by Raymond Moretti, French painter and sculptor (1931–2005).

RIGHT-HAND PAGE
Kallista wristwatch, 1979. A unique piece, it was for a time the most expensive watch in the world. Designed by Raymond Moretti, it is sculpted from a one-kilogram ingot of solid gold, from which 140 grams of its final weight are extracted. The Kallista is enhanced by 118 emerald-cut diamonds representing a total 130 carats. Inv. no. 10150

remain confidential and that only one example would be produced. This jewelry watch, designed by Raymond Moretti, was sold for $5 million (more than $10 million today), which made it the world's most expensive watch at that time. Kallista means "most beautiful" in Greek, a name that was fully deserved: the watch, weighing 140 grams, was carved from a one-kilogram ingot of solid gold. Its bracelet and case were both adapted perfectly to the shape of the wrist and set with 118 emerald-cut diamonds totaling 130 carats. The diamonds were meticulously selected to present the same color, the same level of purity, and the same brilliance. This masterpiece of the watchmaker's art firmly held a place in the long Geneva tradition, requiring no less than 6,000 hours of work.

The appearance of the Kallista watch at that moment perhaps heralded the devastating economic crisis about to unfold. Fine watchmaking, like all sectors of the luxury market, had suffered the effects of the first oil crisis of 1973, and Swiss watch exports went into decline until 1984. Vacheron Constantin had withstood the shock better than others, thanks to its reputation and the loyalty of its clients, but it was still badly affected. In 1974, sales collapsed and the company was forced to put one-quarter of its staff on part-time work. The decision to continue making high-quality mechanical watches was looking hard to justify. Although the company remained in a fragile state for some years, the decision was soon proven right: the Swiss mechanical watch eventually found a profitable niche at the top end of the market.

Georges and Jacques Ketterer had represented the soul of Vacheron Constantin for half a century. When Jacques Ketterer died in 1987, Saudi Sheik Ahmed Zaki Yamani – a friend of Ketterer and a long-time admirer of Vacheron Constantin, who had moved to Geneva to carry out his role in OPEC – became the majority shareholder. It was Sheik Yamani who called in a leading professional to manage the company: Neuchâtel native Claude-Daniel Proellochs, whose family had long been involved in watchmaking.

In 1988, Vacheron Constantin was producing only 3,400 watches annually, and there was fear that focusing on such a small number of clients risked its long-term future. Then a strange

VACHERON CONSTANTIN
GENÈVE

OPPOSITE
Wristwatch, 1992. Behind its sapphire crystal covering, this 18K pink gold minute repeater watch offers a view of the incredible overlapping gears of its ultra-thin 3.28 mm skeletonized movement, entirely hand-decorated and hand-engraved.
Inv. no. 11497

event, one that had nothing to do with watchmaking, helped give it new momentum. A Swiss law that has since been altered, the Lex Friedrich, was enacted in 1985; it seriously restricted the rights of foreigners to acquire real estate. As a result, Sheik Yamani could not remain the owner of the historic Vacheron Constantin building on Rue de Moulins, and it was sold. The company was forced to leave part of its premises and become a tenant of the shop and floor of offices. Proceeds from the sale were immediately used to finance the creation of a new collection of watches, presented at the Basel Watch and Jewelry Fair in 1989. With the Phidias watches – named in homage to the greatest golden age sculptor of Ancient Greece – Vacheron Constantin was opening up to contemporary design in its collections. Yet it also remained traditional by producing a model specifically made to meet demand: a technical sports watch with a self-winding movement and an integrated bracelet that would become another forerunner of the Overseas watch.

The other lines presented that year in Basel drew even more on the company's rich heritage to illustrate this renewal. The Historiques line was the best example: connoisseurs appreciated several evocative reinterpretations of the traditional house style. This collection signaled a return to the company's roots and design codes and influenced new models in the years to follow. In 1989, it created a richly nostalgic timepiece: its railroad track dial was a modern version of the Empire-style pieces "à la Breguet" characteristic of Vacheron Constantin creations in the early nineteenth century and again in the 1940s. The company's technical expertise was demonstrated in other lines and included jewelry watches with complications – a self-winding chronograph and a perpetual calendar with moon phases in a skeletonized version – as well as several beautiful watches designed in the deliberately classic style often used in the 1950s with refined dials, baton-shaped or gently tapering hands and simple hour markers or Roman numerals.

The value of the brand's heritage was also made clear with the care given to the collection of historic watches gradually assembled as of the start of the twentieth century. This was a collection of high-value, but the pieces were mostly unconnected and did not focus on the company's own production. As a result, the policy of selling old but atypical models was instituted in order to finance the acquisition of watches signed Vacheron Constantin. The growing collection soon included several hundred timepieces, each patiently restored to working order. The marvels on display in the windows of the Rue des Moulins location, and occasionally at various public events, included the first known timepiece signed by Jean-Marc Vacheron, magnificent complications, Art Deco watches and small clocks, an accurate model of the Kallista watch, Chinese-style watches, guilloché-embellished hunter-style timepieces, and engraved or artistically enameled watches from the eighteenth and nineteenth centuries. Also featured was the largest collection of watch keys (almost 750), some of which were fine works of art chiefly pre-dating the invention of the pendant winding system in the mid-nineteenth century.

This private collection was kept on the first floor of Rue des Moulins, which also housed a meticulously built scene showing the everyday work of eighteenth-century cabinotiers. It was based on a painting by Christophe François von Ziegler on display in the Art and History Museum of Geneva (page 14). All the elements of a traditional workshop were reproduced in detail: benches, tools, and furniture, while mannequins representing the craftsmen were dressed in period clothing. One of them was an automaton examining the movement of a pocket watch with his loupe then looking around the workshop. Street sounds from eighteenth-century Geneva, complete with horses' hooves clattering on the cobbles, added to the realism of the scene. In 2004, it was transferred to the new manufacture at Plan-les-Ouates and is now regularly displayed at various events the company organizes around the world.

At the same time, Vacheron Constantin intensified its horological activities from 1992 onward by producing increasingly complicated models. For example, it offered a tourbillon caliber outfitted with twin spring barrels. It also developed an exclusive minute repeater caliber

1990

LEFT-HAND PAGE
Structura wristwatch, 1990. Housed in an 18K yellow gold case, the annular dial is paved with brilliant-cut diamonds. For the first time, a watch reveals the heart of its 1.64 mm ultra-thin movement, the side usually hidden on the wrist.
Inv. no. 10335

RIGHT-HAND PAGE
Mercator wristwatch, 1994. Created to celebrate the 400th anniversary of the death of Gérard Mercator, the father of cartography, this platinum watch rests on the pages of an Atlas dated 1607, based on Mercator's cartographic work from the previous century. The watch is fitted with a self-winding mechanical movement. Its dial reproduces the map of Europe in polychrome cloisonné enamel, using the *grand feu* technique. Its creative display presents jumping hours and dragging minutes, indicated by marine compass-shaped hands.
Inv. no. 11473

called the 1755 which was at the time the thinnest in the world (4.2 mm). The watch fitted with this movement was soon thereafter made into a skeletonized version with a specially adapted perpetual calendar. Also in 1992, the company introduced the Vacheron Constantin Prize in collaboration with the University of Neuchâtel and the *L'Homme et le Temps Institute* of the *Musée International d'Horlogerie* to recognize work that has marked the history of watchmaking. In 1995, for its 240th anniversary, the company created a watch expressing the balance between beauty and technical perfection: a tonneau-shaped timepiece available in gold or platinum with movable lugs and fitted with a self-winding movement that drives not only the hour and minute hands but also a power-reserve indicator at 10 o'clock, a date at 2 o'clock and, small seconds at 6 o'clock. That same year, Vacheron Constantin commemorated the 400th anniversary of the death of the great Flemish Renaissance map maker Gerhard Kremer, who was known as Mercator. In 1569, he had published the first flat map of the world for sailors using the projection system he invented, which carries his name. The dial of the Mercator watch produced for this occasion boasts a motif in multi-colored champlevé enamel depicting one of his hemispheric maps. The use of enamel is practically part of the brand's genetic code. The watch features a split time display: two hands joined at the top swing apart, exactly like a compass. The hand on the left indicates the hours, the other indicates the minutes, each moving laterally on a graduated arc and returning immediately (to 0 or to 1) once it reaches the end of its scale. In addition to this display, the watch is fitted with a self-winding movement, making it both a technical and an aesthetic achievement (right-hand page).

In 1996, a unique Mercator watch with an enamel dial depicting the map of his country was offered to King Bhumibol Adulyadej of Thailand to mark the 50th anniversary of his accession to the throne. For Vacheron Constantin, the main event of that year was the offer from the Vendôme group (today Richemont) to purchase the company's total share capital. The fact that this international luxury group based in Switzerland wished to acquire Vacheron Constantin said a great deal about its prestige and reputation for quality: in the watchmaking sector Richemont had already purchased Cartier, Piaget, and Baume & Mercier, and in 2000 it also acquired Jaeger-LeCoultre, IWC, A. Lange & Söhne, and Panerai. Clearly, the group was only interested in the elite of fine watchmaking. Sheik Yamani understood that the future of Vacheron Constantin lay more than ever in the extremely refined, sophisticated sector where Richemont was broadening its expertise, developing its understanding, and acquiring a great experience. He therefore accepted the offer. The company changed ownership, but not management: Claude-Daniel Proellochs remained in charge to complete the work that was underway.

In fact, a new collection developed in total secrecy over several years was revealed: the Overseas watch (page 176). It represented a very contemporary addition to the existing range as an elegant yet sporty companion for anyone actively engaged in exploring the world on land, sea, or air. This simple, beautiful watch had several ancestors, and it restated the hereditary values of the company. But it was not simply beautiful, it offered a style that was both new and contemporary, underscored by the quality of its manufacture and finishing. The Overseas allowed Vacheron Constantin to add a sporty feel to its technical fine watchmaking while adopting the very contemporary theme of travel. The watch was produced in three sizes (men's, women's, and intermediate) in stainless steel or solid gold, with an articulated, satin-finished bracelet, a notched bezel, a blue, ebony, pink or silvered dial, and baton hands with tritium coating for visibility in the dark. The Overseas is an undeniably magnificent object designed with great attention to detail. Its beauty is fascinating, even inside the case. In the same period, and contrary to the Overseas style, Vacheron Constantin quietly developed its rediscovered art of enamel. It created a superb series of men's watches in cloisonné enamel based on the famous illustrations of birds by American ornithologist John James Audubon (1785–1851). In choosing this motif, the company was not simply following a decorative theme: these watches

CONSTANTIN
GENEVE
AUTOMATIC
11

paid homage to a lover of nature and encouraged others to think seriously about the growing threats to the beauty of the natural world.

In 1997, the decision was taken to leave the annual Basel Watch and Jewelry Fair after attending for many years in order to join the SIHH (Salon International de la Haute Horlogerie) in Geneva. The SIHH enabled Vacheron Constantin to confirm its rank alongside the two other leading names in fine watchmaking at the time: Patek Philippe and Audemars Piguet. In a parallel move, it reinforced its status in advanced technical watchmaking by acquiring HDG, a workshop of craftsmen that specialized in designing and producing top-of-the-range watch movements. HDG was located halfway between Geneva and Neuchâtel in the Vallée de Joux. This is a region that had focused on horological micromechanics since the second half of the eighteenth century, and the place where companies such as Audemars Piguet, Breguet, and Jaeger-LeCoultre had developed into powerhouses. HDG was integrated into the small watchmaking division known as Cellule Technique that Vacheron Constantin already had there. In 2013, the various workshops of this new unit were brought together in a custom-built factory in Le Brassus designed by architect Glauco Lombardi. This new facility enabled Vacheron Constantin to produce components for movements that would meet the norms set by the very exclusive Hallmark of Geneva.

This official hallmark was established by the Grand Council of the Republic and Canton of Geneva in 1886 to impose and control a very rigorous standard of quality on the watches made in the canton. The Hallmark of Geneva is practically official recognition of the very highest quality in mechanical watches, achieved by only elite manufactures. To obtain this label of excellence, twelve very precise criteria must be met in making all the components of a movement and any additional mechanisms. These criteria include parts with polished edges, satin-finished surfaces, flat, polished, and chamfered screw heads, and ruby jewels set in polished bushings; other requirements relate to wheels, staffs, and pivots, the pinning of the balance spring,

the winding mechanism, time-setting, and the escapement. In 2011, the Hallmark's technical commission went further, adding tests to the finished watch to verify its functions, water-resistance, power reserve, and precision. As a result, the Hallmark of Geneva now imposes conditions on production to achieve better reliability and appearance, giving the purchaser a quadruple guarantee of provenance, durability, precision, and manufacturing quality. In fact, the examiners, appointed by the Geneva Office of Voluntary Inspection of Watches, demand perfection before they certify a watch, allowing it to bear the prestigious stamp displaying the eagle and key, which are the symbols of the Republic and Canton of Geneva. Vacheron Constantin has submitted a great number of its watches for certification since the start of the twentieth century and has been associated with the Hallmark of Geneva longer than any other watchmaker. While loyal clients and watch connoisseurs do not need the reassurance of this seal, in the case of Vacheron Constantin it is a valuable guarantee for new clients choosing a mechanical watch. Traditionally, Vacheron Constantin had not emphasized the hallmark, viewing it as a natural recognition of its quality. But in the 1990s, when enthusiasm and even passion for top-of-the-range mechanical

LEFT-HAND PAGE
Overseas wristwatch, 1996. The new Overseas collection is an invitation to travel and confirms Vacheron Constantin's commitment to sporting and technical haute horlogerie, as depicted in the 222 model of 1977. This men's watch in stainless steel features a blue sunray satin-finish dial. Inv. no. 11705

OPPOSITE
Advertisement, 1996.

1997

RIGHT-HAND PAGE
Saltarello wristwatch, 1997. This 18K pink gold cushion-shaped watch features a jumping hour in an aperture and a retrograde minute hand on a hand-crafted guilloché pink gold dial. Inv. no. 10740

watches returned, the brand began to draw attention to it among its expanding clientele. As of 2016, all Vacheron Constantin watches carry this symbol of supreme quality.

An exceptional men's watch, stamped of course with the hallmark, was introduced in 1999. The Saltarello (right-hand page) joined the family of complications with a highly original time display: the hour appears in a window at 12 o'clock while a retrograde hand indicates the minutes by moving along an arc marked 0-60, then jumps back (hence the name) to start again. The Saltarello illustrates one of the traditions of the brand: inventing new ways to display the time and the calendar. This self-winding watch is not only the product of extensive technical research, it is also a superbly designed object of great purity with its gentle cushion-shaped case in pink or white gold, its transparent case back revealing the openwork and decoration of the oscillating weight, and its silvered dial with fine guilloché radiating from the base of its single hand. Vacheron Constantin is always ready to offer its clients daringly designed watches. In the same year, it re-issued its famous trapezium-shaped watch, now calling it the 1972 to commemorate the year it was launched and enjoyed its first success. With its unique design, it remains one of the iconic watches of the brand today.

In short, Vacheron Constantin prepared to enter the new millennium by revisiting its heritage and planning a future based on the very highest quality of watchmaking.

0
10
20
30
40
50
60
10
VACHERON CONSTANTIN
GENEVE
AUTOMATIC

VACHERON CONSTANTIN
GENEVE
SWISS MADE

2000–2015...
A VISION, A COMMITMENT

Malte, Patrimony, Traditionnelle, Harmony: a new world of watchmaking was born at Vacheron Constantin with lines that grew steadily more impressive. The company also cultivated its tradition of ornamental watches with its Métiers d'Art collection, and grand complication timepieces made to order or in a small series. The range of its expertise remains simply unique.

2000

PREVIOUS LEFT-HAND PAGE
Harmony wristwatch, 2015. Celebrating the 260th anniversary of Vacheron Constantin, the new Harmony revisits the cushion shape. Combining the elegance of a single single-button chronograph and the prestige of a tourbillon, this watch boasts a 65-hour power reserve. Manual-winding Caliber 3200 features a multitude of technological improvements enhancing precision, reliability, and comfort of use.

RIGHT-HAND PAGE
Patrimony wristwatch, 2004. The icon of this collection, this watch is the embodiment of understatement. Sobriety is a demanding exercise and this model takes its inspiration from the historic piece of 1957 (page 162). With its generous diameter, wide opening on a domed dial enhanced by a pearled minute circle, slender hour markers and baton-shaped hands, it concentrates all the identity codes of the Patrimony collection in one place.

For Vacheron Constantin, the third millennium did not begin on January 1, 2001 as any self-respecting watchmaker would insist. December 1996, the date of its acquisition by the Richemont group, marked the first step toward defining a new horological strategy, which began immediately with a new investment in the future. The year 2000 did have long-term importance for the company, though: a strategic committee was formed to assist the brand's management and, little by little, it put together a new vision and commitment for the future that would lead to the creation of several lines of watches chiefly defined by the shapes of their cases – round, tonneau, cushion – and each in versions that ranged from simple to highly complicated. These lines included Malte (tonneau-shaped), Patrimony (round and thin), Traditionnelle (round, able to accommodate multiple complications), and Harmony (cushion-shaped). There were also two existing collections that had developed their own personalities: Overseas, a fusion of elegance and sport, and 1972 with an asymmetric, off-beat shape. They heralded a wave of bold, creative case shapes from the company's designers.

Like a tree, this new vision was planted in fertile soil and had deep roots. It grew, sprouting new branches, to horological heights. In addition to these classic lines with their dynamic versions, Vacheron Constantin put together collections of more unusual watches: the Historiques reissues vintage models; the Quai de l'Île is like a laboratory of extreme innovation; and the Métiers d'Art illustrates the excellent decorative techniques that have always been one of the brand's priorities. Lastly, it formed two entities that expressed the peak of its creativity and watchmaking expertise: Atelier Cabinotiers, where unique, custom-made watches are produced, and Maître Cabinotier where the most outstanding complications are made, either as a unique piece or in very small numbers. In a new spirit, Vacheron Constantin was building a world focused on consistency and durability that demonstrated its expertise, style, and creativity.

In 2000, the first line was introduced, symbolically called Malte. Today it includes all Vacheron Constantin's tonneau-shaped watches, the "barrel" shape that first appeared in 1912. Flagship of this line is the Malte Tourbillon, fitted – as its name suggests – with this major piece of watchmaking technology. Vacheron Constantin has designed hundreds of tourbillons, one of the most complex of watchmaking devices. Here the company designed a shaped tourbillon: Caliber 1790 is outfitted with a tourbillon adapted to the tonneau shape of the case. A large round window in the dial reveals the splendor of the tourbillon with its carriage in the form of a Maltese cross.

While the third millennium started well for Vacheron Constantin, an economic crisis soon shook the rest of the world, which was made even worse by a tragic event. The euphoria of entering the year 2000 soon evaporated: in the second half of the year, the technology stock bubble – created by illusory growth in many Internet companies – finally burst, leading to a stock market collapse that lasted three years. After a series of spectacular bankruptcies and huge losses, there was a significant slowdown in economic activity. At the same time, on September 11, 2001, the United States suffered a series of terrorist attacks on an unprecedented scale. Carried out by the Islamic extremist movement led by Al-Qaeda, these took the lives of nearly 3,000 people.

The attack had far-reaching consequences: apart from leading to two wars in Iraq and Afghanistan characterized by huge loss of human life, it reinforced the economic slowdown and created a deep sense of insecurity around the world.

Yet in Switzerland, for the first time in thirty years, a higher total value of mechanical watches was produced than quartz watches. In fact, the high-end sector of mechanical watchmaking enjoyed outstanding growth until 2008. Two factors help explain such paradoxical success during a time of global crisis: first, insecurity leads people to prefer well-made objects meant to last, retain their value, and be handed down; second, the spread of the mobile phone meant it was always easy to see the time, wiping out the need for a dedicated time indicator. The watch had to offer more than the digital display on a

VACHERON CONSTANTIN
GENEVE

16''' 164 ART
16''' 162
Remontoir & Finissage
16 162

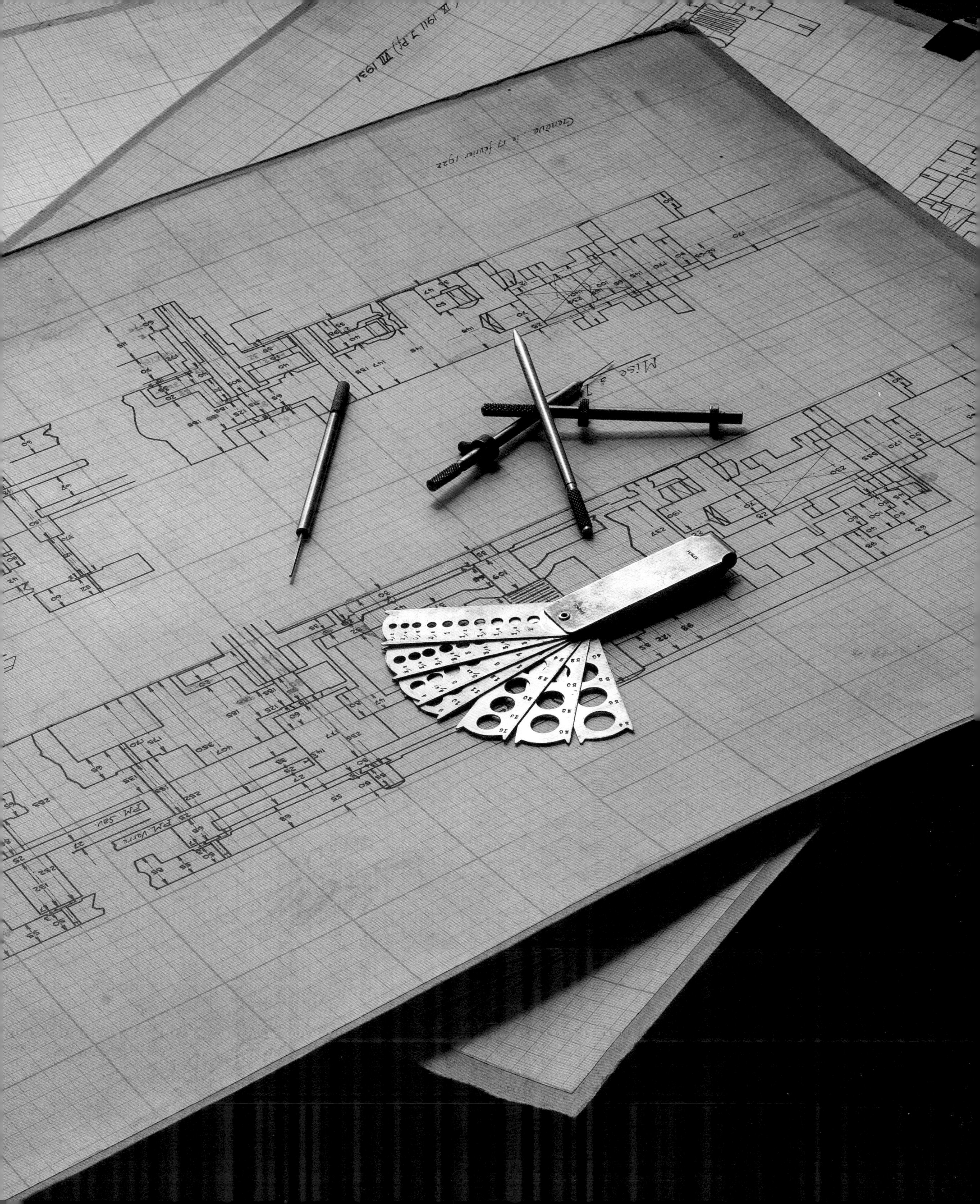

NGLETERRE
YORK B
LLARD N° 27
UILLARD N° 26
SE N° 17
ITALIE.
NEW-YORK du 15 Juillet 1857 au 3
PARIS
HOLLAN
30 Juin 1859 - 30 Juin 1863
PIEMONT.

mobile phone; it had to be something that low-priced watches were not: a beautiful object, a status symbol, an amazing mechanism made with centuries of expertise and drawing on a heritage that gives it a soul.

In periods of uncertainty, traditional values are appealing. Perhaps for that reason, in 2002 Vacheron Constantin decided to open, list, analyze, and organize more than 40 cubic meters of archives stored in wooden crates. They had last been opened in the 1950s, around the time of the company's 200th anniversary. It was a massive task, but eminently valuable at a time when the company was looking to its past for inspiration. It was finally finished with the help of historian and expert in fine watchmaking, Dominique Fléchon. The boxes offered countless treasures: all the company's correspondence since it was founded, including letters between watchmaker Jacques Barthélemy Vacheron and traveling businessman François Constantin in the 1820s; almost all the company accounts since 1811, which it began restore; many administrative documents; precious albums of engraving motifs; and photographs of families and principal managers and staff. In short, countless items that make up a private documentary history of watchmaking that is as rare as it is priceless.

The following year, the company decided to completely reorganize its premises in the historic center of Geneva where it had been founded. The shop and offices on the "île" were transformed in order to publicly display the highlights of the brand's history and current activities. At the new *Maison Vacheron Constantin en l'île*, inaugurated in December 2004 above the shop in a space open by appointment only, its treasures are conserved and displayed with the clarity and elegance of a contemporary museum. They include some of the 1,300 Vacheron Constantin watches that have been amassed so far (two watchmakers authenticate and restore new acquisitions), numerous vintage machines, and old workbenches and documents from the company's rich history such as the famous Ésaïe Hetier apprenticeship contract and Jacques Barthélemy Vacheron's passport. Among the most famous and most valuable watches on display are Jean Marc Vacheron's first-known watch – a pocket watch with a Shepherds of Arcadia-themed miniature enamel painting in Geneva technique – and a ladies' jewelry wristwatch shown at the 1889 Universal Exhibition. The company also organizes regularly changing temporary exhibitions here illustrating a specific theme that underscores the quality and beauty of pieces from the company's long history, such as exceptional repeating watches or chronographs. Also on display are themes illustrating the company's interest in travel and the world's wide array of cultures, magnificently applied to decorative watches.

In a restricted area with controlled temperature and humidity, 140 meters' worth of shelves are loaded with the paper archives. These historical registers are often consulted by watchmakers restoring an old piece at the request of its owner. This area also holds a very rare edition of the Mercator Atlas dating from 1607, which served as the reference for the enameled watch produced in 1995 to mark the company's 240th anniversary.

The preservation of its heritage is of prime importance for Vacheron Constantin: it is the treasure that its watchmakers, designers, and engineers can explore for inspiration. And for apprentices, it is an introduction to the long history of the company they are about to call home. This long, detailed history has been accessible since the publication of the first complete, documented study devoted to the Geneva watchmaker in 2005. *Artists of Time*, published in several languages, is one product of the research and analysis carried out over the course of three years.

Finding harmony between opposites is always a question of balance – exterior vs. interior, for example, or the creativity of Vacheron vs. the commercialism of Constantin. For a long time, the soul of the company had been located in a brain with two perfectly complementary sides. So it is no surprise that, just as masses of old papers were being exhumed, the company started construction on a new, ultra-modern production facility. It was the work of talented architect Bernard Tschumi, who combined metal, wood, concrete,

PREVIOUS DOUBLE PAGE
Technical drawings of calibers dating back to the 1920s.

LEFT-HAND PAGE
Company registers, 19th century. The meticulously managed Vacheron Constantin archives, demanding considerable work in the 2000s, make up an exceptional private horological documentary fund.

RIGHT-HAND PAGE AND FOLLOWING DOUBLE PAGE
The architecture of Manufacture Vacheron Constantin at Plan-Les-Ouates, inaugurated in 2004, at the start of its 250th anniversary celebrations, was designed by Bernard Tschumi. Combining glass, wood, metal and concrete, it offers employees, master watchmakers, and craftsmen an ideal, sun-filled workplace.

and glass in a sort of vast, elongated envelope through which light uninterruptedly streams. His building evokes, in proportion, the cabinets of old Geneva. The new manufacture was built at Plan-les-Ouates, a new Saint-Gervais of sorts on the periphery of Geneva, a location that several other important watchmakers already called home (including Piaget, Patek Philippe, and Rolex). By giving the offices and workshops "a timeless shape that remains of our time" and by aiming to "join the technologies of the twenty-first century with the intelligence of the century of enlightenment," Tschumi provided the company with its integrated *Fabrique*. Today's *cabinotiers* took possession in August 2004, and since then visitors have been able to view them at their benches or circulating, like a perpetual-motion machine, on the stairs and in the glass passageways of an immense atrium. However, after a few years of continuous growth, the inhabitants of the new building began to feel cramped. As a result, after three years of construction, a magnificent extension designed by the same architect was inaugurated in 2015. It follows the concept of the first building but in a different geometric shape and with its central light well linking different levels "to draw in as much light as possible everywhere," to quote Tschumi. Light that is essential to the craft of watchmaking.

In 2004, the year in which the *Maison Vacheron Constantin en l'île* and the new manufacture at Plan-les-Ouates both opened, the company presented what would become an iconic watch, the Patrimony. It had been a company specialty since the 1950s and its bicentennial in 1955: the very first model, born in 1957, was mainly intended for the American market, which gave it its name. Patrimony inaugurated the line of round, classic watches devoted to supreme elegance. While its diameter is a generous 40 mm, it is ultra-thin at a mere 6.79 mm. It offers absolute purity of design with only two baton-shaped hands and fine, tapered hour markers on a circular-grained hour track against the background of a matte dial. At the time, it symbolized a return to watches whose elegance was based on simplicity and purity. With this Patrimony, Vacheron Constantin brought back the fashion for a classic, thin, discreet watch in a wonderful illustration of George Brummel's creed: "True elegance consists in not drawing attention to oneself." Just as this famous dandy spent six hours a day dressing to achieve his elegance, it must have taken a very long time for the designers of this watch to perfect its details and give it a style that appeared to be based on the golden ratio.

The entire Patrimony line inherits this fundamental purity, even if some versions seem much more sophisticated with the addition of complications: like, for example, the Patrimony quantième perpétuel launched in 2011, which was fitted with the famous ultra-thin self-winding Caliber 1120 QP indicating the moon phases at 6 o'clock.

This consummate art of balance and duality was evident in 2004 when the company presented the second generation of Overseas, the top-level sports watch that seems like an invitation to travel. Like the original model, its case back is engraved with the image of a superb three-mast ship sailing the world's oceans: it is the *Amerigo Vespucci*, the famous training vessel of the Italian navy. The watch is chiefly distinguished by a new steel bracelet, recognizable by its links in the form of half a Maltese cross and by a movement entirely protected from magnetism by metal "armor."

Enjoying a huge renaissance and installed in its third-millennium manufacture, Vacheron Constantin celebrated its 250th anniversary by introducing lines that would become the pillars of its new era. It launched five models that each referred to its heritage and paid tribute to all the crafts of watchmaking, particularly watchmaking in the great Geneva tradition. Looking to the future, these models also illustrated the new technical standards that would mark the company's various collections. It took more than four years for the different specialists in the manufacture to complete them. Four of the watches symbolically represent the date 1755 in the number of pieces produced: 1, 7, 55, and 1755.

At the top of the pyramid is a unique timepiece whose name perfectly sums up the history of the company: the Esprit des Cabinotiers. This secret clock takes the form of a pink gold sphere standing on a plinth of lapis lazuli, onyx,

VACHERON CONSTANTIN
GENÈVE
COUPLE DE SONNERIE
HAUT
1/2
BAS

and pink gold. The sphere is formed by eight petals that open up when a secret mechanism, known only to the owner, is activated. Naturally, the clock's movement is worthy of such a superb presentation: it incorporates a spectacular range of complications and astronomic indications.

Together with the Esprit des Cabinotiers, Vacheron Constantin introduced four wristwatches that each relate to the soul of the brand and its standards of finishing. For this unique occasion they all presented a set of distinctive features specific to the 250th anniversary: an exclusive, finely fluted case, specially designed, soldered lugs, original guilloché work on the dial, and hands based on one of the company's iconic designs from 1926.

In addition to their complexity, each watch was fitted with its own new caliber, entirely designed, developed, and produced by Vacheron Constantin. These four movements set the course for the future of the brand. All of them were stamped with the Hallmark of Geneva, the highest-quality certification in fine watchmaking.

The complication developed by Vacheron Constantin in one wristwatch, called the Tour de l'Île, confirmed an extraordinary level of technical expertise. It required more than 10,000 hours of research and development by designers, engineers, production staff, and watchmakers. It was the most highly complicated small-series wristwatch ever made at the time with an astonishing sixteen complications and astronomical indications displayed on two faces. Seven pieces of the Tour de l'Île in a pink gold case were produced, as well as one extra retained for the company's heritage collection. It was the crowning piece of the 250th anniversary, taking a permanent place in the history of watchmaking.

Another expression of Vacheron Constantin's identity is the new Caliber 2250 located in the Saint-Gervais platinum watch with a new-generation perpetual calendar. It incorporates four barrels providing a power reserve of 250 hours (more than ten days). The power reserve indicator is located on the dial between 4 and 8 o'clock. The Saint-Gervais movement with its ethereal tourbillon is a world first. The watch, limited to 55 pieces, is also distinguished by spectacular guilloché.

The "basic" model in the collection is the Jubilé 1755 with a new self-winding movement that includes the power reserve, weekday, and date functions. On both design and technical levels, it reflects the company's values of simplicity and classicism. Of the 1755 numbered pieces in the limited edition, 500 were each available in yellow, pink, and white gold and 250 in platinum, including a dial with guilloché work. One model in each metal has been kept for the Patrimony collection and one piece has found a place in the watchmaking and enameling collection of the Geneva Museum of Art and History.

Lastly, the Métiers d'Art collection demonstrates mastery of engraving, gemsetting, and different enameling techniques; it presents the time in windows without hands. This form of display is entirely in line with the tradition of the company, which had already shown an interest in it at the beginning of the nineteenth century. The 18-karat gold dial is decorated with the colors of each season and combines sculpture, fine engraving, gems, and the techniques of refined enameling. At its center is a delicate appliqué of Apollo in his chariot drawn by four horses. The case back, coated with translucent enamel, shows a sun and a golden moon. This refers to the legend of Apollo crossing the sky each day in his chariot and symbolizes the circular concept of time in ancient civilizations. On parts of the chariot, carefully applied plant motifs for each season appear. Twelve sets of the four watches were produced for the occasion, one of which is part of the Vacheron Constantin Heritage collection.

On April 3, 2005, as part of the 250th anniversary celebrations, the Antiquorum auction house organized a prestigious sale of some of the most famous historical Vacheron Constantin watches as well as pieces specially designed for the event. The world's leading collectors were present, and total sales amounted to 18 million Swiss francs, setting a record for this kind of themed auction. King Fouad of Egypt's watch fetched more than three million francs, making it the fifth most expensive pocket watch ever sold. At more than 1.8 million francs, the Tour de l'Île

2005

LEFT-HAND PAGE
Tour de l'Île wristwatch, 2005. The most complicated wristwatch ever made at the time, produced in a limited edition of 7 individual numbered watches. Designed to celebrate the 250th anniversary of Vacheron Constantin, the Tour de l'Île includes 16 complications visible on a double-sided display. Inv. no. 11474

OPPOSITE AND RIGHT-HAND PAGE
Tour de l'Île wristwatch, 2005. This masterpiece of watchmaking technology comprises 834 components in a 47 mm diameter case. Caliber 2750 controls the following functions and indicators, besides hours, minutes, and seconds at 6 o'clock: hour, quarter and minute repeater on demand, power reserve indicator, second time zone, moon phases and ages, couple de sonnerie, perpetual calendar with day, date, and month indicated by hands, leap year in an aperture, perpetual equation of time, sunrise, sunset, and map of the sky. Inv. no. 11474

VACHERON CONSTANTIN
GENÈVE

became the most expensive serial wristwatch ever sold up to that point. As for the unique Esprit des Cabinotiers, it was bought for more than 2.2 million Swiss francs.

It was during the 250th anniversary celebrations that Claude-Daniel Proellochs, president of the company since 1988, officially passed the baton to his successor, Juan-Carlos Torres, assistant director-general at the time. The son of a cabinet maker, he was hired in 1981 and progressively learned all the traditional crafts of watchmaking. He worked to achieve technical independence for Vacheron Constantin, which had to quickly master all the specialties of watch manufacturing in order to design and produce every component of every watch bearing its name – as required by the Hallmark of Geneva. In addition to this commitment to autonomy and excellence, his other objectives were to remain a human-sized organization with a spirit of craftsmanship; to increase the number of Vacheron Constantin boutiques around the world (about fifty in 2015); and to exploit the value of its heritage as the oldest watchmaking brand in continuous operation.

Although platinum has been used in the company since 1820, working with it on the 250th anniversary watches sparked the idea to develop more models in this pure, rare, eternal metal. The reason was not so much prestige but rather to harness its beauty and simplicity to highlight the design and technical quality of a watch. The result was the Excellence Platine collection, launched in 2006 and unique in the world of watchmaking. It is a superb homage to this unalterable metal of which not just the case is crafted (as is common in watchmaking), but virtually all the external parts: the sanded dial, the hands, the winding mechanism, the clasp, and even the platinum wire that is mixed with silk thread to stitch the midnight blue alligator skin straps of these exceptional watches. They are still produced in limited series of 10 to 150 pieces depending on the model.

For some, even within the company, the Patrimony Excellence Platine, which joined the collection in 2006, is the most beautiful watch Vacheron Constantin has ever made. The reason is perhaps that its supremely refined elegance, sculpted in the purest metal (platinum is 95 percent pure), has an effect like the spirituality of a Zen garden. But the collection also includes highly complicated watches such as the Traditionnelle Calibre 2253 launched in 2010. Its combination of complications is unique in watchmaking: an equation of time, times of sunrise and sunset, a tourbillon, and an extraordinary power reserve of approximately 336 hours (14 days).

This new Traditionnelle line was introduced in 2007. The company had begun to realize that certain complications could not be fitted into the very fine, usually ultra-thin cases of the Patrimony models. Another look was called for, another more technical expression of the classic round watch represented by the Patrimony.

The adjective *traditionnelle* was used right from the start since this model utilizes the company's design codes of the 1930s and 1940s such as certain finishes applied to the dial. The railroad minute track, the type of hands, and the hour markers known as *baton de Genève*, as well as an overall appearance seeming more robust than the Patrimony, echo a certain tradition of Geneva watchmaking. Yet, inside the watch, the calibers are at the forefront of innovation. Particularly notable is Caliber 2755, which lends its name to one of the models. It brings together three major complications: a tourbillon, a perpetual calendar, and a minute repeater. This repeater mechanism was entirely updated with the development of a new silent regulator governing the striking speed. Although this regulator remains invisible unless the watch is completely dismantled, the designers kindly gave it the form of a Maltese cross. During the years of development, the watchmakers took the principle of this regulator to create Caliber 1731 (the founder's year of birth): at 3.9 mm it is the world's thinnest repeater movement, and it was fitted into an ultra-thin Patrimony (8.09 mm case height) in 2013. Creating a beautiful chime in such a thin watch is an impressive technical achievement – especially in a watch with a sapphire crystal case back that resonates less than one with a thicker, all-metal case.

In another market segment opposite that of the Patrimony, Traditionnelle, and Malte

LEFT-HAND PAGE
Métiers d'Art Les Quatre Saisons wristwatch, 2005. In line with its long tradition of producing a wide variety of displays, Vacheron Constantin upholds the art of horology by displaying time without hands, using instead four windows. Stamped with the Hallmark of Geneva, the self-winding mechanism, Caliber 2460, is fitted with an oscillating weight in 22K gold like all its mechanical components. A limited edition of twelve sets including four timepieces, each illustrating a season (winter in this case), individually numbered.

2007

RIGHT-HAND PAGE
Métiers d'Art Les Masques Congo wristwatch, 2007. The Métiers d'Art Les Masques collection puts a special focus on another watchmaking craft, that of the engraver. The idea is to represent an authentic mask, reproduced and miniaturized on the dial of a watch. The original masks inspiring this collection are all from the private collection of the Barbier-Mueller museum in Geneva, the world's largest private collection of primitive art. Each watch is fitted with self-winding Vacheron Constantin Caliber 2460 G4 and bears the prestigious Hallmark of Geneva. This movement allows the time to be read without hands. A set of wheels and gears move four disks that reveal hours, minutes, day, and date in separate windows, thus freeing the center of the dial. The craftsmen's creativity was given free rein to produce the mask.

classic watches – available in a large variety of models from the simplest to the most complicated – Vacheron Constantin appeals to those who love watches that are different or unique. It uses its greatest expertise in the three domains of excellence that form its identity: centuries of tradition (with the previously discussed Historiques line), artistic crafts, and extreme innovation.

From its earliest days, Vacheron Constantin watches were embellished by crafts traditionally linked to the watchmaker's art: enameling, engraving, guilloché, and gem-setting. In 2004, the company made this aesthetic approach official by creating the Métiers d'Art collection. It was inaugurated in a limited series of enameled watches called *Métiers d'Art Hommage aux Grands Explorateurs*, featuring, in this case, Magellan and Zheng Hé. Several series were added to this collection in the following years, some involving crafts that were completely new to watchmaking, such as maki-e, a traditional Japanese lacquering technique, and wood marquetry.

Each series illustrated the two values that run through the entire history of Vacheron Constantin: the excellence of its craftsmen and its openness to the world and to other cultures. This was illustrated spectacularly in 2007 with the *Métiers d'Art Les Masques* series, which had an extraordinary impact. The brand was looking for a decorative, multicultural theme on some aspect of the human adventure to decorate the dials of a limited series of watches, and the idea of primitive masks from different civilizations was proposed. Representatives from the brand met with Jean-Paul Barbier-Mueller, a great art collector who kept a magnificent collection of tribal masks in the Geneva museum he had founded. He allowed twelve of these masks to be reproduced in miniature on the dials of a series of exceptional watches. Miniature versions of these masks from every continent except Europe were sculpted in wood, gold, copper, and basalt, providing an extraordinary example of the engraver's art. Caliber 2460 G4 allows the mask to be placed on a dial without hands, showing the time, day, and date in four windows. A set of four watches limited to 25 pieces was proposed each year from 2007 through 2009. This adventure of the *Métiers d'Art Les Masques* continued in a partnership between Vacheron Constantin and the Cultural Foundation of the Barbier-Mueller Museum. The objective was to present little-known cultures in order to preserve their legends and their cultural or social traditions.

Several other partnerships were formed in those years: with the Paris National Opera, the Orchestra of the Swiss Romande, the National Institute of Artistic Crafts in France, the Royal Ballet School of London, the New York City Ballet, and the Grand Theater of Geneva. These partnerships were a symbolic tribute from Vacheron Constantin to all its clients who love watches, art, and culture. Each of them was in support of the principles they shared with the company: investing the rigor and passion required to create great work, preserving the artistic crafts, drawing contemporary inspiration from a long heritage, and, lastly, passing down expertise.

The last of these is fundamental to the future of Vacheron Constantin. In the training center, 24 apprentices as young as 15 years of age spend three or four years with experienced masters, learning the principal crafts of watchmaking. Stints in different departments of the company alternate with courses at the Geneva School of Watchmaking and time spent in other companies as they prepare to qualify for the Professional Certificate of Capacity as a practicing watchmaker. All apprentices at Vacheron Constantin qualify. And since the training center was opened, only one has chosen to leave the company after qualifying. But he can always return if he chooses.

This important principle is at the heart of an unusual partnership with the Criar Institute of Sao Paulo. This non-governmental organization was set up by a famous name in Brazilian television, Luciano Huck. Every year it carefully selects 150 young Brazilians aged 17 through 20 from disadvantaged backgrounds to train for eleven different jobs in radio and television broadcasting.

Some of these partnerships are linked to the creation of watches in the Métiers d'Art

VACHERON CONSTANTIN
GENÈVE
On a voulu approfondir
mieux de leurs flèches pour
soleil ou de flammes pénètrent
votre visage et la peau de tout votre corps
yeux pour que les éclairs de
l'ombre où vous logerez vos
tatouer non seulement
mais les secrets de votre nuit
VEN
SAM
10
11
20
15

VACHERON CONSTANTIN
GENÈVE
PHILOSOPHIA

Chagall & l'Opéra de Paris series. For example, in 2010 it was the Chagall & l'Opéra de Paris series – twelve pieces in grand feu enamel produced in a single example, each dedicated to one of the composers depicted by artist Marc Chagall in his magnificent ceiling at the opera. The first of these watches represented the entire ceiling: a 200 m^2 fresco reduced to the size of a watch dial only 31.5 mm in diameter. Today, this unique piece remains with Vacheron Constantin.

Following the Métiers d'Art collection, other unique watches were introduced in 2008 within the Quai de l'Île collection, which forcefully express the passion for innovation at Vacheron Constantin. This avant-garde concept renews the spirit of fine watchmaking by enabling the client to personalize his or her watch using more than 400 possible combinations, choosing from three metals – gold, titanium, and palladium – three styles of dial, and two finishes for the movement. The case, inspired by the cushion shape and whose case band comprises seven distinct elements, allows for such extreme personalization.

These highly technical Quai de l'Île watches are also notable for their semi-transparent dials, which reveal the details of the three calibers specially developed for them (a self-winding movement, a day/date with power reserve, and since 2011 a retrograde annual calendar). In addition, a transparent security film is applied under the sapphire crystal. Using the techniques of security printing developed for banknotes, it is laser-engraved with symbols that are invisible to the naked eye – such as a replica of the Maltese cross or concentric circles – to protect against counterfeiting. For the first time anywhere, a brand began to combat counterfeiting not by repression but by prevention and in a way that is also aesthetically non-intrusive. This system, like the modular concept of the watch itself, was patented.

The watch industry suffered somewhat from a major economic event: the bankruptcy of Lehman Brothers in September 2008, which triggered a worldwide stock market collapse. The underlying causes were the burst real estate bubble and the subprime crisis a year earlier. This crash provoked the most serious economic crisis the world had known since the Great Depression of 1929. Most countries went into recession and were unable to prevent a massive increase in unemployment. In Europe, the growing public deficits created by recovery policies and a very expensive bailout of the banking system soon led to drastic austerity measures. These further increased unemployment and delayed a return to growth. The problem spread around the world and, in some developing countries like Brazil and China, the previously spectacular growth rates began to decline. Brazil even went into recession in 2014.

The luxury industry, including fine watchmaking, could not escape this crisis that had no end in sight, but suffered less dramatically than other sectors of the economy. There occurred a return to watches with more restrained, classic designs and a surge in the popularity of vintage models, particularly those from the 1950s. At Vacheron Constantin, however, these crisis years did not stop innovation in the design of new watches and calibers. The extraordinary Calibers 1731 and 2253 numbered among the developments, as previously mentioned, as well as Caliber 2260, which includes a tourbillon and the same fourteen-day power reserve: in 2012 this movement was fitted into a Traditionnelle, with a version also appearing in the Excellence Platine collection. Caliber 2460 QRA, became the heart of the Quai de l'Île watch with a retrograde annual calendar that was introduced in 2011.

In fact, 2011 was a particularly successful year for the company with the National Museum of Singapore mounting a major exhibition called "Treasures of Vacheron Constantin." One hundred eighty of the most beautiful watches from its past were presented alongside documents from the archives, vintage machines, and old workbenches.

Beyond producing watches that have become classics, in versions with varying degrees of complexity such as Overseas, Traditionnelle, Patrimony, and Malte, and even the unique watches of the Historiques, Métiers d'Art, and

LEFT-HAND PAGE
Philosophia wristwatch, 2009. This special commission named Philosophia by its owner brings together haute horlogerie and philosophic time. The idea behind this design was based on the postulate that humans did not need to permanently know the precise time to the nearest minute. The watch, inspired by a model in the Traditionnelle collection, has only one central hand - an hour hand - offering a 24-hour display. If the owner needs a more accurate idea of the time, he would simply need to activate the minute repeater. An opening in the dial reveals a tourbillon, performing a complete rotation in 60 seconds. 552 components comprise the manual-winding mechanical movement.

OPPOSITE
Ceiling of Opéra Garnier in Paris, painted by Marc Chagall in 1964.

RIGHT-HAND PAGE
Métiers d'Art Chagall & l'Opéra de Paris wristwatch, 2010. This unique piece, part of a series of 12 unique pieces in *grand feu* enamel, is an identical reproduction of the complete ceiling of the Paris Opera using the ancestral Geneva technique of *grand feu* enamel miniature painting. In its 18K yellow gold case, the dial of this piece presents a 31.5 mm diameter reproduction of the original that covers more than 200 m^2. An amazing feat that is now part of Vacheron Constantin's heritage.

VACHERON CONSTANTIN
GENEVE

VACHERON CONSTANTIN
GENEVE

Quai de l'Île collections, Vacheron Constantin continues to cultivate what it has done consistently for 260 years: create marvelous, unique watches produced to order as a single example (or a very limited series to beef up the client's service stock of spare parts).

Customized, made-to-order watches have become rare in the world of watchmaking. But at Vacheron Constantin, a special entity was devoted to them in 2006: the so-called Atelier Cabinotiers. The idea, and the name of the first watch it produced, occurred to Juan-Carlos Torres that same year after a friendly discussion with a leading Geneva collector on a beautiful summer's day in Provence. This loyal client of the company began to muse on the ideal holiday watch, one that would show the time approximately, but which, if necessary, would indicate it with great precision. After three years of development and manufacturing, the first custom-designed watch emerged from the Atelier Cabinotiers and its owner named it Philosophia. It presents a single hand on a dial marked only with the 24 hours. On demand, a minute repeater strikes to indicate the exact time. Accuracy is provided by a tourbillon, visible in a window at 6 o'clock. A personalized, precise moon phase display is located at 9 o'clock. The power-reserve indicator is on the back of the watch, decorated with the interlinked Ursa Major and Ursa Minor constellations.

After the Philosophia, the Atelier Cabinotiers carried out many other special orders with various complications and ornamentation. Each order received is submitted to a review committee to ensure that it respects the brand's principal identity codes. Even if the order is highly original, it must remain a Vacheron Constantin watch.

Today, some thirty to forty watches are being manufactured at any given time in the Atelier Cabinotiers, which has its own research and development team. The simplest of them, made from existing components, takes about a year to complete. However, because some very complicated or highly decorated pieces take much longer, the overall average is two years with the record being eight years. Throughout development and manufacturing stages, the client is kept informed of progress and is often welcomed to Geneva by the watchmakers in charge of the order.

In this same galaxy of pieces designed and produced without the constraint of time, Vacheron Constantin decided to offer Maître Cabinotier watches. These are the purest expressions of the art, with grand complications entirely designed and made by a single person who possesses the highest set of watchmaking skills and who works independently with complete freedom, with zero time constraints. Created in 2014, the Astronomica is one of the world's most complicated wristwatches, produced in a single example comprising 839 components and 15 complications including some of the most demanding in fine watchmaking. As its name suggests, astronomical indications occupy the largest part of this double-sided watch. Some of these are very rare in watchmaking: a sky chart, the solstice, the equinox, sidereal time, the seasons, and signs of the zodiac. All this in a white gold case measuring 47 mm in diameter. The beating heart of this piece is not only its unique caliber but also the years of watchmaking brilliance that were devoted to it, from the original concept to its final fine adjustment. The watch found a buyer as soon as it was presented in 2014.

Another key date in the history of Vacheron Constantin was 2015: its 260th anniversary. At the Salon International de la Haute Horlogerie (SIHH) in January, it presented pieces so innovative that they were an event in themselves.

Together with the team from the Métiers d'Art collection, the movement designers used all the expertise gained through years of reflection, research, and development to be finished in time. At the SIHH, they presented a set of twelve unique table clocks, each produced as a single example, all inspired by an extraordinary small clock that Vacheron Constantin created in 1933. They use the same material – natural rock crystal (or translucent crystal produced by master crystal-makers for eight of the clocks) – as well as the same design features of the case, visible movement, and onyx base. They are a tribute to the magnificent table clocks that Vacheron

2011

LEFT-HAND PAGE
Malte Tourbillon Collection Excellence Platine wristwatch, 2014. Vacheron Constantin has long established its expertise in the tourbillon movement. Often combined with another complication, Vacheron Constantin tourbillons reveal rare know-how and unrivaled daring. A new interpretation of this sublime complication is expressed in the Malte Tourbillon Collection Excellence Platine model.

2015

BELOW
Métiers d'Art Arca table clock, 2015. Inspired by a 1933 Vacheron Constantin table clock, this piece is part of a series of 12 clocks each issued as a unique piece. The transparency of the case gives real perspective to the new manual-winding mechanical movement (using a key) by Vacheron Constantin: skeletonized Caliber 9260. Its openworked construction reveals the inner beauty of the movement, which is structured around seven patiently hand-chamfered bridges. Combining a 30-day power reserve and constant force mechanism, Caliber 9260 has exceptional functional qualities that are part of the Vacheron Constantin horological tradition.

Constantin has created throughout its long history, always with very refined decoration.

Several artistic crafts were involved in achieving the subtle yet sumptuous impact of these table clocks: the enameling of the Roman hour numerals, the enameling and guilloché work on the base, and the cutting and engraving on crystal in forming the shape and decoration of the "cabinet." Eight of them are enhanced by an engraved motif in translucent crystal inspired by the great architectural movements of the twentieth century. The other four clocks are sculpted from blocks of very rare natural rock crystal, found only after several months of searching around the world. They pay tribute to this timeless mineral while honoring the art and culture of our time. Shining through the transparency of the rock crystal is an outstanding new hand-wound caliber in a pyramid shape that echoes the original piece, but is specifically designed to offer a power reserve of 30 days at constant force for extreme precision.

In March of this commemorative year, the company presented twenty examples each of three clocks at the European Days of Arts and Crafts in Paris called Métiers d'Art Savoirs

Enluminés. The Métiers d'Art collection, always reflecting the world of art and culture, is the result of long research and almost miraculous encounters. This time, the designers' first idea was to explore the vast world of calligraphy. But after combing museums and libraries, they opted instead for medieval illuminated manuscripts, texts that include miniature paintings. It was their beauty and sheer magnificence that persuaded the designers, and medieval illumination became the theme of the new anniversary series. Then followed a long search for the most beautiful examples of this subject thought to resonate with all cultures of the world. They finally found them in a famous twelfth-century manuscript, the *Aberdeen Bestiary*, kept in the library of that Scottish city's very old university. Considered one of the ancestors of the ubiquitous encyclopedia, using illustrations it counts and describes all known animals from the common to the exotic, although the latter appear more often than not purely fantastical.

Apart from the beauty of the illuminations on a gold background, this homage to nature and its diversity featured something that immediately fascinated the researchers: the unfinished manuscript still has the margins that would have been removed when the work was finished. Notes were written on these margins for the various craftsmen who were required to contribute their skills: the calligraphers, who specialized in lettering or ordinary text or headings, the gilder, and the illustrator. The illuminated manuscript and the watch in this prestigious collection both involve several artistic crafts, and it almost seems as if the two were always destined to meet.

Vacheron Constantin chose an animal for each of its watches from the illustrations in the manuscript: the halcyon, a mythological bird sometimes thought to be a swan and a symbol of water and serenity; a pair of vultures symbolizing air and longevity; and a goat, symbol of the earth and judgment. The crucial task was the miniature reproduction of the illustrations on the dial of a watch using the special Geneva-born technique of miniature enameling in addition to engraving and gilding. Meanwhile the company's watchmakers

OPPOSITE
Métiers d'Art Savoirs Enluminés wristwatch, 2015. With this Métiers d'Art collection, Vacheron Constantin highlights the importance of combining talents while taking inspiration from a masterpiece from the Middle Ages, an ancient manuscript dating back to the 12th century known worldwide for its beautiful illuminations, the *Aberdeen Bestiary*. This model dedicated to the earth shows a dark blue goat with piercing eyes. The enameling work is long and meticulous.
The colors are applied under the microscope, one after the other, before several trips to the kiln. In the background, the golden enamel background is hand-textured using fine brushes and gums to accurately reproduce the gold leaf effect. The time is indicated in Arabic numerals mounted on satellites: the hours pass one after the other to the left of a 120° semi-circle depicting the minutes on the left side of the dial.

VACHERON ✠ CONSTANTIN

were creating a caliber that could display the hour as well as ten-minute intervals on the right half of the dial without hands.

This anniversary was also highlighted by the presentation of a new horological triumph, just like the Tour de l'Île ten years earlier, made to order. One of today's leading watch collectors set Vacheron Constantin a challenge in 2007 to push back the known boundaries of watchmaking art and produce a piece defying the imagination and the historic record of complications. Vacheron Constantin not only accepted the challenge but exceeded it. This incredible adventure involved eight years of intensive labor in the manufacture by a trio of brilliant watchmakers, Jean-Luc Perrin and brothers Micke and Yannick Pintus, under the aegis of the Atelier Cabinotiers.

The Reference 57260 pocket watch, a supreme masterpiece of horological art, was therefore presented on September 17, 2015 – the symbolic date upon which Jean-Marc Vacheron took on his first apprentice. This double-face pocket watch contains no fewer than 57 complications, a stupendous number that almost doubles the existing record for a pocket watch featuring some 30 complications. But it was not this number in itself that excited the collector and the watchmaking team. It was the innovative way in which they were designed and integrated. The production of all the existing complications is, in fact, based on a new concept. But the watch is also notable for some totally original complications, such as a perpetual Hebrew calendar and a night mode for the chiming mechanism, both requested by the collector. These innovations resulted in several patents being filed. This amazing movement integrates seven major areas of watchmaking: timekeeping regulated by a tri-axial tourbillon with a spherical spring, both invented for this watch; two perpetual calendars, Hebrew and Gregorian; an astronomical calendar with a dozen indications including the seasons, the signs of the zodiac, an equation of time, times of sunrise and sunset, a sky chart, and several others; a lunar calendar with the age of the moon and its phases; chronograph functions with a retrograde second hand; an alarm with its own gong or the possibility to link to the chimes of the repeater; a repeater mechanism with a grand and small strike as well as Westminster chimes on five gongs.

To accommodate this awesome mechanical micro universe, a special extra-large gold case had to be designed and produced. The watch is a supreme masterpiece of watchmaking and will be the subject of a beautiful book all on its own. These extraordinary pieces, paying tribute to a

LEFT-HAND PAGE AND BELOW
Reference 57260 pocket watch, 2015. Double-sided watch comprising 57 horological complications and a large number of filed patents, this special order took 8 years to research and develop.

RIGHT-HAND AND FOLLOWING DOUBLE PAGE
The Reference 57260 pocket watch, the ultimate masterpiece in the art of watchmaking.

special anniversary, are all produced as single examples or limited series. At the same time, Vacheron Constantin also presented several versions of the line that seemed to have been missing so far, like Harmony. The round Overseas, Patrimony, and Traditionnelle watches along with the tonneau-shaped Malte watches are now complemented by the Harmony timepieces in a revisited cushion shape. This original, elegant shape, a symbol of modernity and much appreciated by connoisseurs, was first introduced by Vacheron Constantin in 1917. It has reappeared regularly in unique models that have marked the history of the brand, such as the Saltarello in 1997 and the Quai de l'Île in 2008.

The seven Harmony watches presented in 2015 come in limited editions all carrying the Hallmark of Geneva. As a tribute to the founder, the movement is engraved with the same classic flourish of delicate arabesques that decorate the first watch attributed to Jean-Marc Vacheron. It symbolizes the fusion of a 260-year heritage with the technical excellence and innovation of the twenty-first century.

Two of these watches are fitted with innovative single-button chronograph movements with a dynamic release system developed and produced by the company over a period of seven years: Calibers 3200 and 3300. Caliber 3200 is equipped with a spectacular tourbillon positioned at 12 o'clock: housed in a platinum case and offering a 65-hour power reserve, the manually wound movement comprises 292 components – all naturally decorated by hand – and incorporates a multitude of technological advancements reinforcing this exclusive timepiece's precision, reliability, and ease of use.

In choosing to put a chronograph into a cushion-shaped case, the watchmakers drew once again on the rich heritage of the company, specifically one of its first wristwatch chronographs, produced in 1923 and further developed in 1928. They followed its essential design codes – a round bezel within a cushion-shaped case, elegant Arabic numerals, Stuart pear-shaped hands, and a pulsometer on the single-button chronograph model – but gave them a contemporary touch. The result is a watch that blends sophistication, technical expertise, elegance, and dynamism in perfect harmony. The symbiosis between a formal structure on a series of interwoven levels and sculpting time gives it its name. Harmony is a work of art produced by rigorous design and expertise, a science of tuning several elements simultaneously. Among the other models, the Harmony line represents another technical and design achievement: the single-button split-seconds chronograph is ultra-thin, measuring only 8.4 mm in height – a world record.

Fifteen years after its universe was redefined, the oldest continuously producing watchmaker sprouted new shoots to grow and flourish. It is a clear demonstration of its faith in the future. Harmony represents a logical addition to the other lines, which already have a strong horological identity cemented in numerous versions. The seven Harmony models are the first in a long series to reinforce Vacheron Constantin's determination to perpetuate its name and its insistence on excellence. Each Harmony is a mirror of three centuries. And each one captures what E.M. Forster, author of *Passage to India*, called when describing a flash of lightning "an eternal moment."

PISCES
ARIES
TAURUS
GEMINI
CANCER
LEO
VIRGO
LIBRA
SCORPIO
SAGITTARIUS
CAPRICORN
AQUARIUS
WINTER
SPRING
SUMMER
AUTUMN
EQ
SOL
JAN
FEB
MAR
APR
MAY
JUN
JUL
AUG
SEP
OCT
NOV
DEC
N
E
W
GRE
SAT
SUN
MON
TUE
WED
THU
FRI
SUNRISE
DAY LENGTH
SUNSET
NIGHT LENGTH
Au750

29½
N C A
M

MASTERS OF THE ART

OPPOSITE
Diderot and d'Alembert, *Encyclopédie ou Dictionnaire raisonné des sciences, des arts et des métiers*, Vol. III of Illustrative Plates: Plate X, 3rd set, "Watch with alarm and watch with equation, with concentric seconds, marking the months and the date." Martin Bodmer Foundation, Cologny (Geneva), Switzerland.

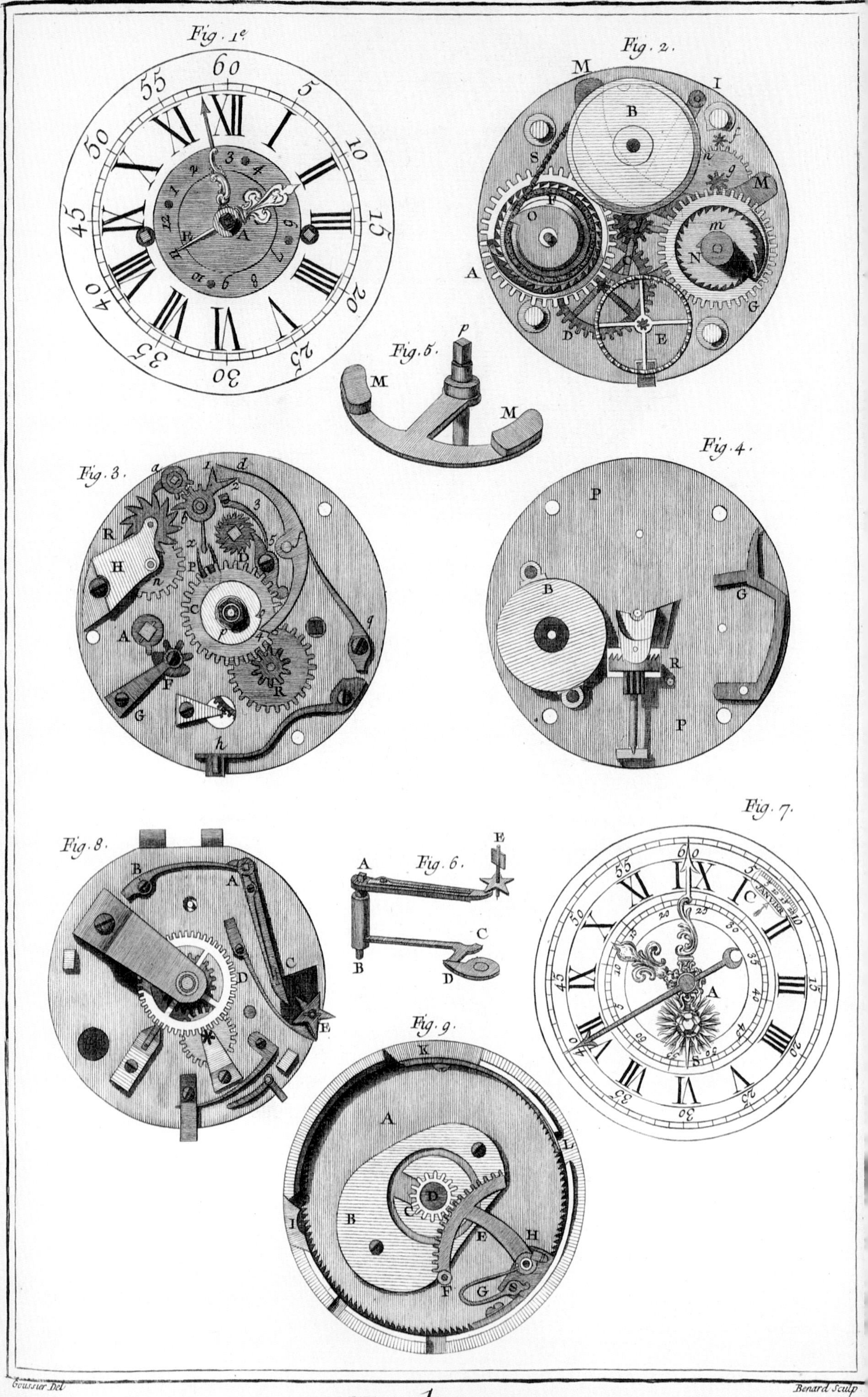

In the *Encyclopédie, ou dictionnaire raisonné des art et des métiers (Encyclopedia, or a Systematic Dictionary of the Sciences, Arts, and Crafts)* by Denis Diderot and Jean le Rond d'Alembert, a great symbol of the Age of Enlightenment, articles on watchmaking describe the craft as follows: "[Horologist] is the name given to artists who create clocks and watches and, in general, to all those who work in horology." The image of a man whose "craft" is to master time would have certainly appealed to the rationalists of the enlightenment. And, yet, the mention of "artists" suggests something more (and different) than just admiration or partisan support. The authors of the *Encyclopédie* were, in fact, already asking whether some human activities are more than simply "crafts" or "trades," and they saw watchmaking as a profession that undeniably included some element of artistry.

But where does craft end and art begin? Is there a way to define the borderline? And what exactly is an "artistic craft"? Watchmaking provides a way to understand this. It is, and always has been, a pendulum that swings between creativity and technical expertise, making it an example of an artistic craft. In previous centuries, clocks were very often works of art, but could only be made with the support of wealthy patrons. They stood apart in that they were not only works of art: they had a function that, because of their importance and great value to the community, needed to be performed as precisely and reliably as possible. That is why, right from the start, a clockmaker had to combine art and science. He had to design an extremely sophisticated machine with a mechanism close to perfect, which is at once beautiful, elegant, and highly decorative. Contemporary watchmaking has not strayed from these requirements, whether in restoring monumental clocks, producing the most modern and valuable watches for big Swiss brands, or training the "masters of art" who turn an idea into an object by designing and producing unique pieces deep inside their workshops.

Another aspect of the profession merits attention in that it represents a particularly interesting point of view: that of an artistic craft as a network of connections between various skilled artisans and the knowledge that distinguishes them. Designing and producing a watch is, in fact, always the result of several branches of expertise coming together, some of which call upon the artistic crafts (engraving, jewelry, goldsmith work, enameling, guilloché, etc.).

By bringing together artistic mastery and technical perfection – now guaranteed by the very stringent requirements of the Hallmark of Geneva – Vacheron Constantin has become the ultimate benchmark in this tradition. Master watchmakers, designers and specialists in the artistic crafts all work a few steps apart in the same building and are continuously in contact.

Together with this close harmony, a time-tested dynamic helps to explain the company's longevity: a passion for handing on traditions and knowledge, coupled with a thirst for innovation in every area. At Vacheron Constantin, the apprentice is as important as the master, and understanding the company's heritage is as important as the development of an entirely new caliber or decoration.

This is a glimpse into the grand mechanism of marvels that is Vacheron Constantin, its secrets and discoveries and its traditions and innovations, both technical and aesthetic. A distinction particularly difficult to make in a company where the calibers are as beautiful as the cases that house them. And where the great art practiced by its watchmakers meets the technical virtuosity of its designers and embellishers. All of this can be summarized in François Constantin's 1819 instructive motto: "Do better if possible, and it is always possible." Doing better means taking all the time required.

VACHERON CONSTANTIN
GENEVE
SWISS
TWENTY-ONE (21) JEWELS
ADJUSTED FIVE (5) POSITIONS

MASTER WATCHMAKERS

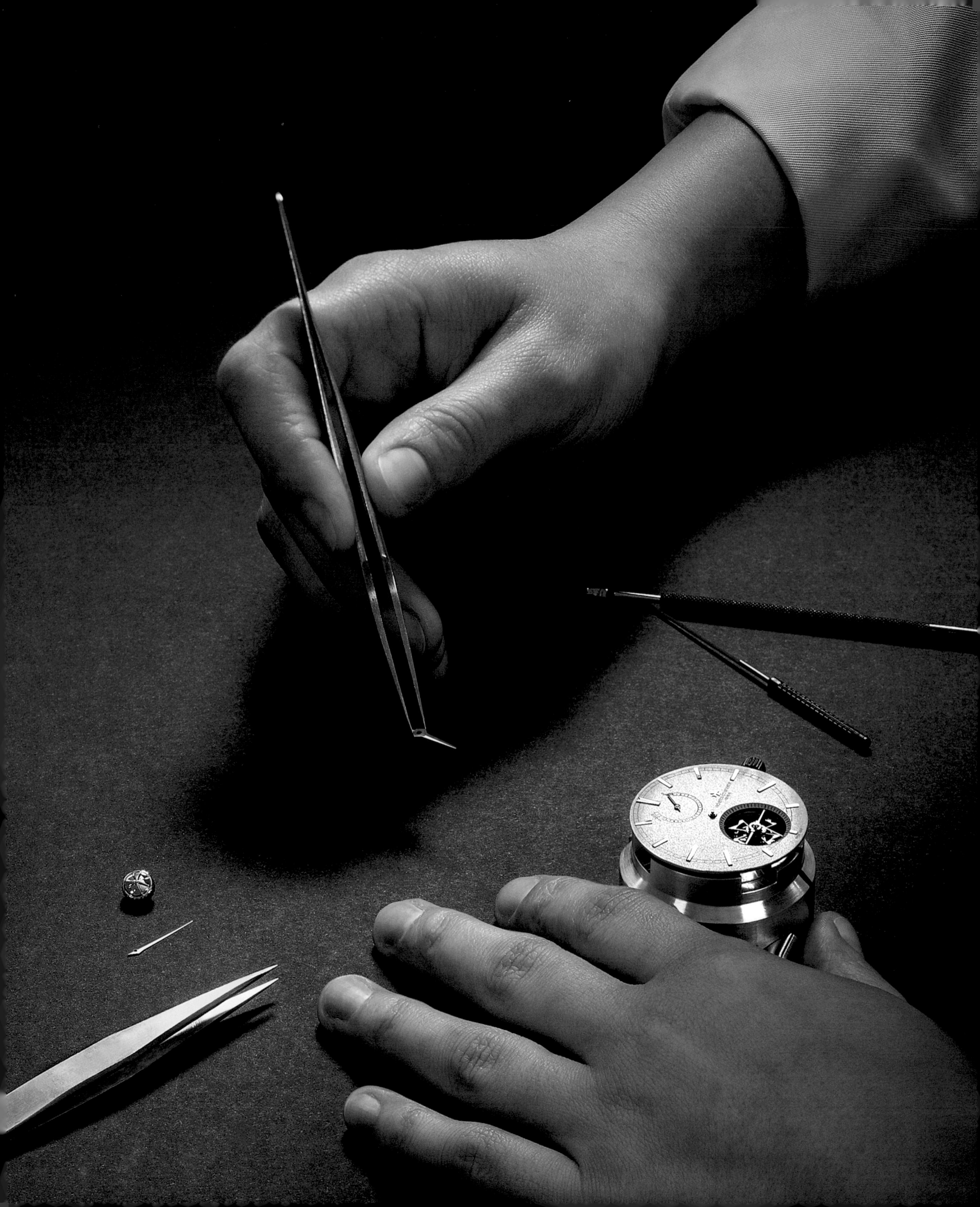

No other sector of industry can claim to bring together such a range of skills as fine watchmaking, which is almost a world of its own. Where else but in a watch manufacture are so many talents found side-by-side: designers, scientists, technicians, artists, craftsmen, and workers? A number of watchmakers acquire several of these skills, often performed by a single specialized professional. At Vacheron Constantin, this versatility is encouraged: a watchmaker can know how to assemble, regulate, and encase a movement. And master watchmakers can design a movement, perform the technical or decorative finishing on its components, assemble and adjust it, fit the dial and hands, and insert it into the case.

Looking through the windows of the various workshops in the Vacheron Constantin manufacture at Plan-les-Ouates located in the canton of Geneva, visitors can't help but be struck by the large number of skills being performed with intense concentration. More than a hundred watchmakers stationed in different workshops lean over benches personally adjusted for height, entirely focused on assembling a movement, piece by microscopic piece. In the complications workshop, the most highly qualified among them assemble tourbillons that compensate for the negative effect of gravity, resulting in even greater precision; perpetual calendars that indicate the date, taking leap years into account; minute repeaters that chime the time; and skeletonized movements that reveal all the complexity and delicacy of a movement.

Seventy kilometers from Plan-les-Ouates, on the other side of the 1447-meter Marchairuz pass in the Swiss Jura mountains, is another ultra-modern Vacheron Constantin manufacturing site housing some 200 of the Vallée de Joux's watchmakers and craftsmen. This second temple of beautiful watchmaking is devoted to machining, finishing, and hand-decorating caliber components such as plates, bridges, balances, and tourbillon bridges. Several minutes of care are given to finishing a one-millimeter screw head, requiring what Vacheron Constantin calls a "good hand." It is the indispensable tool for fine watchmaking.

PREVIOUS LEFT-HAND PAGE
Vacheron Constantin calibers, stamped with the Hallmark of Geneva. From left to right and from top to bottom: Caliber 1400, Caliber 1300, Caliber 2475, Caliber 1120, and Caliber 4400.

LEFT-HAND PAGE
Slender and graceful, designed according to technical and aesthetic criteria, watch hands are immediately visible examples of the watchmaker's art. They must be placed and attached in a specific position with extreme care and attention to ensure an impeccable appearance and functional efficiency.

THE ART OF PRECISION

RIGHT-HAND PAGE
Consisting of a balance wheel and spring to regulate its oscillations, a mechanical watch's regulating organ is suspended from a bridge usually referred to as the balance cock. Traditionally, the balance cock is decorated with delicately engraved patterns.

FOLLOWING DOUBLE PAGE
Patented in 1801 to compensate for the effects of the earth's gravity, the tourbillon is a sophisticated device that is simultaneously one of the most difficult watch subassemblies to produce. At Vacheron Constantin, this mechanism's characteristic rotating carriage takes the shape of a Maltese cross, the emblem of the brand. It is attached to a bridge of traditional design, but slim and elongated in shape, known in watchmaking parlance as a *barrette*.

"When I am timing certain movements, time itself stops," says Michel Keller, the doyen of master timers at Vacheron Constantin. This poetic paradox illustrates the degree of concentration required for timing, one of the most delicate stages in adjusting the watch so that it runs perfectly. It involves a series of minuscule operations performed on the regulating organ (the balance and its spring) to ensure a precise rate, taking account of the different parameters that can affect it, notably gravity in certain positions of the watch. These operations, carried out on infinitely small and fragile parts using tiny tools and meeting microscopic measurements, require great dexterity, high spatial awareness, and a well-developed capacity for thought and analysis.

Over the last twenty years, the work of the master timer has evolved considerably. The acceptable tolerance at Vacheron Constantin (between zero and a few seconds per day) used to be measured by ear and by comparison with a calibrated chronometer over a 24–hour period. Today, electronics and digital technology can instantly measure a variation of as little as one-tenth of a second per day in six positions. The average of these six values determines the precise adjustment to be made. The role of the timing itself, however, has not fundamentally changed.

The art of precision is applied most rigorously in the area of timing and this has been the case at Vacheron Constantin since the middle of the nineteenth century. Some fifty years later, Queen Consort Marie of Romania and King Peter I of Serbia, as well as the Wright Brothers in the United States, acquired Vacheron Constantin chronometers. In 1935, Albert Pellaton, the company's chief technician, presented a portable recording machine designed for sports events that was capable of measuring time to one-tenth of a second. Its lightness, precision, and the fact that it preserved the measurements on a metallic tape would revolutionize timing at high-level competitions. Four pieces were ordered in the first year, two by the Swiss Automobile Club and two by the Swiss Aero Club.

In 1907, the company unveiled the Royal Chronometer, offering a level of precision and reliability that made it an international success. Its centennial was celebrated by a special, valuable edition of the Royal Chronometer 1907 with the double certification of the Hallmark of Geneva and the C.O.S.C. (the official Swiss institute of chronometer testing), in addition to the company's own 30-day running test confirming the superb quality of the Royal Chronometer predicate.

BERGEON No.

MANUAL DECORATION AND FINISHING

The manual finishing of different watch components gives the term "manufacture" its original meaning and distinguishes brands working at a fine watchmaking level from the rest.

Until recently, this craft of finishing had a practical value in watchmaking. Parts that had just been machined often showed minor imperfections that, over time, could deteriorate the metal and impair the smooth running of the watch. At the time, hand-finishing was one of the guarantees of supreme watchmaking quality. Today, modern machines produce flawless parts; hand-finishing is used to remove all traces of machining and to apply decoration. But even before the arrival of these advanced machines, hand-finishing for a master watchmaker was more than just a criterion of technical excellence: it was also an artistic process that gave a movement its beauty. Beveling and polishing by hand transform a highly complex mechanism into a sparkling jewel, an endlessly fascinating marvel.

Lastly, these finishes are a craftsman's signature, a personal mark that involves his professional conscience, respect for tradition, and pride in work well done. This even includes the invisible parts whose secret decoration is only revealed by disassembling the watch completely. Discovering this decoration is surely one of the greatest joys in fine watchmaking.

LEFT-HAND PAGE
The traditional preserve of fine watchmaking, hand-finishing creates contrasts and light effects that give the movement an appearance of unrivaled magnificence. In skeletonized watches, which reveal all the beauty of their interior, many components, some made of solid gold, are entirely openworked, then beveled, drawn, and delicately engraved by master craftsmen of exceptional skill.

BEVELING BY HAND

OPPOSITE
To bevel a part, the sharp edges are removed to form perfectly polished bevels or chamfers along its contours. This work is patiently carried out by hand at Vacheron Constantin, whose craftsmen are specialists in the interior corner, the most difficult beveling technique to perfect. It takes four or five days to bevel one of the brand's emblematic tourbillon carriages in the shape of a Maltese cross.

Beveling removes the sharp edges at the point where the top surface and the side of a component meet. Using a binocular magnifier and a file, the edge is chamfered to produce a 45-degree bevel. This bevel itself is then polished. The component then gives off a stunning impression of volume, and its reflections join in the play of light across the entire movement. While ordinary beveling can be achieved mechanically, beveling intended for fine watchmaking requires the hand of a craftsman; no machine, for example, could achieve one of the criteria of the Hallmark of Geneva: the interior corner. This is the concave angle formed where two sides come together: the result of a long, difficult operation in which the intersection must be clean, presenting a single vertical line. Exterior corners must also be sharply defined.

Eight steps are required to go from the initial sharp edge to the perfect bevel, thereby removing the last trace of almost invisible file marks and creating a perfectly polished surface. The craftsman uses a grinding stone, then several increasingly fine *cabrons* (wooden sticks covered with abrasive fabric like a buffer) to produce a soft feel. Various polishers, some in fabric impregnated with diamond paste, are then used to polish the entire component. A meticulous inspection might require the craftsman to repeat one of these steps to achieve a perfect result. Beveling can then be finished off with a final touch by brightening with a brush. Hand beveling involves up to ten hours of work for various components, while it takes four or five days for a complete tourbillon carriage.

It takes two years to train a beveler. Within the company, someone noted for having good manual dexterity as well as excellent concentration and patience is chosen to learn the subtleties of the art, including the most demanding and spectacular effects, namely what is known as mirror polishing and rounding-off.

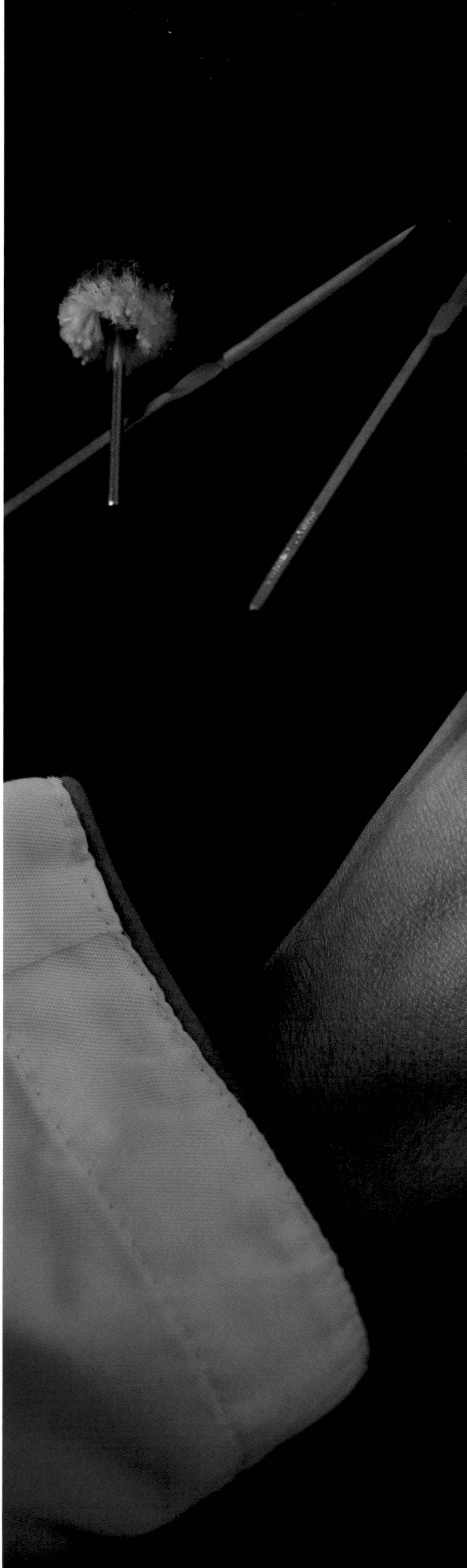

MIRROR POLISHING

"Black polish" (also known as "mirror polish") is the highest level of polishing used at Vacheron Constantin for certain parts, such as screws, indexes, and hammers in striking watches. "Black" because the polish is so perfect that, at a certain angle, the surface does not reflect the light; "mirror" because at another angle it perfectly reflects whatever is in front of it. The reason for black polishing is purely aesthetic: it is the key to creating the wonderful play of light in a movement.

Despite numerous experiments, no machine has been able to achieve this degree of perfection. Polishing a piece in this way requires several hours of work. It starts with preparing a block of zinc, making it as flat as possible with a file, then spreading on a thin layer of diamond paste. The piece is subsequently turned by hand on this paste for as long as necessary. This is where manual dexterity and experience play a vital role. "After some time," explains the polisher, "it slides on its own. This means it is probably done, but we check it with a microscope."

OPPOSITE
Black polish is the result of perfect polishing without the slightest flaw, obtained after several hours of handwork and checked with a microscope. It is a quality standard to which Vacheron Constantin is strongly attached for purely aesthetic reasons.

BELOW
A black-polished Maltese cross forming part of the structure of a Vacheron Constantin tourbillon.

ROUNDING OFF

OPPOSITE
At Vacheron Constantin, the bars upon which tourbillons are placed have their ends rounded off, a technique carried out by the brand's two specialists requiring more than twelve hours of work per part.

Manually polishing the bridge that holds the tourbillon in place calls for a slow, curved, rocking motion.

Rounding off consists of filing the two ends of the bridge evenly to give them a semi-cylindrical, conical shape while respecting the shape of the center and the heels. This half-moon shape requires applying a flat file using a motion that approximates rocking a cradle. To finish the operation, the polisher "softens" the metal by using wooden buffers and finishing paste, thereby obtaining a perfectly polished surface. To be accepted at Vacheron Constantin, the entire length of the component must reflect a single, straight thread of light.

Rounding-off a tourbillon bridge is a challenging technique that requires more than twelve hours of work to meet the finishing criteria. In the Vacheron Constantin Vallée de Joux workshops, the task is entrusted to two experienced, extremely meticulous bevelers. They both prepare their own tools, which they receive unfinished: files, buffers, and polishing woods. And they both use their own methods, choosing what they deem to be the best tools and the best pastes for each stage of work, depending on the quality of the steel and the bridge. This freedom and trust in the craftsman represents one of the brand's keys to excellence.

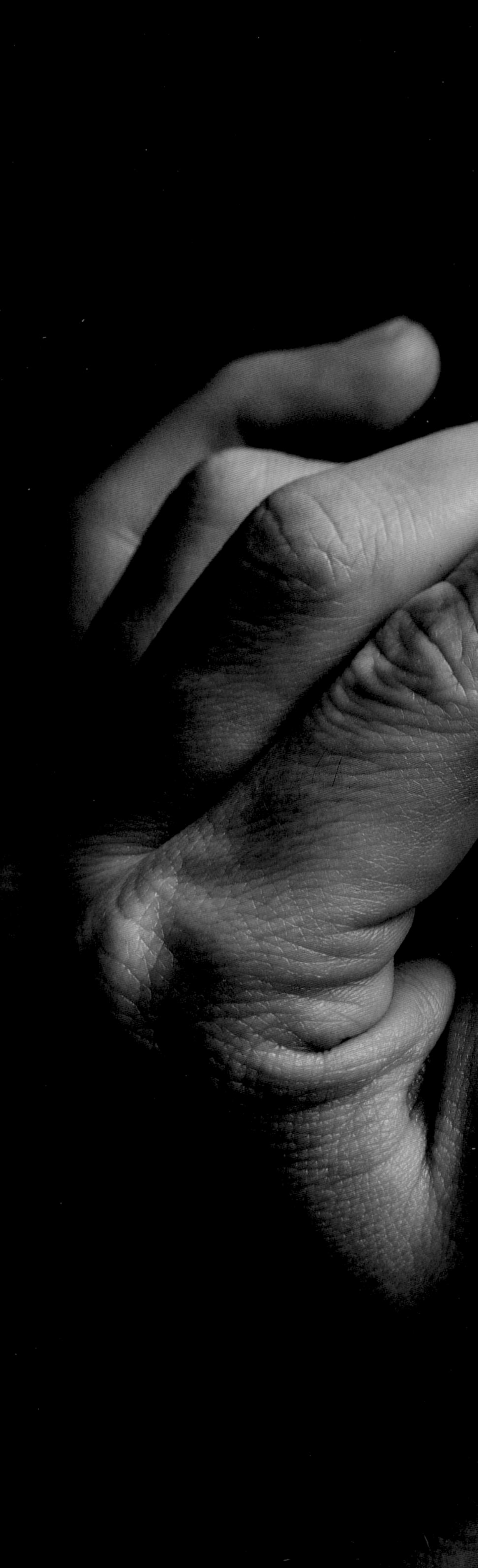

SWISS
VACHERON CONSTANTIN
GENEVE

CÔTES DE GENÈVE

As with circular graining, the company has its own tradition of Côtes de Genève decoration. One of the best known motifs in watchmaking, it forms waves of lines that are applied to bridges and plates in particular. The legend is that it imitates the waves lapping on the shore of Lake Geneva in the early morning before boats disturb its calm waters.

Here, again, the design must be totally mastered so that each movement contributes to the beauty of the overall piece through a subtle play of contrasts. Sometimes they are very visible if the watchmaker has decided to highlight the crafts of manual decoration. But on other models they hardly appear, or seem completely absent, if they risk disrupting the harmony of this part of the movement.

In the world of watchmaking, Vacheron Constantin stands out with Côtes de Genève that are quite special: they are applied very lightly. The reason for this is primarily aesthetic: the company feels that the waves in fashion today lack elegance – they are too deep with overly pronounced edges. Relatively flat, the Vacheron Constantin Côtes de Genève are softer, finer, and more graceful, which means, of course, they are much harder to produce. They are applied by hand using a regular motion with a lathe of sorts and scaled with a ruler.

OPPOSITE
A traditional decoration usually applied to movement bridges and plates, côtes de Genève, sometimes referred to as Geneva stripes, are formed by a series of undulating lines hollowed out of the surface. Vacheron Constantin's Côtes de Genève are particularly refined, crafted as they are by traditional methods using lathes and straight-edge rulers.

CIRCULAR GRAINING

OPPOSITE
Circular graining is a traditional decoration formed by concentric circles of pearl-shaped beads. Vacheron Constantin applies "pearls" of different sizes, even including quarter-sized "pearls." These shapes are produced by applying pressure with an abrasive buffer. The craftsman turns the part to be decorated by hand under the machine bearing the buffer.

The first reason for applying this type of decoration on the components of a movement is to remove all traces of machining, while the second is to give the movement a beautiful, traditional, horological appearance. At one time, before watches were so well sealed, this decorative technique comprising small concentric circles also helped to trap any dust that might have found its way in.

At Vacheron Constantin, the tradition of circular graining is unique. According to the company's criteria of excellence, this decoration is also applied to the parts of a movement that are not visible from the outside. At the same time, the application of the decoration is done by hand: the craftsperson moves the component under the circular graining machine and decides how much pressure to apply. He or she is completely in control of the decoration.

However, the company's criteria are very specific. In order to create beautiful contrasts that highlight certain finishes or components, the circular graining must, as much as possible, be matte in appearance to clearly distinguish it from brilliantly polished parts. In addition, to create a vibrant visual, the overlapping "pearls" may not all be the same size. For this same reason, the company's tradition is that, when possible, quarter-pearls should be included. Naturally, this means that decorating the piece takes four times as long. This sophisticated circular graining, which exceeds the criteria of the Hallmark of Geneva, contributes to the magic of movements signed by Vacheron Constantin. Some consider them to be the most beautiful in the world.

Constantin
R
Platine 1120 sous

HOROLOGICAL COMPLICATIONS

In a watch or clock, a complication is an extra function added to the visual display of hours, minutes, and seconds. "Complicated" watches, sometimes including "grand complications" combining several horological specialties, are one of the special fields mastered by Vacheron Constantin. The first known horological complication dates from the end of the eighteenth century: a calendar providing the date and weekday. The most amazing of the company's series of wristwatches with grand complications is the Tour de l'Île, which combines sixteen complications. Seven examples of it were produced in 2005. In the Plan-les-Ouates building, two workshops are devoted to complications. In one, the most commonly used mechanisms produced by the manufacture are assembled: tourbillons, annual calendars, perpetual calendars, skeletonized perpetual calendars, chronographs, and certain original displays. In the other, grand complications are assembled that are produced in very small series or even as unique pieces, and here we also find the Maître Cabinotier and Atelier Cabinotiers departments.

LEFT-HAND PAGE
Reference 57260 pocket watch, 2015. A world record in terms of watch complications, and an impressive timepiece produced on special commission.

CALENDARS

BELOW
Traditionnelle Perpetual Calendar Openworked wristwatch, 2007. Ultra-thin Caliber 1120QP.

RIGHT-HAND PAGE
Toledo wristwatch, 1952. Made of 18K yellow gold, its curved, square case houses a complete calendar. Inv. no. 10933

In calendar watches, the date is indicated by a hand or appears in an aperture. Vacheron Constantin offers three kinds of calendar watches, each of which is quite complex to produce.

- A date watch displays just that; it does not take the different number of days in some months into account and has to be corrected five times a year (at the end of months shorter than 31 days). This simple calendar watch may also indicate the day of the week and the month. It often includes a moon phase display as well.
- An annual calendar watch indicates the date and automatically adjusts 30- and 31-day months. It has to be corrected only once a year, on March 1.
- A watch with a "perpetual calendar," one of the most intricate watch complications, indicates the month and date besides the hours and minutes. The perpetual calendar automatically takes into account irregular months, moon phases and leap years. For example, the mechanism advances from September 30 to October 1 with no need for manual adjustment. The calendar is "perpetual" because it needs no adjustment, except for the last years of the century which are not leap years. For instance, a current perpetual calendar will not need to be adjusted until 2100. Vacheron Constantin is known for creating perpetual calendars that are ultra-thin: among the most recent is Caliber 1120 QP, one of today's most famous movements with a height of just 2.45 mm. It also displays the phases of the moon, while the day, month, and date are indicated by hands on subdials located at 9, 12 and 3 o'clock.

VACHERON & CONSTANTIN
GENEVE

GRADUE POUR 30 PULSATIONS

MEASURING SHORT PERIODS OF TIME

A chronograph is a particularly difficult timepiece to design and produce due to the large number of moving parts it contains. For a long time it was one of the brand's horological specialties. "One of the chief problems with chronographs is the very small margin for error," explains a master watchmaker, looking at Caliber 3300 presented in 2015 within the Harmony collection. "Because there are so many moving parts, the slightest modification to any one of them can affect the whole mechanism."

At the start of the twentieth century, the company's single-button pocket chronographs measured one-fifth or one-tenth of a second, even a hundredth of a second when requested by some industrialist clients. All through the century, it developed new chronograph movements for pocket watches and wristwatches. Some were given a graduated scale used for measuring a pulse. One of these was a 1928 model that inspired the single-button chronographs in the Harmony collection. Only very experienced watchmakers can assemble the 254 parts of its particularly innovative Caliber 3300.

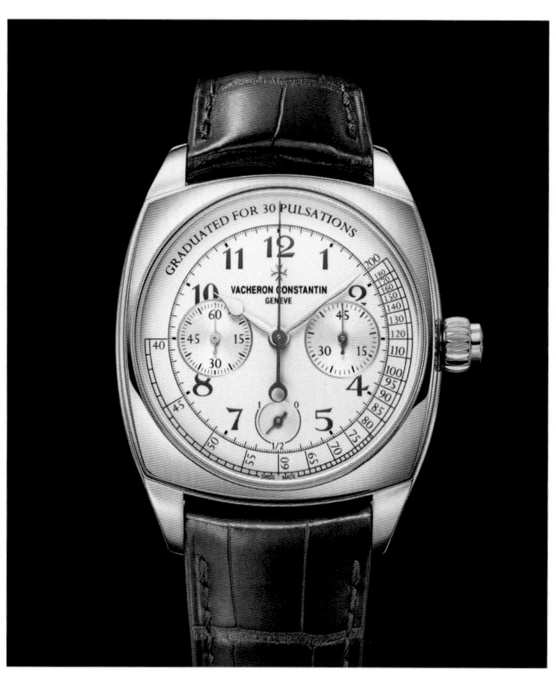

LEFT-HAND PAGE
Monopusher chronograph wristwatch with pulsometer graduated for 30 pulsations, 1928. This cushion-shaped watch in 18K yellow gold was the inspiration for the Harmony collection presented in 2015.
Inv. no. 11059

OPPOSITE
Harmony Chronograph wristwatch, 2015. A new collection launched during the celebratory year marking the 260th anniversary of uninterrupted creativity at Vacheron Constantin. Stamped with the Hallmark of Geneva and crafted in pink gold, it houses a unique chronograph caliber.

STRIKING WATCHES

BELOW
Pocket watch, 1827. Made of 18K pink gold, this model is fitted with a grande sonnerie striking mechanism that repeats the quarter-hours upon request. Inv. no. 10715

RIGHT-HAND PAGE
Patrimony Ultra-Thin Caliber 1731 wristwatch, 2013. This timepiece pulls off the twin feat of being both the thinnest caliber and the thinnest minute repeater watch on the market.

Before the introduction of electric lighting, watchmakers were always looking for ways to indicate the time in the dark. One solution was the repeater watch, a complication with a chiming mechanism that "repeats" the time when activated by pressing a button or moving a lever.

Starting in 1675, this type of watch struck the quarter hours; later, the half-quarter, and finally it chimed every five minutes. Around 1710, the first minute repeater watch was presented in Germany, then in England by Thomas Mudge in 1750.

Vacheron Constantin steadily developed its expertise in quarter-repeater pocket watches then in minute repeaters, which became one of the specialties of Jacques Barthélémi Vacheron. These exceptional pieces introduced the "grand strike," which automatically chimes the hours and quarters by repeating the hour at each quarter and, on demand, the hour, the quarter, and the minute. The "small strike" that sometimes accompanies it automatically chimes the hours and the quarter hours. Both types are normally equipped with a "silence" lever that locks the striking mechanism.

Around 1925, Vacheron Constantin succeeded in fitting the complex repeating mechanism into a wristwatch case, and even together with a perpetual calendar, all while preserving a soft, melodious chime. "See the watch sing" was the invitation from the company's master watchmakers at their creative peak in the early 1990s upon creating a minute repeater wristwatch with a beautifully engraved and polished skeletonized movement visible in all its glory through a transparent case back. In 2007, the company transformed the minute repeater with a new, totally silent governor: the musicality of the chimes was no longer disturbed by the noise of the mechanism. They then took on another challenge: to make the beautiful tones of the gongs resonate properly in a watch as thin as a Patrimony. After years of development, the solution was unveiled in 2013: it was Caliber 1731 (celebrating the year of Jean-Marc Vacheron's birth) with a 65-hour power reserve. Measuring just 3.9 mm in height, it is the thinnest minute repeater movement in the world. Yet it produces a clear ringing tone in this watch that is not only extremely thin (8.09 mm) – in fact, the thinnest on the market at that time – but features a sapphire crystal case back, which theoretically resonates less than a classic, all-metal case.

VACHERON CONSTANTIN
GENEVE

ASTRONOMICAL COMPLICATIONS

Any watch that indicates the time is already a small astronomic complication in itself. However, Vacheron Constantin has been producing astronomical complications for quite some time that are much more sophisticated. The most common is the moon phase indicator, generally displayed in an aperture. More complex is the equation of time that indicates the difference between mean time (the civil time in common use) and solar time. It is slightly different every day, with the difference varying from zero (four times a year) to sixteen minutes. Another technical achievement is the indication of time in different cities of the world. This complication is useful for travelers and has been a tradition of the company since the introduction of the Cottier system of universal time zones in 1932. The most common complication is dual time, which indicates two time zones, but the company is also famous for its Traditionnelle heures du monde watch representing the time in the 37 zones, half zones, and quarter zones across the planet represented by principal cities or geographic points. It is a world record for which a patent has been filed.

Other astronomical indications are rarer: the signs of the zodiac, sunrise and sunset times at a given location, a map of the sky viewed from a given location, the solstice and equinox for the current year, the seasons, and the age of the moon (the number of days elapsed since the last full moon). All these complications, among others, have been brought together in the extraordinary Astronomica: the unique piece developed as a demonstration of Vacheron Constantin's expertise, which includes fifteen complications and is part of the Maître Cabinotier collection. Presented in 2014, it was quickly acquired by a lover of astronomy.

LEFT-HAND PAGE
Maître Cabinotier Astronomica wristwatch, 2014. This unique model combines 15 complications and gives pride of place to the astronomical functions.

OPPOSITE
World time pocket watch, 1946. Made of 18K yellow gold, it houses a silvered dial divided into three segments. The inner section is fitted with hour markers; the 24-hour scale represented with Arabic numerals turns with the movement; and the outer section indicates the names of the world's great cities to represent their time zones. Inv. no. 11182

THE TOURBILLON

BELOW
Malte Tourbillon Collection Excellence Platine wristwatch, 2014. Caliber 2795.

RIGHT-HAND PAGE
Manually-wound Caliber 3200, 2015. This new movement combines a monopusher chronograph and a tourbillon characterized by the famous carriage in the form of a Maltese cross. Although it has a conventional structure, it is equipped with technological innovations that make it particularly accurate and reliable.

The tourbillon is one of the most beautiful and useful complicated elements that can be added to a watch movement. It was invented and patented by Abraham Louis Breguet in 1801 and, basically, it houses the regulating organ of the watch – the balance, the balance spring and the escapement – in a carriage that rotates permanently around its own axis. This rotation cancels out the effects of terrestrial gravity that can perturb the balance and negatively affect the accuracy of the watch.

Vacheron Constantin's watchmakers consider the tourbillon a principal element to take into account when designing a beautiful dial, either alone or paired with complications such as the chronograph, the perpetual calendar, and a power reserve indicator. Today, the movement may be in classic or skeletonized form, but it is ultimately distinguishable by its carriage in the shape of a Maltese cross, the brand's emblem.

For a master watchmaker, it is a challenge to work on a tourbillon, assembling about fifty parts that weigh no more than half a gram in total. But it is also a pleasure. "Placing a tourbillon correctly in its carriage, then into the movement, and finally turning the crown a few times to start it running is a magic moment. The watch comes to life!" Another notable technical achievement is Caliber 2795, a hand-wound mechanical movement with 169 components, which drives the Malte tourbillon Collection Excellence Platine. This tonneau-shaped movement, perfectly adapted to the case of the watch, has been entirely developed and produced in-house. The tourbillon carriage, inspired by the brand's emblematic Maltese cross, showcases the outstanding level of finishing on each component, including several interior corners beveled by hand. Rounding off the single tourbillon bridge is a demanding challenge that requires more than twelve hours of manual work to meet Vacheron Constantin's finishing criteria.

MULTIPLE COMPLICATIONS

Watches and clocks combining several complications are the masterpieces of elite watchmaking, and have appeared regularly throughout the history of Vacheron Constantin. Combinations have included perpetual calendar and tourbillon, chronograph and tourbillon, and perpetual calendar and minute repeater.

Even rarer are the grand complications that include at least three of these – or up to several dozen. Vacheron Constantin is one of only a handful of companies with a long tradition of master watchmakers passionately devoting at least five years of development and production to the creation of extremely complicated pieces, often as a single unique piece. In the history of the company, examples include watches such as the Packard (1919), the Fouad (1929), the Farouk (1934), the Tour de l'Île (2005), as well as clocks such as L'Esprit des Cabinotiers (2005), the Traditionnelle calibre 2755 (2010) and the Traditionnelle calibre 2253 (2011), and the Reference 57260 (2015).

At Vacheron Constantin today, grand complication watches are produced in units where brilliant watchmakers and outstanding craftsmen use the intelligence of the combined mind and hand to display all that is mechanically measurable. Their work can be appreciated in the unique and extraordinary timepiece, the Reference 57260, presented at the 260th anniversary of the company.

LEFT-HAND PAGE
Pocket watch, 1929.
This unique piece was offered by the Swiss community in Egypt to King Fouad I.

OPPOSITE
Reference 57260 pocket watch, 2015.
This piece, the only one of its kind, combines 57 watch complications.

ULTRA-THIN MOVEMENTS

The elegance of finesse is in the genetic makeup of Vacheron Constantin, one of the few horological manufactures that has never stopped developing ultra-thin movements despite fluctuations in their popularity. The company started producing them in the early nineteenth century to meet a strong demand in France and Italy for pocket watches that do not create a bulge in clothing. One hundred years later, the "thinness race" led Vacheron Constantin to develop increasingly slender pocket watch movements that set records at the time: 2.25 mm in 1917; 1.88 mm in 1924; 0.94 mm in 1931.

As for wristwatches, after three years of development, the company introduced Caliber 1003 in 1955. This famously beautiful and reliable hand-wound caliber was, at the time, the thinnest wristwatch caliber in the world at 1.64 mm in height. Still in use in 2010, it equipped the Historiques Ultra-fine 1955 watch, which set a world record with a height of only 4.13 mm.

Vacheron Constantin likes to apply its taste for slim silhouettes to wristwatches with complications, particularly perpetual calendars and repeaters. In 1930, the company launched its first repeating wristwatch. Ultra-thin designs were very popular at the time and Vacheron Constantin Reference 4261 no doubt made a great impression. This pursuit of the extraordinary continued throughout the next decades and produced, among others, a minute-repeater caliber in the 1950s with a height of just 3.25 mm. Then came Caliber 1755 in 1992, a minute repeater movement with a height of 3.28 mm that was endowed with a large power reserve. Continuing in this direction, Caliber 1731 was introduced in 2013: at a height of just 3.9 mm, it was fitted in the Patrimony Ultra-Thin Calibre 1731, a masterpiece of technical virtuosity and delicacy named for Jean-Marc Vacheron's year of birth.

In 2015, the Harmony collection, introduced for the company's 260th anniversary, welcomes the Harmony chronographe grande complication ultra-plat watch, an automatic split-seconds chronograph movement, Caliber 3500. This model holds a dual record: the world's thinnest caliber and the world's thinnest watch to contain this complication.

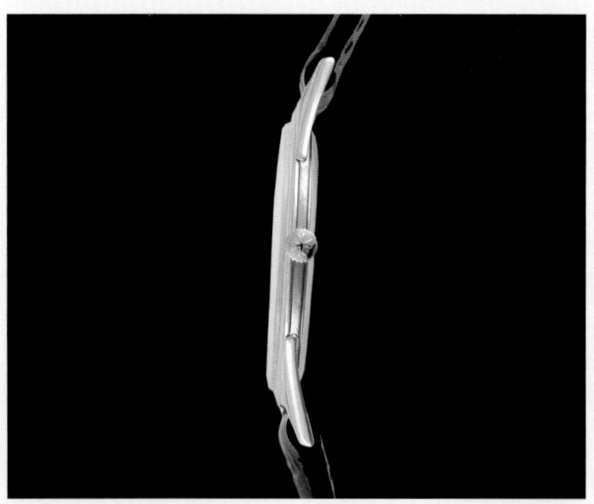

BELOW
Wristwatch, 1955. Made of yellow gold, this ultra-thin piece houses a mechanical movement that is only 1.64 mm thick. Launched to mark the brand's bicentennial, it features strap attachments shaped like Maltese crosses. Inv. no. 11422

RIGHT-HAND PAGE
Harmony Ultra-Thin Grande Complication Chronograph wristwatch, 2015. The self-winding split-seconds chronograph movement, Caliber 3500, is only 5.20 mm high, and its cushion-shaped case only 8.40 mm. Some of the movement's 459 components are only 3/100th of a millimeter thick.

RESTORATION

Twenty-five of the company's watchmakers work exclusively on repair and restoration. Their mission is to preserve the body of expertise, whether it dates back two centuries or just a few years. The three workshops in this service center effectively take care of the most valuable pieces made by the company since the eighteenth century. Two of them repair pieces brought in by their owners: one focusing on recent complication watches or grand complication watches, the other on pieces of any kind made from around 1930 to 1980. The third workshop restores the oldest pieces, unique examples belonging to private individuals or kept in the company's heritage collection. What was the oldest piece restored in recent years? An 1824 quarter-repeater pocket watch sent in from Italy, which was probably sold by François Constantin. Its balance cock is beautifully engraved with the name Vacheron.

Two watchmakers, a timer and a pivot maker – who is responsible for reproducing original balance springs, balance staffs, and pivots – take care of these historic watches. Their task is to reproduce the original balance springs, balance staffs, and pivots in every detail. The fundamental rule is to work with materials dating from the particular era and reproduce the finishes of the time using the machines and tools from that epoch. For example, the workshops use old fixed chisels, various milling cutters, and Vacheron Constantin heritage machines in order to decorate pieces that are almost a century old but still in working condition. They are kept lubricated and ready to use.

The work begins by consulting the company archives to find the original description of the watch that must be meticulously reproduced. Then the watchmakers start searching for similar parts, either within their own stock or on the market. If a defective component cannot be found, it must be copied exactly. The work is not limited to the movement but includes the external components, which can at times be very valuable. This sometimes leads the workshops to call in Vacheron Constantin's jewelers, guilloché artists, and gem setters from other departments.

It is clear that special qualities are needed to be successful at repairing and restoring old watches: a deep interest in watchmaking history and the company's heritage in particular, the instincts of an archaeologist, and a fascination with traveling back in time. It is comparable to a rescue service that restarts a heart that has failed, because every piece that comes through these workshops is returned to its owner in perfect working order.

LEFT-HAND PAGE
In the repair and restoration workshops, watchmakers work on timepieces from all periods. In the case of the oldest models, identical reproductions are made of parts that can no longer be found, using machines and tools from the period.

OPPOSITE
The watchmaker's tools.

MASTER ARTISANS

PREVIOUS LEFT-HAND PAGE
Pocket watch, 1905. Made of 18K yellow gold, engraved and decorated with a miniature landscape painting in enamel, this piece features a silvered guilloché dial. Inv. no. 10792

RIGHT-HAND PAGE
"Scarab" jewelry pendant watch, 1910. Made of 18K yellow gold engraved, enameled, and decorated with guilloché, this jewelry piece is set with rose-cut diamonds and rubies. Inv. no. 10556.

FOLLOWING DOUBLE PAGE
Book by Danielle Plan, published in 1930 in Geneva under the auspices of the Société des Arts. This monograph is dedicated to the life of Abraham Constantin, a reputed painter in the field of porcelain and enamel, and the brother of François Constantin.

What first distinguishes a Vacheron Constantin from other brands' offerings is the feeling of harmony it radiates. This arises from creativity tempered with the criterion of elegance that makes the company unique. Its long heritage in Geneva design is a springboard for exploring new ideas, and it has constantly reinvented the refined, sophisticated wristwatch. Conscious of its 260 years of history, the company's designers work for months on a new watch, defining the tiniest details of its dial, its hands, its lugs, and its strap or bracelet, trying out the effect of new materials and experimenting with the subtleties of different textures. All these are essential steps to creating a Vacheron Constantin watch today.

At the same time, maintaining mastery of all the artistic crafts of ornamentation within the manufacture is rare in the world of fine watchmaking. At Plan-les-Ouates, in a series of intercommunicating workshops with large windows, top experts in guilloché, enameling, engraving, and gemstone-setting pass their art on to apprentices in order to preserve Geneva's tradition of precious, ornamental watches: an unbroken tradition of more than two and a half centuries in which decoration was applied by hand with tools made by the craftsman himself or with highly complex old machines guided by hand such as rose engines.

The artistic crafts, which combine technical expertise with creativity, have been deeply involved in the long history of fine watchmaking in Geneva, particularly at Vacheron Constantin. The artistic crafts and horology came together early on as a result of the religious reform of 1541, when Calvin banned the wearing of ornamental and religious objects. This decision forced goldsmiths, jewelers, and other artisans to apply their skills and knowledge to an art form that was still tolerated: watchmaking. Since the late seventeenth century, Geneva has been recognized as the center of technically advanced, high-value watchmaking.

As such, the manual dexterity of Vacheron Constantin's craftsmen and -women is essential. Using skills passed down over generations, they master materials and, with patience and concentration, pursue perfection in the smallest elements of a caliber. Whether decorated or skeletonized movements, engraved or chased cases, dials with enamel or guilloché, or timepieces set with gemstones – since 1755, the artists of time at Vacheron Constantin have remained true to the spirit of the eighteenth-century cabinotiers of Geneva, lavishing as much care on the interior of their creations as on the exterior.

Traditional crafts practiced in an ultra-modern facility behind large bay windows overlooking the historic neighborhood of Saint-Gervais – this could be one of the key images of the world of Vacheron Constantin today. It symbolizes drawing on the treasure of tradition and gaining energy from looking out over the world while engaging in permanent dialog with designers and master watchmakers as a guide and superb craftsmanship as a tool. Without forgetting the support of independent specialists working in areas that are still unseen in watchmaking in the spirit of invention that is one of the features of the company. This is what is required to produce watches that are incontestable masterpieces of the art. The virtuosity of their decoration is unique in watchmaking today, using imagination just as much as extraordinary, re-imagined techniques.

A. Constantin, dessin d'Ingres.
(A Mlle A. Boissonnas.)

MELLE PLAN

NSTANTIN

TRE SUR ÉMAIL
SUR PORCELAINE

BLIÉ SOUS LES AUSPICES
DE LA
OCIÉTÉ DES ARTS

DITIONS DE GENÈVE
1930

12 Juillet 30

THE DESIGNER

The satin finish of a platinum dial, the finesse of a gold hour marker, the sheer nobility of a blue numeral, the balanced arrangement of displays in a grand complication watch, the gracious curve of a lug, and the subtle play of colors and textures in different metals...these are some of the many details of the elegance that distinguishes a Vacheron Constantin watch from all others. What is the secret of this aesthetic excellence? Quite simply it is the taste and skill of designers who can draw on a 260-year heritage as a basis for innovation.

Three examples, three iconic watches from the world of Vacheron Constantin: the Patrimony, the Overseas, and the Quai de l'Île.

Its simplicity, purity and minimalism makes the Patrimony the essential classic of the brand, the most delicate watch highlighting the perfection of the circle – the theme that has guided the designer's inspiration. The starting point is the simple time display of the most traditional pieces, and the heritage of more than two centuries of round and thin watches at Vacheron Constantin. A circular-grained minute track, four elongated, triangular hour markers, and eight very delicate baton markers make for perfect symmetry that dictates the rest of the design. This harmony is echoed on the various areas of the dial between empty spaces and those occupied by these few elements. The watch, which must be thin and very elegant, requires all the other elements to be in proportion: delicate, discreet hands; a narrow bezel that does not interfere with the displays on the dial; and simple, more contemporary lugs whose width and positioning are carefully chosen to match the diameter and width of the bezel.

There is perfection in every detail: an ultra-thin, curved case highlights the wrist rather than distracts from the dial and the bezel. The gently domed crystal prolongs the curve of the bezel and the dial, which itself is domed. But since one feature doesn't stand out, the design boasts a magnificent harmony that starts with the unique hour circle and its affinity with the case. Ironically, the elegant perfection of this supreme simplicity required years of development and dozens of sketches and mock-ups.

Another great design success was the elegant sports watch Overseas, inspired by models the company created in the 1930s and in particular the famous 222 of the 1970s. It originally launched in 1996 and enjoyed a second surge of interest in 2004. Particularly notable is its new, highly contemporary bracelet with a uniquely wide link and prominent polished bevels that suggest the Maltese cross. Echoing the watch with its strong design codes, including the Maltese cross engraved on the winding mechanism, the new bracelet perfectly integrates with the case and helps confirm the overall identity of the watch. Highly distinctive and evocative of the company emblem, the Maltese cross bracelet, now easily recognizable from a distance, has made a major contribution to the success of this new Overseas around the world. Other versions with leather or rubber strap are housed in gold, titanium, or two-tone (pink gold and steel) cases.

The year 2008 saw the arrival of the Quai de l'Île watches that have revolutionized the concept of fine watchmaking. The designers' idea was to reach out to younger clients who appreciate both beauty and technology. After much discussion, a style was set for the whole watch: a shape somewhere between tonneau and cushion, a round dial, and very thin, fluid lines directly inspired by certain

LEFT-HAND PAGE
The secret of the elegance of Vacheron Constantin watches lies in a multitude of details that have long been studied by designers imbued with the culture and stylistic history of the brand.

RIGHT-HAND PAGE
Each detail is imagined by the designer and gives rise to a study.

sports cars. Just as certain automobile brands invent increasingly complex shapes to discourage copying, it was decided to make the sides of the watch case deliberately complicated.

After many mock-ups and three-dimensional drawings, the design of the case was finalized. Its complexity ruled out a classic construction and soon led the designers to consider a play of different materials. Elements like the lugs, the spaces between the lugs, and the sides were located around a central case containing the movement, the dial, the hands, etc. This suggested the idea of personalization, enabling the client to compose his or her case using a selection of different materials, some of which were completely new to Vacheron Constantin: titanium, tantalum, and palladium. Pink gold and white gold were natural additions to this list.

Complexity was also designed into the dial. The designers decided to show the top of the movement while making it easy to read the indications of the complications it incorporated. They wanted to create different levels for the eye as well as a nearly invisible world to explore with a loupe. To achieve this, the sapphire crystal dial was given a polymer filter that makes it possible to read the indications as well as to see the entire movement. The fineness of this filter is adjustable, thanks to the hundreds, or even thousands, of Maltese crosses micro-printed on it. The technical and design innovations in the Quai de l'Île watches make it a "laboratory" line at Vacheron Constantin. They are still, however, beautifully elegant and have nothing to envy in the timeless classicism of a Patrimony.

CREATIVE DISPLAYS

BELOW
Pocket watch, 1825. This ultra-thin model features jumping hours and a silver guilloché dial. The case back and pendant are decorated with floral motifs in black champlevé enamel.
Inv. no. 11744

RIGHT-HAND PAGE
Métiers d'Art Tribute to Great Explorers - Marco Polo Expedition wristwatch, 2004. With magnificent dials crafted in *grand feu* enamel and reproducing maps of the journeys of the greatest explorers in history, this watch completes a collection that offers what is referred to as a "dragging" hour indication, thanks to the self-winding manufacture Caliber 1126AT.

With its skill in making external components that are both daring and elegant, Vacheron Constantin often sought to indicate the time in a way other than the traditional revolution of hands around the dial. During the twentieth century, one of the company's most amusing creative displays was its "arms in the air" (*bras en l'air*) watches. When activated by a pushbutton, a figure indicated the hour with its right arm and the minutes with its left. In 1955, on its watch paying tribute to the cartographer Mercator, the company developed the "divergent display" with two watch hands linked at the top like a navigator's compass. The left hand indicated the hour and the right hand the minutes.

More recently, creative displays have mostly appeared in the Métiers d'Art collection, which is designed to display the decorated dials in uninterrupted splendor. For the Métiers d'Art Hommage aux Grands Explorateurs series, launched in 2004, the company developed a moving display of the hours on a revolving enameled disc, visible in an aperture extending 120 degrees. This principle was used again in 2015 with the Métiers d'Art Savoirs Enluminés series. In 2007, the Métiers d'Art Les Masques watches presented the time and date in four apertures: the hour at 10 o'clock, the minutes at 1 o'clock, the date at 4 o'clock, and the day at 7 o'clock. This discreet display, which does not disturb the decoration, was inspired by the Métiers d'Art watches for the 250th anniversary, and was used again in 2014 for the Métiers d'Art La Légende du Zodiaque Chinois and the Métiers d'Art Eloge de la Nature.

Creative displays also appear in the technical watches of pure time-only collections: for example, the day and date indications by retrograde hands on a Patrimony, or the sapphire crystal day and night disc that revolves above a second disc engraved with a map of the world in the Traditionnelle Heures du Monde watch.

VACHERON CONSTANTIN
GENEVE
RUSSIA
MONGOLIA
PERSIA
Kashgar
Tokto
Khotan
Shachow
Cambaluc
Mare Giallo
Kerman
Hormuz
Himalaya
Indus
Yangtse
Mare Cinese Meridionale
Mare
Gange
Mekong
Golfo del Bengala
60
50
Ceylon
40
30
4
20
10
0

THE ENAMELER

The art of enameling was already valued by the pharaohs in 1500 BCE; for 4,000 years, this ancient art has been used to decorate a wide range of decorative items. It was adopted by watchmakers in the seventeenth century to enhance and embellish their pieces, putting Geneva at the center of the art. Particularly difficult to master, it includes several different techniques: champlevé enamel, cloisonné enamel, and miniature painting. The techniques of both champlevé and cloisonné enamel show the outlines of the motifs. In the first, the design is traced on a gold plate and the outlines formed by "excavating" each field to form cavities, which are then filled with enamel. In the second, the enameler traces the design with gold wire then seals it to a first coat of enamel by firing it in a kiln: the "cells" formed in this way are then ready to receive their individual enamel.

In all the *grand feu* (high fire) techniques, a few grains of enamel in the chosen color are laid down with an extremely fine brush. The color is obtained by mixing glass and metallic oxides according to a traditional alchemist's formula. After the first color is applied, the piece is fired at around 800°C. The artist then adds a second color, which must also be fired, continuing in this way for as many as ten firings and sometimes even more. Once the motif is complete, several coats of translucent enamel are applied, each requiring another firing. This stage provides the protection that ensures the enamel's permanence. It also brings out the intensity and brilliance of the colors and highlights the subtle vibrations and depth of the work.

This rare artistic craft, which has been used and developed by Vacheron Constantin since its early days, is only practiced by a handful of specialized artisans around the world. Mastering it requires total discipline at all times as it is one of the most demanding of all artistic techniques. The collection of vintage Vacheron Constantin watches decorated with enamel represents a wide range of techniques and themes, including travel, nature, floral designs, figurative scenes, landscapes, and even miniature reproductions of paintings by famous artists.

LEFT-HAND PAGE
Ladies' pendant watch, 1922. This watch in 18K yellow gold features a case back delicately enameled with a floral decoration that applies the ancestral technique of miniature painting in enamel. Inv. no. 10840

OPPOSITE AND FOLLOWING LEFT-HAND PAGE
Decorative enamel work is achieved through the use of different techniques but always involves the application of successive layers fired in a kiln. Consisting of glass and metal oxides, enamel is applied in small quantities using extremely thin brushes. Following a tradition created in Geneva, the work is completed by the application of fondant, i.e. layers of translucent enamel that enhance and protect the finished motifs. Vacheron Constantin calls upon the services of craftsmen with exceptional and increasingly rare skills in order to thus embellish its creations.

FOLLOWING RIGHT-HAND PAGE
Métiers d'Art Les Univers Infinis wristwatch, 2012. Paying tribute to the centuries-old art of tessellation, with regularly repeated motifs, this collection celebrates the work of Dutch artist Maurits Cornelis Escher through its engraving, guilloché, gem-setting, and *grand feu* enameling.

SWISS
MADE

ET IN
RCADI
EGO
Gall

GENEVA TECHNIQUE OF *GRAND FEU* ENAMEL MINIATURE PAINTING

Developed around 1760, the Geneva technique of miniature painting in *grand feu* enamel under a translucent coating is the peak of the enameler's art. Today, it is only practiced by a very few independent enamelers. Vacheron Constantin has been helping to keep this tradition alive since the early nineteenth century as illustrated by the magnificent pocket watch from 1923 representing the famous painting by Nicolas Poussin, *Les Bergers d'Arcadie.*

In 2007, the company again highlighted this extraordinary technique with the Métiers d'Art Chagall et l'Opéra de Paris series. The dial of one of these watches reproduces Marc Chagall's 200-square-meter painting on the ceiling of the Paris Opera.

With a diameter of 31.5 mm and a height of 1 mm, the enameler started by applying a white base coat and firing it at 900°C so that it could withstand the numerous firings to come. On this background, he drew the outlines of the subjects using a brush with just two or three sable hairs. With the help of a very powerful binocular magnifier, he gradually painted the oeuvre: the colors were placed point by point in a precise order moving from the softest tones to the most vibrant. After some twenty firings between 800°C and 850°C, the motif began to appear. During these critical stages, as the heat vitrifies the colors, they change, shrink, and become more intense. This is where the experience of the enameler plays a key role. The duration of the firing is carefully calculated according to the type and quantity of material applied. It is one of the enamel artist's trade secrets. The last stage of the process is particularly hazardous: the enamel is fragile, sometimes unpredictable, and threatens to explode each time it comes out of the oven. The cooling stages must be very carefully managed to avoid any sudden changes of temperature. The slightest mishap can cause irreversible damage and force the enameler to abandon the piece and start again. When a miniature painting on enamel is fired for the final time, a finishing layer, consisting of two or three coats of transparent enamel, is normally applied to protect the work against the ravages of time. This finish, in turn, is fired at 800°C after which the enameler rubs down and polishes the painting to bring out its full visual impact.

At least three months of intense work is required to decorate a single watch.

LEFT-HAND PAGE
Pocket watch, 1923. This model in engraved yellow gold is embellished by a reproduction of the famous painting *The Arcadian Shepherds* by Nicolas Poussin using the ancestral technique of miniature enamel painting. The watch's back cover features the engraving *Summer Reapers Arriving in the Pontine Marshes* by Léopold Robert and an extract from Beethoven's *Pastoral Symphony*. The movement is engraved with two small cherubs inspired by the ceiling of the Sistine Chapel painted by Raphael (also see pages 302 and 353). Inv. no. 10659

BELOW
Métiers d'Art Chagall et l'Opéra de Paris wristwatch, 2010.

GRISAILLE ENAMEL

BELOW
Pocket watch, 1905.
Inv. no. 11659

RIGHT-HAND PAGE
Métiers d'Art Hommage à l'Art de la Danse wristwatch, 2013. To mark the tricentennial of the Paris Opera Ballet School, Vacheron Constantin revived the ancestral technique of *grand feu grisaille* enamel to spotlight the art of classical ballet in the form of various masterpieces painted by Edgar Degas.

In 2013, Vacheron Constantin presented three watches with dials inspired by three paintings of dancers by Edgar Degas. They were the first in the Métiers d'Art Hommage à l'Art de la Danse series, which soon grew to include twelve watches. All were produced as a single piece, with a level of quality that was equally unique.

The paintings were reproduced in grisaille enamel, a technique that dates back to the ninth century. Extremely difficult to apply, it has only been mastered by small number of craftsmen. Normally it begins with a coat of black enamel on a gold base, then the motif is created by a succession of spots in *blanc de Limoges* white paint spread using needles and very fine brushes to obtain the desired shades of gray. Each coat is fired for a precise length of time, measured to the second, depending on the quality and amount of material being applied; three seconds too long and the motif disappears – which happens from time to time, and when it does, three weeks' worth of work is wiped out. Apart from great expertise, a master enameler needs nerves of steel. With ten successful firings, a large range of gray is produced, enabling the artist to create very delicate motifs with shadows and shimmering reflections.

The challenge for Vacheron Constantin's enamelers was to give the grisaille enamels as much relief, sensitivity, and softness as the brightly colored paintings by Degas. After a good deal of trial and error, they managed to invent a new version of grisaille by using a base coat of translucent enamel instead of black enamel. This method, which includes other technical innovations that remain secret, gave the decoration what they were looking for. The result is that a Vacheron Constantin grisaille can be recognized by its depth of color and variations in brightness.

VACHERON CONSTANTIN
GENEVE

MAKI-E, JAPANESE ART OF LACQUER

BELOW AND RIGHT-HAND PAGE
Métiers d'Art La Symbolique des Laques wristwatch, 2010. The lacquer used, known as *urushi*, is a natural product, obtained by cutting notches in the bark of the urushi trees that grow in Japan. This art flourished during the Heian era (794-1185).

Following the international success of the Métiers d'Art Les Masques series in 2007, one of the oldest Japanese lacquer companies, Zohiko (founded in Kyoto in 1661), proposed a collaboration with Vacheron Constantin. Years of work and thought finally produced the Métiers d'Art La Symbolique des Laques series between 2010 and 2012: three boxes of three watches in a limited production of twenty pieces. The series illustrates one of the fundamental values of the company: opening up to others and to other world cultures with the beauty they have to offer.

Once the two companies had agreed on the motifs taken from Japanese traditions of design and symbolism, the Zohiko craftsmen decorated the dials with the most sophisticated technique of Japanese lacquering: *maki-e*. This term means "seeded image." The freshly painted motif is placed on a background of dry black lacquer and sprinkled with a fine gold or silver powder while it is still wet. The valuable powder only adheres to the wet parts, highlighting the motif in all its delicate beauty. The different stages of this manual technique are generally performed freehand without support, which requires considerable dexterity as it has for more than ten centuries.

THE *GUILLOCHEUR*

An art that brings together hand and machine, guilloché was successfully utilized in watchmaking throughout the nineteenth century. Vacheron Constantin has used it since 1780 to enhance its watches with an endless variety of guilloché patterns, as shown in a yellow gold pocket watch with an embossed engraving on the case and guilloché work on the dial around a floral center in champlevé enamel. Straight or curved patterns, measured in tenths of a millimeter, are engraved on gold using a "straight line" machine or a lathe. Unlike industrial guilloché work, at Vacheron Constantin the operation is carried out from beginning to end by artists who use the machine simply as an extension of their hands.

They give free rein to their imaginations by playing with shapes, spaces, and intersections to create rosette motifs, broken lines, ripples, and waves. Whatever pattern they choose, it is composed of a series of symmetrical motifs created with great dexterity and artistic sensitivity. With one hand, the artists turn the handle advancing the piece to be decorated, and with the other they manipulate the frame holding the graver tool that engraves the fine, regular lines. Combining several guilloché patterns adds richness to the dial and improves its readability.

Clous de Paris (hobnail), *grains d'orge* (barleycorn), *rayons de soleil* (sunburst), *gros grains* (large beads), and *pannier* (basket weave) are among the countless variations that create their own play of light and enable the guilloché artist to emphasize the watch functions.

Guilloché is sometimes enameled to form a shimmering decoration where the play of light gives a beautiful impression of depth.

The wonderful creativity of one of its specialists enabled Vacheron Constantin to revolutionize this traditional art with "figurative" guilloché work. This unique process utilizes the same traditional guilloché machines, but replaces the network of lines with a pattern of minuscule points, rather like pixels, that can be used to draw any kind of motif. A drawing made with this technique radiates incomparable strength and resonance. In 2009, Vacheron Constantin used this technique in the Métiers d'Art Les dragons limited series of watches: three Chinese dragons in several colors of gold, engraved with manually applied guilloché. Nine examples of each were produced. It took a master guilloché artist an entire year to produce these extremely valuable watches, which were a major success and received a great amount of attention...and also inspired many crude fakes. This revolutionary technique made a rare reappearance in 2013 combined with translucent enamel in the Métiers d'Art Florilège collection.

LEFT-HAND PAGE
Chronomètre Royal pocket watches, 1907. The case in 18K yellow gold features delicate guilloché work with a sunburst finish. A series of guilloché plates from the 19th and 20th centuries testify to the wide variety of guilloché designs.
Inv. nos. 11238 and 11268

OPPOSITE
Métiers d'Art Les Dragons wristwatch, 2009. It took the master *guillocheur* concerned one year's work to perfect the application of the guilloché technique to the dial of this timepiece.

RIGHT-HAND PAGE
Guilloché on the dial of a Métiers d'Art Florilège wristwatch.

FOLLOWING LEFT-HAND PAGE
At Vacheron Constantin, guilloché is carried out by applying the methods of traditional craftsmanship using machines such as rose engines, which are constantly guided by hand. With one hand the craftsman turns the piece to be decorated, while the other pushes the carriage that carries the graver tool.

FOLLOWING RIGHT-HAND PAGE
Ultra-thin pocket watch, 1929. Designed in the Art Deco style, this watch in 18K yellow and white gold features jumping hours and a silvered dial with a sunburst-effect guilloché center. A triangular hour marker in onyx indicates the minutes, while the hour is displayed in an aperture.
Inv. no. 10152

12H

90 72 48

VACHERON & CONSTANTIN

THE ENGRAVER

A master engraver at Vacheron Constantin has a wide variety of tools available to bring a material to life. Two traditional techniques in particular are used to create an infinite variety of a decorations. Engraving in relief (embossing) is inspired by low relief sculpture. Intaglio engraving, also known as "line engraving," is borrowed from the printing of postage stamps and banknotes as well as the reproduction of old engravings.

The artist working in relief uses a graver or chisel to progressively remove material around the outline of the design until it emerges in three dimensions. A variation of this – used for ornamental engraving of precious metals – is *la taille de joue*, in which the engraver tilts the tool to make a larger incision that will reflect the full sparkle of light. This technique involves removing shavings to create furrows of varying widths and depths that form the decoration or the scene. In conjunction with the craft of engraving is that of chasing, a symbol of extreme refinement that is increasingly rare today. Instead of removing material it pushes and shapes it, using tools developed over the centuries: *boutrolles*, blunt-tipped chisels, and hammers.

Vacheron Constantin has always used the delicacy of engraving to decorate its watches. In the late eighteenth and early nineteenth centuries, its watch cases often displayed Moorish-style motifs in relief or intaglio engraving created with gravers. In the 1820s, the chaser worked the metal with chisels and hammers to create the decoration in relief. The second half of the nineteenth century was marked by a fashion for displaying one's initials on the case of a pocket watch. They were applied as a cut-out, chased, polished, inlaid, or simply beautifully engraved. The arrival and spread of wristwatches substantially reduced the call for engraving since the only spaces they offered were the bezel and possibly the case band. However, Vacheron Constantin ensured the survival of the craft with increasingly subtle and sophisticated decoration on its most beautiful movements, cases, and dials.

The supremely gifted master engravers at Vacheron Constantin apply their art to all the parts of the watch that can be engraved, in relief or intaglio, then beveled and polished by hand: dials, case backs, covers, hands, clasps, and skeletonized parts can be decorated using their gravers and chisels – tools that have not changed since the fourteenth century – which they personally "finish" before starting their work.

The engravers also innovate and invent new techniques that make certain Vacheron Constantin watches unique in the world of watchmaking. For example, in the Métiers d'Art Mécaniques Ajourées collection introduced in 2014 they transformed one of the great company traditions: the art of skeletonization. In skeletonizing one of its iconic calibers, the hand-wound 4400, they took their inspiration from architecture and proceeded to sculpt the movement. Rather than the usual hacksaw method of removing areas of the plates' and bridges' flat surfaces with a small saw then drawing and beveling them, the master engravers carved out the entire components around the edge, creating genuine sculptures with volume and relief. Copying the vaulted arches of railway stations from the end of the nineteenth century, they created delicate arches on the caliber in a fascinating curved design. Its roundness broke away from the straight lines of classic skeleton movements and involved more complex beveling and drawing than ever. In the intertwining of interior angles that only the

LEFT-HAND PAGE
Pocket watch, 1897. The Art Nouveau style can be seen here in the scrolls of delicately engraved yellow gold with a floral motif carved in openworked components. Inv. no. 11248

OPPOSITE
Métiers d'Art Mécaniques Ajourées wristwatch, 2014. This model forms a link between two fields that developed in a similar way during the 19th century: architecture and watchmaking. Developed from one of the brand's key movements, Caliber 4400, this creation takes inspiration for its ethereal structure from the great European railway stations of the golden age of the industrial revolution, transcending the art of skeletonization.

RIGHT-HAND PAGE
The master engraver employs a wide range of tools, in particular chisels and gravers, to decorate timepieces held in place with a clamp.

FOLLOWING DOUBLE PAGE
Pocket watch, 1910.
This hunter-style timepiece in 18K yellow gold features a bas-relief engraving representing *L'Audition en tête-à-tête* inspired by a work of the 17th century.
Inv. no. 10559

hand of man is capable of finishing, polished finishes captured the light while the matte-finished drawn surfaces offered a striking contrast. A blend of different finishes created by hand to enhance the vaulting arches required more than three days of work on each caliber and accorded each one a unique personality.

2
6

SKELETONIZED MOVEMENTS

OPPOSITE
Pocket watch, 1953. The Art Deco-style rock crystal case is surrounded by a platinum bezel. The case band and flange are set with sapphires, highlighting a skeletonized movement in pink gold.
Inv. no. 11123

RIGHT-HAND PAGE
After placing the skeletonized plate in wax to keep it in place, the master craftsman prepares to decorate it to highlight the beauty and structural complexity of the movement.

Creating the perfect fusion of technology and design is more than a policy at Vacheron Constantin: it has been an obsession for at least two hundred years. A perfect example of this is the skeletonized watch in which all the parts are opened and decorated by hand to highlight the functional beauty of the mechanism. The first known Vacheron Constantin movement to be entirely skeletonized dates from 1924. Ever since that time, the company has continued to increase transparency in its designs, becoming a master of this most challenging technique. It is one of the very few manufactures capable of skeletonizing such complicated calibers as minute repeaters, perpetual calendars, tourbillons, and ultra-thin movements. The decoration that its master engravers apply to these openworked mechanisms can reach a degree of sophistication that is probably unique in fine watchmaking.

THE GEM-SETTER

Completely devoted to the art of time, Vacheron Constantin's gem-setters fully appreciate the volume of the piece being created. They work the material with their hands and prepare it for setting. Connoisseurs of precious stones and their cuts, strengths, and ability to catch the light, gem-setters choose the technique that will respect the design of the piece most effectively. In a close setting, the stone is encircled by metal that the setter folds tightly all around it. The claw, grain, and *clous* settings display the stone optimally by showing it more completely. Lastly, the pinnacle of the gem-setter's art is the invisible setting, in which the metal structure is completely hidden so as to not distract from the stone.

In watchmaking, gem-setting is a relentlessly rigorous discipline. Working with extremely fine layers of gold, master gem-setters adapt to the limits imposed by the functional nature of the watch while working with the stones and the metal. Using traditional tools, they take great care not to use excessive force to avoid the risk of scratching or even chipping a precious stone.

At Vacheron Constantin, watchmaking and jewelry have been intimately linked since the very beginning. Like two facets of the same work of art, the fine gold of a watch case is often enhanced by precious stones and enameling. But it was only in the nineteenth century that watches truly became pieces of jewelry – status symbols for owners who were much more concerned with fashion than with function. Diamonds, rubies, sapphires, emeralds, turquoise, pearls, onyx, garnets, and many other stones were used to soften the curve of a pair of glasses, form the petals and pistils of a flower, enhance an enamel miniature, or embellish an engraved or finely chased decoration. Gradually, however, instead of simply highlighting a shape, fine and precious stones became the decoration itself.

Experimenting with style is a constant feature of Vacheron Constantin collections of jewelry watches. It demonstrates a powerful creativity that anticipates new trends. In the search for ultimate refinement, from the middle of the nineteenth century the company used platinum to create very delicate decoration that showed off the brilliance of diamonds as never before. After the decades devoted to Art Nouveau and Art Deco, a wave of creative freedom dominated the post-war years, particularly in an unexpected emphasis on gold. Over time, Vacheron Constantin's gem-setters have revealed the many facets of their art, most spectacularly in 1979 with a watch that would make its mark in history: the Kallista, which boasts 118 emerald-cut diamonds totaling 130 carats.

In 2009, to celebrate the 30th anniversary of this exceptional creation, Vacheron Constantin launched the Kallania. Once again the company made headlines by setting a new world record: this modern jewelry masterpiece, distinguished by its essential lines, is decorated with 186 very pure emerald-cut diamonds, totaling around 170 carats. The diamonds were certified both by the independent laboratory of the Swiss Institute of Gemology and by the GIA (Gemological Institute of America). Their sourcing was also an important achievement; apart from the secrecy that had to surround the making of the watch, Vacheron Constantin was determined to respect

LEFT-HAND PAGE
At Vacheron Constantin, watches can be customized by means of initials set with precious stones.

OPPOSITE
Métiers d'Art Lady Kalla Flame wristwatch, 2009. This jewelry piece is embellished with flame-cut diamonds, used here for the first time ever in watchmaking.

RIGHT-HAND PAGE
The invisible setting is one of the most sophisticated gem-setting techniques. It ensures that all metal disappears completely from view beneath the precious stones.

FOLLOWING DOUBLE PAGE
Jewelry wristwatch, 1923. The Art Deco style is revealed here amid the combined brilliance of diamonds and sapphires, which enhance a geometrical dial divided by glittering Arabic numerals. Inv. no. 10981

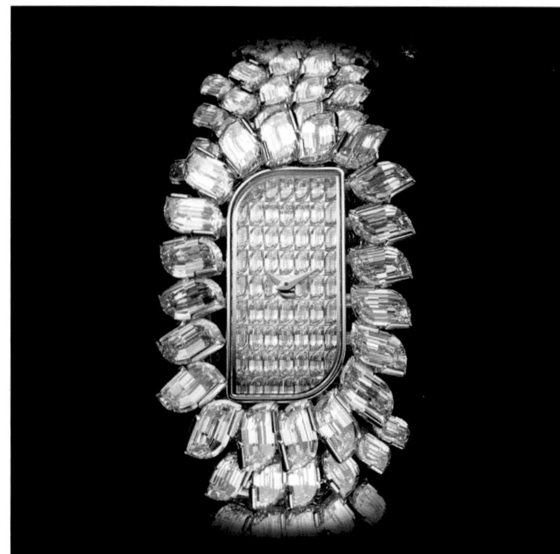

the Kimberley Process prohibiting the import of precious stones from countries in conflict.

Two other watches, the Métiers d'Art Lady Kalla Flame and the Métiers d'Art Lady Kalla Haute Couture à Secrets (which were followed two years later by the Kalla Haute Couture à Pampilles), are covered in diamonds of a cut that was unique in watchmaking, and still is: the flame cut. Vacheron Constantin is the only watchmaker using flame-cut diamonds, a cut recently approved by the GIA. Asymmetrical with a thin profile and comprising 57 facets, the flame-cut diamond has a dynamic femininity, evoking a naked flame and revealing the sparkling brilliance of the stone. It requires a specific, complex setting, known as the semi-closed claw setting.

The principal master setter at Vacheron Constantin has forty years' experience and is entrusted with these exceptional stones. He oversees all the settings including the very complicated invisible setting: every stone is "clicked" into a foil cup about one tenth of a millimeter in diameter, which must be individually adjusted. In the case of the Malte tourbillon haute joaillerie, limited to eight examples, more than 500 diamonds were involved, each with a microscopic slot that had to be individually adjusted. Six or seven weeks' worth of work were needed.

SYMPHONIE PASTORALE
923. Souvenir de l'affection de deux frères.
1864

COMBINING ARTISTIC CRAFTS

The various artistic crafts practiced at Vacheron Constantin are located in the same area of the manufacture to form a solid team. This special arrangement facilitates the development of decorations involving different virtuoso specialties and fosters a permanent dialog between the artists.

The Métiers d'Art Les Univers infinis series, inspired by famous embedded motifs taken from the traditional mosaic art of Escher, is an excellent example of this arrangement at work. One watch in this series, the Lézard produced in 2013, involves a rare combination of the four major artistic crafts used in watchmaking: engraving, grand feu enamel, gem-setting, and guilloché. The engraver begins the work by chasing the motifs in a base of yellow gold. The enameler fills the south-facing lizards with taupe-colored enamel and those heading west with crimson red. The setter then dresses some of them in a costume of round-cut diamonds. To avoid cracking the enamel, he cuts the cavities that hold the stones before the enameling is carried out. Lastly, the master guilloché artist works on the other lizards. With amazing dexterity, he creates their scales, which are measured in tenths of a millimeter. It is very rare for guilloché to be carried out as the last stage on an enameled piece because of its great difficulty and the risk, in this case, of damaging the engraved threads that create the enamel sectors making up the lizards.

That same year, another series, Métiers d'Art Florilège, presented a dazzling world first: figurative guilloché on grand feu enamel. The decoration was based on the famous botanical drawings in the *Temple of Flora* by Robert John Thornton, published in 1799. The vibrant sense of life that radiates from the plants is a double feat of unique craftsmanship. It makes these ladies' watches some of the most fabulous models that Vacheron Constantin has ever produced.

LEFT-HAND PAGE
Pocket watch, 1923. Referred to as "The Arcadian Shepherds," from the name of the painting by Nicolas Poussin that it reproduces, this exceptional model perfectly illustrates the constant link at Vacheron Constantin between artistic crafts and watchmaking skills (see also pages 276 and 353).

MARQUETRY IN WOOD, GOLD AND MOTHER-OF-PEARL

OPPOSITE AND RIGHT-HAND PAGE
Métiers d'Art Les Univers Infinis - Horseman wristwatch, 2013. The marquetry specialist has produced a particularly complex creation by working with two materials that are diametrically opposed. Each horseman is first carved out in gold or mother-of-pearl before being carefully applied to a gold base as though in a jigsaw puzzle. The two sections are seamlessly joined, which is an impressive feat.

In the Métiers d'Art collection, the very exclusive Éloge de la Nature series consists of three unique pieces introduced in 2014 that celebrate the beauty and freedom of wild animals. Two of them use a decorative technique almost unknown in watchmaking: wood marquetry. Ninety minuscule fragments of wood are assembled individually in one, and 130 in the other, to create a landscape background. Different species of raw wood, tinted or lightly charred, produce a delicate range of colors. The art of marquetry lies not only in choosing the species of wood but also in sensitively orienting the grain to fit the scene as it gradually emerges. For example, the steepness of a mountainside is emphasized by a descending grain. Each fragment is cut with very precise movements of a tiny saw: no cracks or chips are acceptable. The smallest mistake can ruin the whole piece and the work has to start again. The decoration must fit perfectly into the dial and the fibers must be properly aligned. And like any work of art, each piece is unique and fundamentally influenced by the master craftsman who created it.

Another marquetry, this time in gold and mother-of-pearl, decorates a watch in the Métiers d'Art Les Univers infinis series: the Cavalier model is a tribute to Maurits Cornelis Escher and was produced in twenty examples in 2013. Each of the Ottoman cavalrymen on the dial have been cut from fine sheets of gold or mother-of-pearl and fit together without the slightest gap. The combination of two totally different materials and the cutting of the highly fragile mother-of-pearl with all its irregularities required some exceptional craftsmanship. The two materials were meticulously engraved to depict the horsemen and their mounts.

VACHERON CONSTANTIN
GENEVE
SWISS MADE

ART AND TECHNIQUE: A SINGLE WORLD

The ornamental tradition that has existed at Vacheron Constantin since it was founded, and has been a large part of its identity as a Geneva-based watchmaker, is not limited to the Métiers d'Art collection. And, indeed, it would be wrong to think that all the company's watches belong in one of two worlds: artistically decorated or technical. The fact is that the collections devoted to advanced watchmaking often benefit from the artistic crafts. For example, the cases of certain grand complication watches are completely engraved by hand. The dials of the Traditionnelle watches are now frequently decorated with manually applied guilloché. Another example is the Moon phase indication on the Traditionnelle chronographe quantième perpétuel introduced in 2010: its two moons – one sad, the other laughing – are manually engraved on a golden disc.

There is only one world at Vacheron Constantin: one that is committed to achieving both technical perfection and beauty. It is guided by talent, experience and imagination, where craftsmen's hands have worked their magic for more than 250 years. Yet this world is still young, alert, expert, and bold, always ready to explore. To explore our planet and time. I once asked a master *guillocheur* at Vacheron Constantin how long he would need to decorate the dial he was working on: He answered quietly with a little smile. "As long as it takes," he said. He seemed to enjoy the sensation of passing time, not concerned that he would have to finish one day. He also seemed to be traveling within the space of his dial at the same time as he discovered new areas of his knowledge, technique, and talent.

Vacheron Constantin was built on this idea of continuous unlimited exploration that pushes every boundary: geographic and cultural, technical and artistic and, of course, temporal. Much like the writers and artists in previous centuries who left on a "grand tour" with no fixed date to return, sometimes staying away for years. They left in search of the unknown but also to find their cultural roots and develop a spirit of imagination and invention. To reinvigorate their art through the revelations of ancient worlds and the discovery of new ones. While they traveled, time was unlimited. This is how Vacheron Constantin works and how it creates: "for as long as it takes." Its only horizon is infinity and each new watch it develops is simply another stage on the journey.

LEFT-HAND PAGE
Harmony Tourbillon Chronograph wristwatch, 2015. Equipped with Caliber 3200 and stamped with the Hallmark of Geneva, this timepiece houses an ample tourbillon carriage in the shape of a Maltese cross.

Doit — N.Sr Constant

Année	Mois	Jour		Compte
1820	Décemb^re	31	à	Lui-même Cie March^ses
"	"	"	à	Bijouterie de Cte à ½
"	"	"	à	Meschini
"	"	"	à	Veenozzi
"	"	"	à	L^s Baldini
"	"	"	à	F^s Carlieri
"	"	"	à	F^s Sena
"	"	"	à	Fanagli & Mariani
"	"	"	à	F^ns Bourkart
"	"	"	à	F^s Dani
"	"	"	à	L^s Bianchi
"	"	"	à	J. Luigy
"	"	"	à	F^ch D'Ivernois
"	"	"	à	Jaq^s Serre
1821	Février	7	à	Lui-même Cie March^ses
"	"	"	à	Bijouterie de Cte à ½
"	"	"	à	D^me Piccardi
"	"	"	à	Caputi
"	"	"	à	J. Allodi
"	"	9	à	Lui-même Cie March^ses
"	"	22	à	Bijouterie de Cte à ½
"	"	"	à	G. Zanoni
"	"	"	à	L^s Nenci
"	"	"	à	L^s Bartolini
"	"	"	à	J. Serre
"	Mars	20	à	Lui-même Cie M^ses
"	"	"	à	Bijouterie de Cte à ½
"	Avril	20	à	Lui-même Cie M^ses
"	"	"	à	Bijouterie de Cte à ½
"	"	"	à	L^s Lacroix
"	"	"	à	G^me Capuccio
"	"	"	à	Vve Marchisio
"	Mai	31	à	Caisse
"	Juin	13	à	Lui-même Cie M^ses
"	"	"	à	Bijouterie de Cte à ½
"	"	"	à	D'Ivernois &
"	"	"	à	F^ch D'Ivernois
"	"	"	à	F^ns Bourgard
"	"	30	à	Lui-même Cie M^ses
"	"	"	à	Bijouterie de Cte à ½

Transport du F° 110

Montant	Détail
F 83120.75	ses ventes en Toscane
16294.70	idem
19114	qu'il a reçu du dern^r
210	idem
200	idem
68.70	idem
130	idem
603.20	idem
590	idem
310	idem
40	idem
75	idem
215	idem
107	idem
27.50	ses ventes à Rome
21014.50	idem
21748	qu'il a reçu du dern^r
420	idem
106	idem
215	ses ventes à Florence
7563.05	idem
9491.95	qu'il a reçu du dern^r
315.85	idem
117	idem
176	idem
78	ses ventes à Bologne
9736.45	idem
3914.10	ses ventes à Turin
11461.15	idem
12157.50	qu'il a reçu du dern^r
1227	idem
297	idem
41	payé à Paschoud f. ^lo
45	ses ventes à Livourne
11092.20	idem
7884.65	qu'il a reçu du dern^r
176	idem
100	idem
96.25	ses ventes à Florence
15744.15	idem
12997.80	

184 1 13
184 98
184 1 15
184 1 15
184 1 15
184 1 15
184 1 15
184 1 04
184 1 15
184 1 15
184 1 15
184 1 15
184 1 15
184 1 15
189 1 13
189 1 07
189 1 16
189 1 16
190 1 00
191 1 13
191 1 07
191 1 16
191 1 16
191 1 16
194 1 13
194 1 07
196 1 13
196 1 07
197 1 16
197 1 16
197 1 16
202 80
202 1 13
202 1 07
202 1 16
202 1 16
202 1 16
204 1 13
204 1 07

F 272084 | 55

Transporté au F° 112 — F 16801

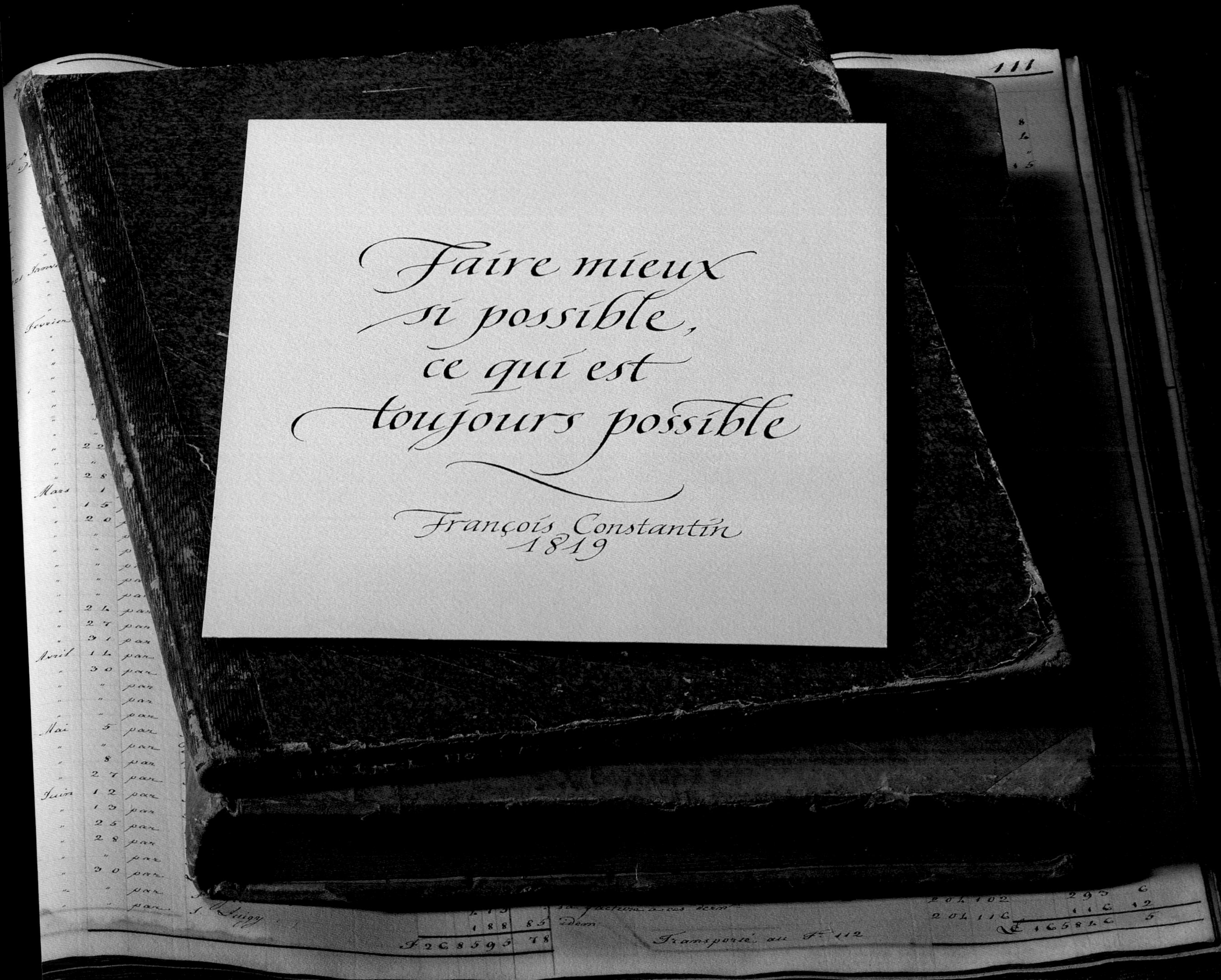

*Faire mieux
si possible,
ce qui est
toujours possible*

*François Constantin
1819*

GENEALOGY OF THE VACHERON AND CONSTANTIN FAMILIES

THE VACHERON FAMILY

PIERRE VACHERON

JEAN-JACQUES
Lugnorre, 1685 - Geneva, 1773. 1711 married Étiennette Mauris.

JEAN-MARC
Geneva, 1731 - Geneva, 1805. 1755 married Judith Suzanne Derogis.

LOUIS ANDRÉ
1755 - 1814.
1777 married Adrienne Gallet.
He succeeded his father Jean-Marc in 1805.

JEAN-MARC ABRAHAM
1760 - 1843 Geneva.
1786 married Anne Élisabeth Girod.

JACQUES BARTHÉLÉMI
1787 - 1864. 1810 married Catherine Étiennette Chossat. Jacques Barthélémi joins his brother-in-law. Charles François Chossat in 1816, and with François Constantin on April 1, 1819.

CHARLES CÉSAR
1812 - 1868. 1840 married Louise-Françoise-Laure Pernessin.

CHARLES
1846 - 1870

THE BRAND'S COMPANY NAME

J M VACHERON, GENEVA

VACHERON FRÈRES, GENEVA
ANDRÉ VACHERON, GENEVA
AB. VACHERON GIROD & CIE, GENEVA

VACHERON CHOSSAT & CIE.
VACHERON & CONSTANTIN
from 1819.

CÉSAR VACHERON & CIE.

CHARLES VACHERON
until 1870.
V^VE^ CÉSAR VACHERRON & CIE,
from December 21, 1870.

VACHERON & CONSTANTIN
1883.
ANCIENNE FABRIQUE VACHERON & CONSTANTIN,SOCIÉTÉ ANONYME (OR ANCIENNE FABRIQUE VACHERON & CONSTANTIN, LIMITED)
from 1887.

VACHERON & CONSTANTIN SA
1947.

VACHERON CONSTANTIN HOLDING SA
1977.

VACHERON CONSTANTIN, SUCCURSALE DE RICHEMONT SUISSE SA
1998.

VACHERON CONSTANTIN, BRANCH OF RICHEMONT INTERNATIONAL SA
2003.

THE CONSTANTIN FAMILY

JACOB CONSTANTIN
1755 - 1835. 1783 married Élisabeth Charlotte Rival.

ABRAHAM
Geneva, 1785 – Vernaz, 1855
Established porcelain painter in Paris and well known in the 19th century
French society.
He worked for the Sèvres Manufacture where he appears in the records from 1813 to 1849.

FRANÇOIS
Geneva, 1788 – Geneva, 1854
Joined with Jacques Barthélémi Vacheron in 1819.

JEAN NICOLAS
Born in 1792. 1823 married Eug. Cabrol.
Master artisan.

JEAN-FRANÇOIS
1829-1900. Married J. Pernette Plan. He commissioned the rue des Moulins building in 1880.

MARC EUGÈNE
1868 - 1922. Married M. Duvillard.

CHARLES
1887 - 1954. Married P. Chaix. Great nephew of François. He edited the records of Vacheron Constantin in 1927-1928. Won second prize in the 1929 Concours Colladon organized by the Society of Arts.

SELECTIVE CHRONOLOGY OF TIMEPIECES

1755

POCKET WATCH
1755
Inv. no. 10198 (pages 20 and 22-23)

1800

POCKET WATCH
1780
Inv. no. 10718 (page 29)

POCKET WATCH
1812
Inv. no. 10302 (pages 33 and 34)

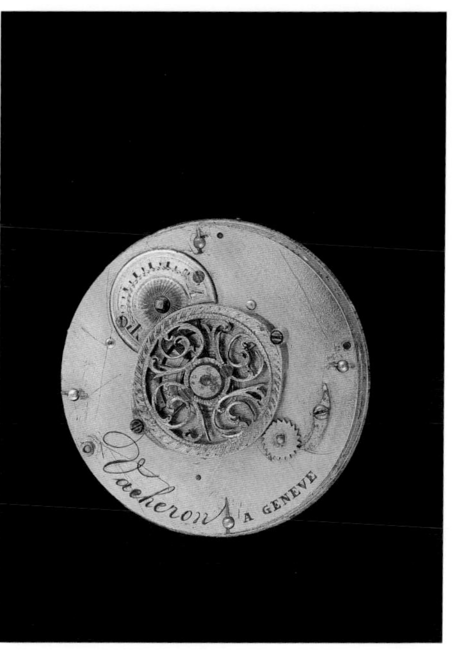

POCKET WATCH
1790
Inv. no. 10870 (pages 24 and 26-27)

POCKET WATCH
1815
Inv. no. 10128 (page 30)

POCKET WATCH
1817
Inv. no. 10436 (page 37)

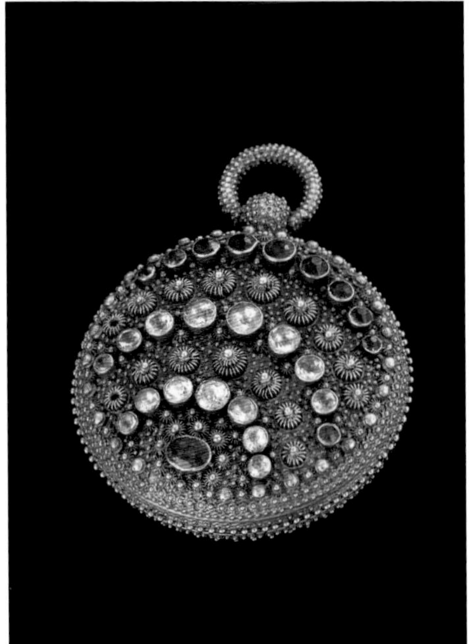

POCKET WATCH
1822
Inv. no. 10469 (page 47)

POCKET WATCH
1824
Inv. no. 11324 (page 48)

POCKET WATCH
1825
Inv. no. 11744 (page 268)

POCKET WATCH
1827
Inv. no. 10715 (page 244)

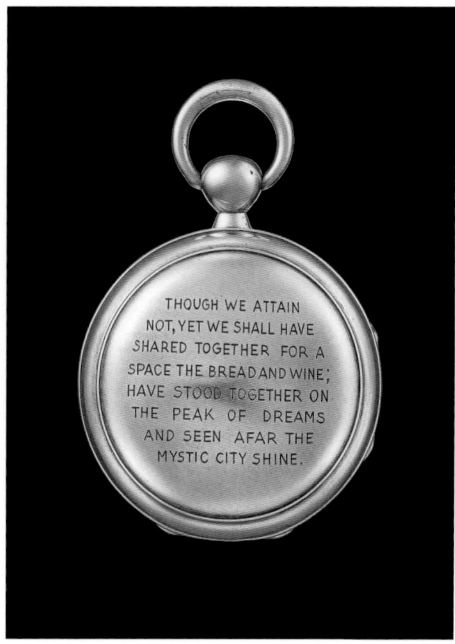

POCKET WATCH
1827
Inv. no. 10713 (page 38)

POCKET WATCH
1827
Inv. no. 11281

POCKET WATCH
1836
Inv. no. 10311 (page 51)

1855

POCKET WATCH
1855
Inv. no. 10329 (pages 68-69)

DOUBLE-SIDED POCKET WATCH
1884
Inv. no. 10155 (pages 80-81)

LADIES' PENDANT WATCH
1887
Inv. no. 10554 (page 79)

LADIES' WRISTWATCH
1889
Inv. no. 10531 (page 91)

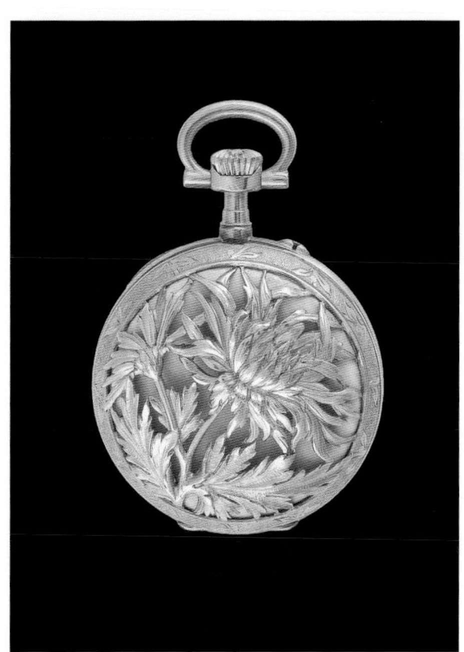

POCKET WATCH
1897
Inv. no. 11248 (page 288)

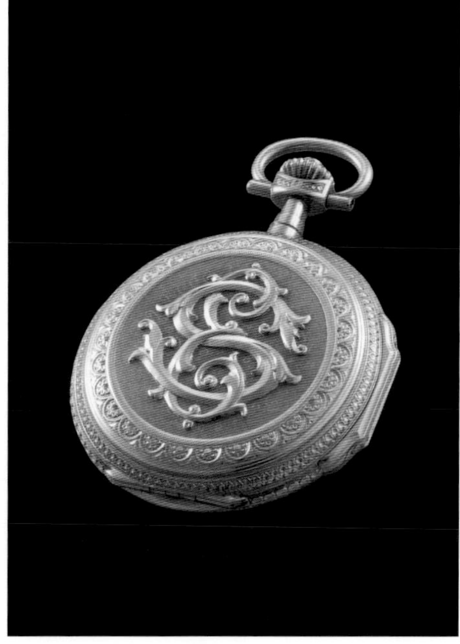

POCKET WATCH
1899
Inv. no. 10926 (page 84)

1900

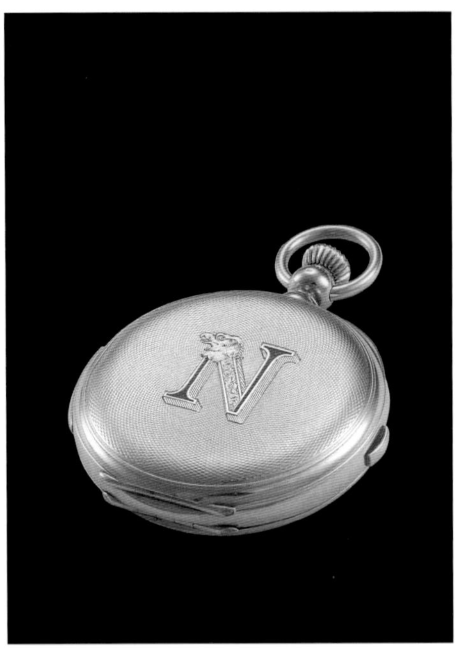

POCKET WATCH
1900
Inv. no. 10803 (page 93)

POCKET WATCH
1901
Inv. no. 10158 (pages 96-97)

POCKET WATCH
1901
Inv. no. 10536 (pages 96-97)

AVIATOR WATCH
1904
Inv. no. 10756 (page 101)

POCKET WATCH
1905
Inv. no. 11659 (page 278)

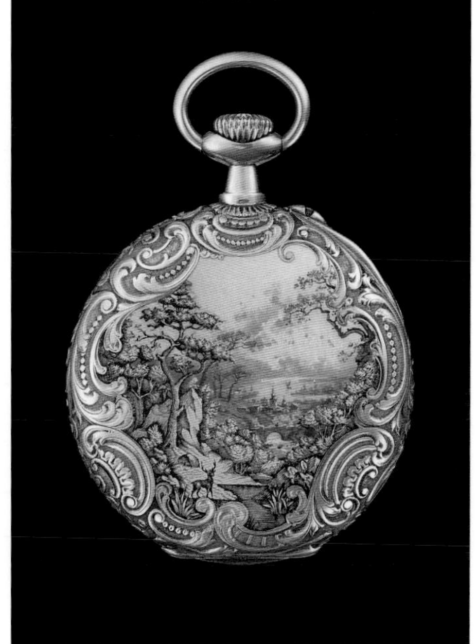

POCKET WATCH
1905
Inv. no. 10792 (page 258)

1910

POCKET WATCH
1906
Inv. no. 10655 (page 90)

POCKET WATCH
1910
Inv. no. 10559 (pages 292-293)

CHRONOMOMÈTRE ROYAL POCKET WATCH
1907
Inv. no. 11035

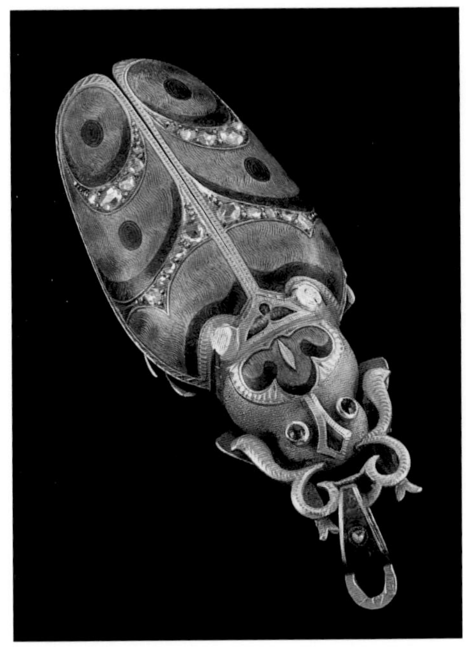

"SCARAB" JEWELRY PENDANT WATCH
1910
Inv. no. 10556 (page 261)

LADIES' PENDANT WATCH
1910
Inv. no. 10184 (page 98)

LADIES' WRISTWATCH
1912
Inv. no. 10668 (pages 106-107)

PENDANT WATCH
1915
Inv. no. 11696 (page 105)

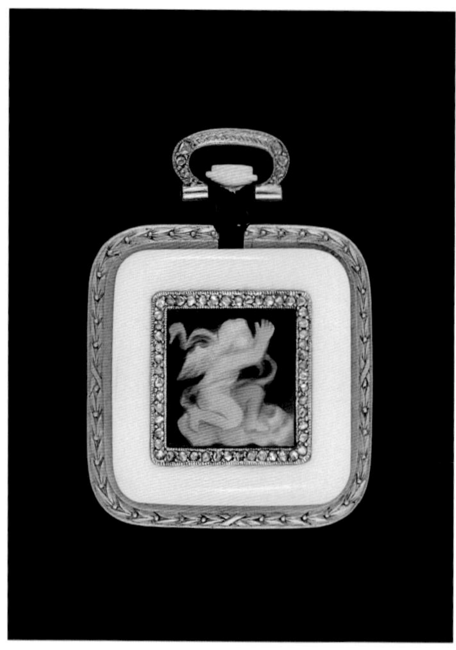

WRISTWATCH
1915
Inv. no. 10144 (page 114)

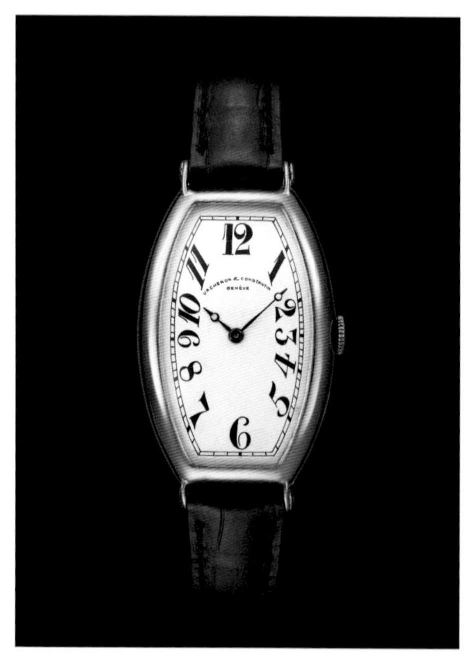

WRISTWATCH
1915
Inv. no. 10594 (page 114)

LADIES' JEWELRY WRISTWATCH
1916
Inv. no. 10939 (page 108)

"CORPS OF ENGINEERS USA" CHRONOGRAPH POCKET WATCH
1918
Inv. no. 10237 and 11093 (page 111)

POCKET WATCH
1918
Inv. no. 11527 (page 113)

1920

WRISTWATCH
1921
Inv. no. 11677 (pages 116-117 and 349)

LADIES' PENDANT WATCH
1922
Inv. no. 10840 (page 270)

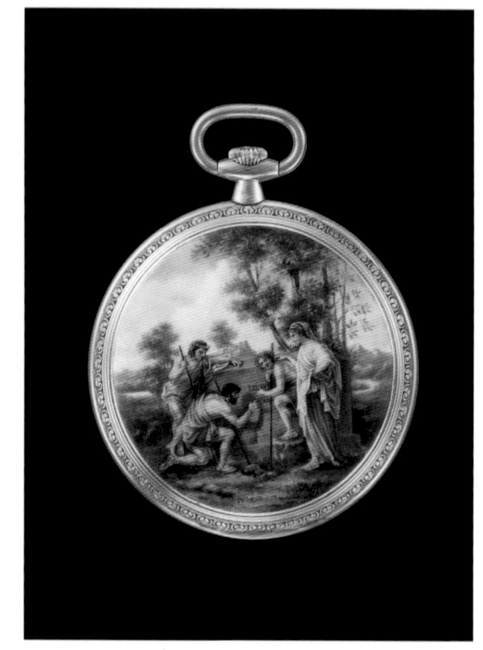

JEWELRY WRISTWATCH
1923
Inv. no. 10981 (pages 300-301)

POCKET WATCH
1923
Inv. no. 10659 (pages 276, 302 and 353)

OPEN POCKET WATCH
1923
Inv. no. 10659 (pages 276, 302 and 353)

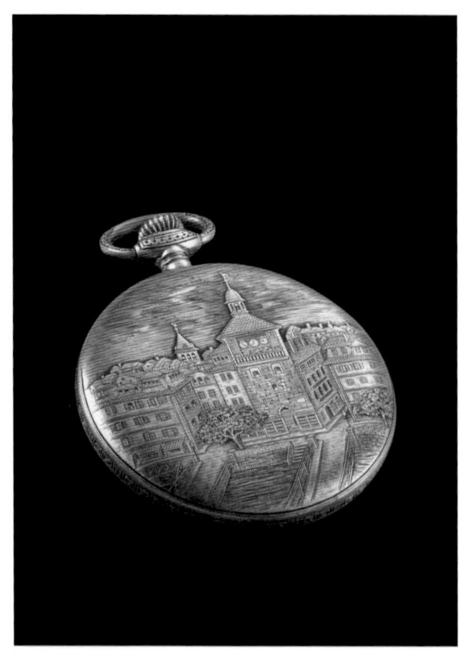

POCKET WATCH
1926
Inv. no. 10656 (pages 12-13)

SKELETON POCKET WATCH
1926
Inv. no. 11131 (page 118)

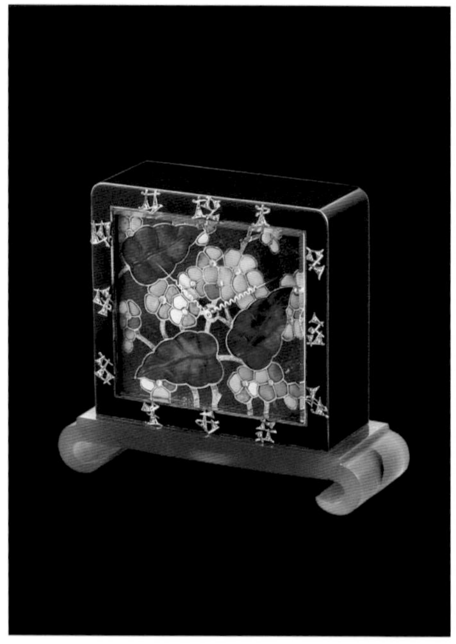

ART DECO-STYLE CLOCK
1926
Inv. no. 10547 (pages 122-123)

POCKET WATCH
1928
Private collection

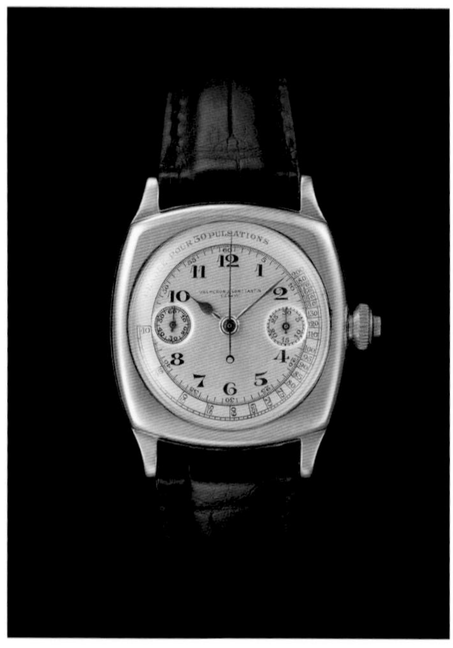

CHRONOGRAPH WRISTWATCH
1928
Inv. no. 11059 (page 242)

"SURPRISE" POCKET WATCH
1928
Inv. no. 10252 (page 119)

ULTRA-THIN POCKET WATCH
1929
Inv. no. 10152 (page 287)

POCKET WATCH
1929
Private collection (pages 126-127 and 250)

1930

WRISTWATCH WITH SHUTTERS
1929
Inv. no. 10405 (pages 120 and 121)

WRISTWATCH WITH SHUTTERS
1930
Inv. no. 10194

WRISTWATCH WITH SHUTTERS
1930
Inv. no. 10572

WRISTWATCH
1930
Inv. no. 11243 (page 130)

ULTRA-THIN POCKET WATCH
1931
Inv. no. 10726 (page 129)

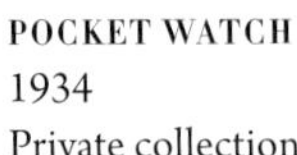

POCKET WATCH
1934
Private collection

MEN'S WRISTWATCH
1935
Inv. no. 10794 (page 139)

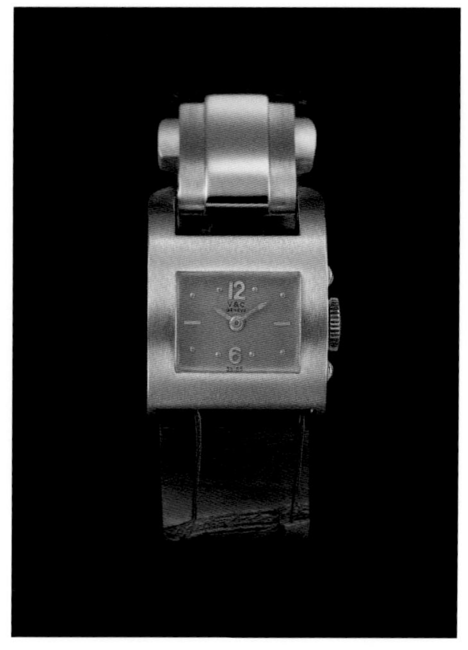

LADIES' DRIVER WRISTWATCH
1939
Inv. no. 10387

DRIVER WRISTWATCH
1939
Inv. no. 11164 (page 140)

DRIVER WRISTWATCH
1939
Inv. no. 11155 (page 140)

1940

AIR FLOW WRISTWATCH
1940
Inv. no. 11198 (page 143)

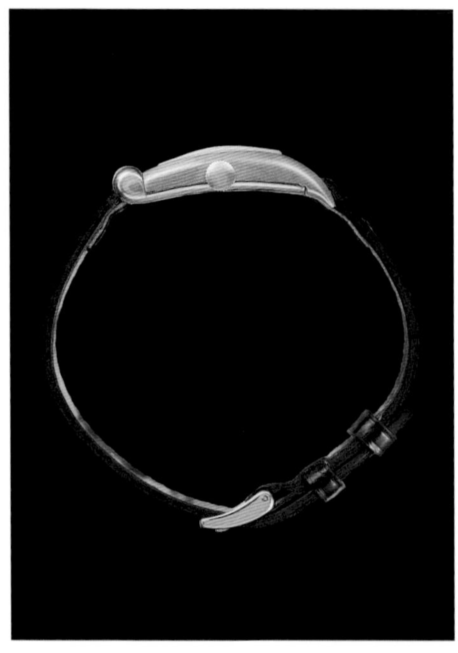

ALUMINUM POCKET WATCH
1945
Inv. no. 10167 (pages 146 and 147)

WORLD TIME POCKET WATCH
1946
Inv. no. 11182 (page 247)

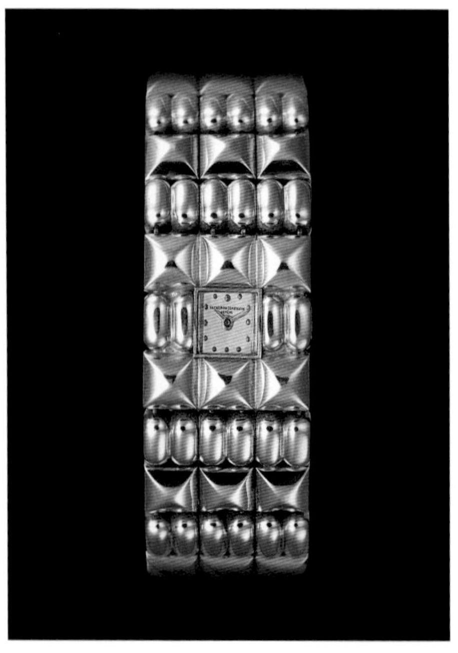

LADIES' WRISTWATCH
1946
Inv. no. 10771

LADIES' JEWELRY WATCH
1948
Inv. no. 10353 (page 149)

1950

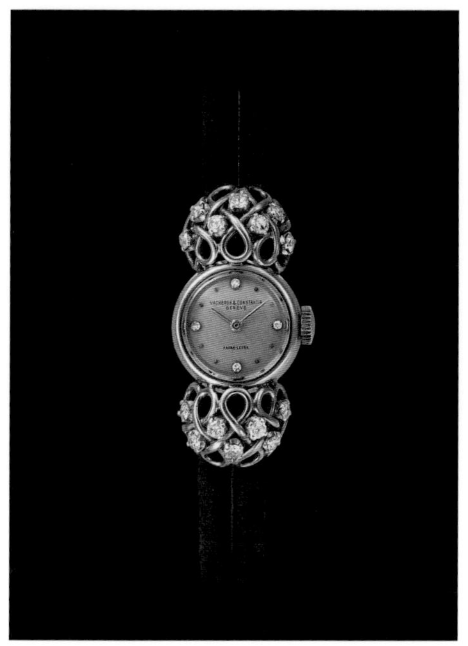

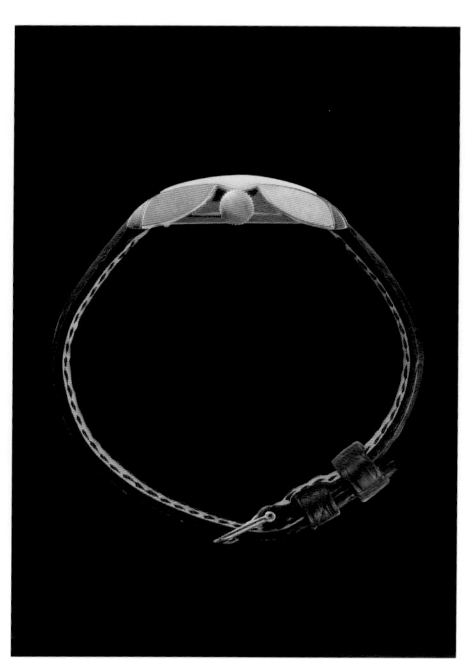

LADIES' WRISTWATCH
1948
Inv. no. 10795

BUTTERFLY WRISTWATCH
1952
Inv. no. 10974 (pages 150-151)

POCKET WATCH
1953
Inv. no. 11123 (page 294)

WRISTWATCH
1954
Inv. no. 11056 (page 153)

TOLEDO WRISTWATCH
1954
Inv. no. 10933 (page 241)

CINCHED RECTANGLE WRISTWATCH
1955
Inv. no. 10416 (pages 156-157)

WRISTWATCH
1955
Inv. no. 11422 (page 252)

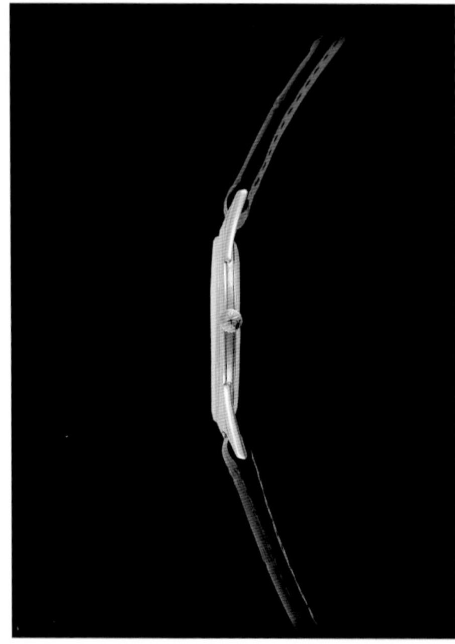

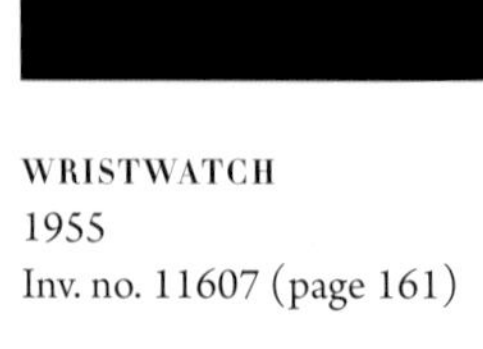

WRISTWATCH
1955
Inv. no. 11607 (page 161)

WRISTWATCH
1957
Inv. no. 11818 (page 162)

WRISTWATCH
1957
Inv. no. 10146

WRISTWATCH
1957
Inv. no. 6213 (page 163)

WRISTWATCH
1957
Inv. no. 11381

1960

1970

CHRONOMOMÈTRE ROYAL WRISTWATCH
1966
Inv. no. 10984

WRISTWATCH 1972
1972
Inv. no. 11671 (page 165)

WRISTWATCH 1972
1972
Inv. no. 11689 (page 165)

WRISTWATCH
1968
Inv. no. 11481

1972 "PRESTIGE DE LA FRANCE" WRISTWATCH
1972
Inv. no. 10766 (page 165)

WRISTWATCH 222
1976/1977
Inv. no. 11524 (page 166)

1980

KALLISTA WRISTWATCH
1979
Inv. no. 10150 (page 169)

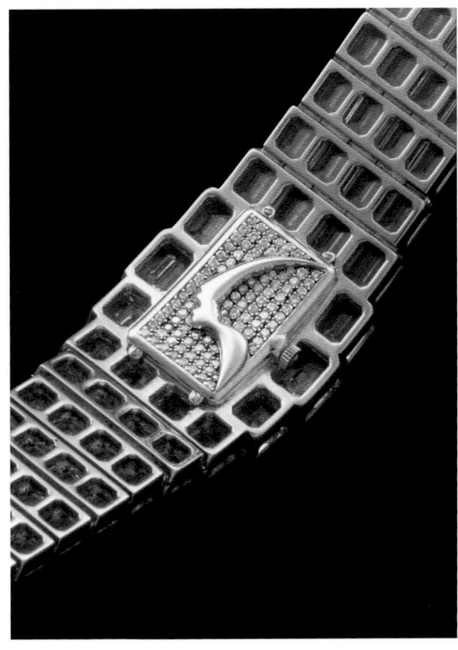

WRISTWATCH
1982
Inv. no. 10337

LADIES' WRISTWATCH
1984
Inv. no. 10120

1990

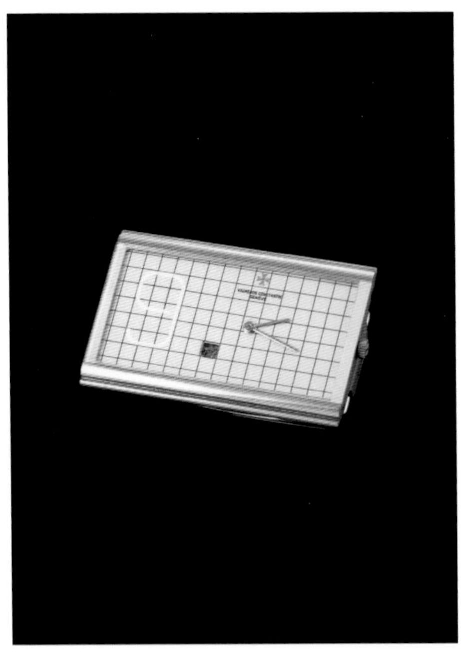

MEN'S CUFFLINK CLIP WATCH
1985
Inv. no. 10491

WRISTWATCH
1990
Inv. no. 11497 (pages 170-171)

STRUCTURA WRISTWATCH
1990
Inv. no. 10335 (page 172)

LADIES' WRISTWATCH
1986
Inv. no. 11502

MERCATOR WRISTWATCH
1994
Inv. no. 11473 (page 175)

OVERSEAS WRISTWATCH
1996
Inv. no. 11705 (page 176)

2000

SALTARELLO WRISTWATCH
1997
Inv. no. 10740 (page 179)

PATRIMONY WRISTWATCH
2004 (page 183)
Ref. 81180/000R-9159

MÉTIERS D'ART TRIBUTE TO GREAT EXPLORERS - MARCO POLO EXPEDITION WRISTWATCH
2004 (page 269)
Ref. 47070/0005-9086

1755 JUBILEE WRISTWATCH
2005
Inv. no. 11374

SAINT-GERVAIS WRISTWATCH
2005
Inv. no. 11475

TOUR DE L'ÎLE WRISTWATCH
2005
Inv. no. 11474 (pages 192, 194 and 195)

MÉTIERS D'ART LES QUATRE SAISONS WRISTWATCH
2005
Inv. no. 11389

TRADITIONNELLE PERPETUAL CALENDAR OPENWORKED WRISTWATCH
2007 (page 240)
Ref. 43172/000P-9236

MÉTIERS D'ART LES MASQUES CONGO WRISTWATCH
2007 (page 199)
Ref. 86070/000P-9296

PHILOSOPHIA WRISTWATCH
2009 (page 200)
Ref. 80173/000R-9483

MÉTIERS D'ART LES DRAGONS WRISTWATCH
2009 (page 284)
Ref. 86990/000R-9498

2010

MÉTIERS D'ART LA SYMBOLIQUE DES LAQUES WRISTWATCH
2010 (page 280)
Ref. 33222/000R-9701

MÉTIERS D'ART CHAGALL & L'OPÉRA DE PARIS WRISTWATCH
2010 (page 203)
Ref. 86090/0005-6664

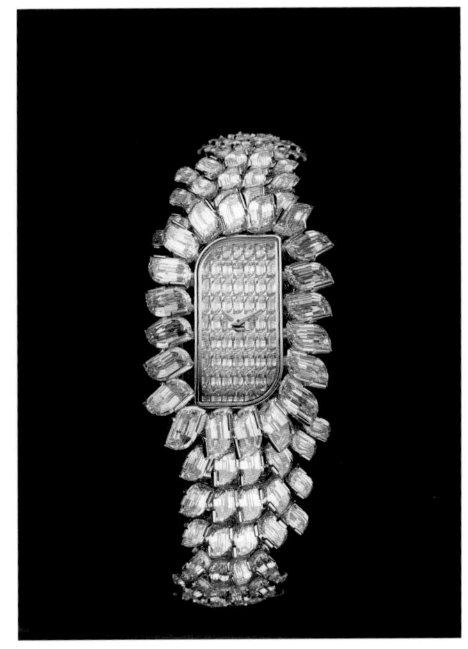

MÉTIERS D'ART LADY KALLA FLAMME WRISTWATCH
2011 (page 298)
Ref. 17620/511G-9478

MÉTIERS D'ART LES UNIVERS INFINIS WRISTWATCH
2012 (page 275)
Ref. 86222/000G-9689

MÉTIERS D'ART LES UNIVERS INFINIS - HORSEMAN WRISTWATCH
2013 (pages 304 and 305)
Ref. 86222-000G-9833

PATRIMONY ULTRA-THIN CALIBER 1731 WRISTWATCH
2013 (page 245)
Ref. 30110/000R-9793

MÉTIERS D'ART HOMMAGE A L'ART DE LA DANSE WRISTWATCH
2013 (page 279)
Ref. 86090/000G-9987

MAÎTRE CABOTIER ASTRONOMICA WRISTWATCH
2014 (page 246)
Ref. 80174/000G-9995

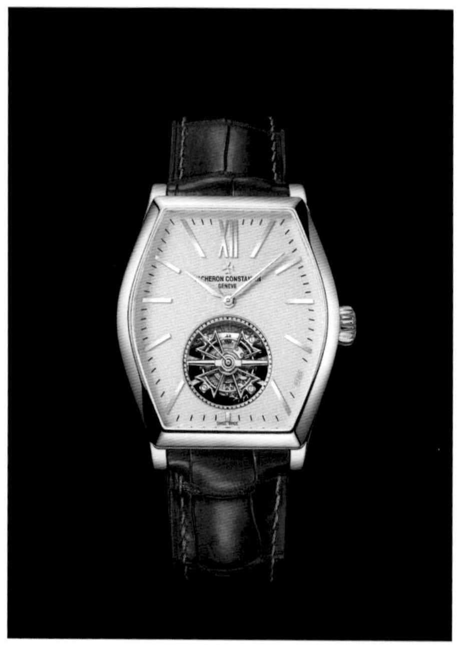

MALTE TOURBILLON COLLECTION EXCELLENCE PLATINE WRISTWATCH
2014 (pages 204 and 248)
Ref. 30130/000P-9876

MÉTIERS D'ART MÉCANIQUES AJOURÉES WRISTWATCH
2014 (page 290)
Ref. 82020/000G-9925

HARMONY ULTRA-THIN GRANDE COMPLICATION CHRONOGRAPH WRISTWATCH
2015 (page 253)
Ref. 54005/000P-B057

REFERENCE 57260 POCKET WATCH
2015 (pages 208, 209, 211, 212, 213, 238 and 251)

MÉTIERS D'ART SAVOIRS ENLUMINÉS WRISTWATCH
2015 (pages 207)
Ref. 7000S-000B-B002

MÉTIERS D'ART TABLE CLOCK
2015 (page 206)
Ref. 99900-001-B034

INDEX

VACHERON & CONSTANTIN
GENÈVE-SUISSE

11"115
17 BAISSE
17 12/12
8
19 CHRON
19194
16162
17 MOY
16 164
9 92
9"95

SELECTIVE BIBLIOGRAPHY

PUBLICATIONS ON VACHERON CONSTANTIN

Annales de la maison d'Horlogerie Vacheron et Constantin 1914-1938
Charles Constantin, 1938

Les Maîtres des Heures
Vacheron Constantin, 1955

L'Univers de Vacheron Constantin,
Lausanne - Geneva
C. Lambelet / L. Coen.
Scriptar SA/Vacheron Constantin, 1992

Vacheron Constantin
Franco Cologni
Assouline, Paris, 2000

Secrets of Vacheron Constantin
François Chaille / Franco Cologni
Flammarion, Paris, 2005

Treasures of Vacheron Constantin: A Legacy of Watchmaking since 1755
Hazan, 2011

Calibre 2755
Assouline, Paris, 2011

Calibres 2253 & 2260
Assouline, Paris, 2012

Calibre 1731
Assouline, Paris, 2013

Calibres 3200 & 3300
Assouline, Paris, 2014

PUBLICATIONS ON THE HISTORY, TECHNIQUES AND ART OF WATCHMAKING

Les Montres-bracelets
H. Kahlert / R. Mühe /
G.L. Brunner.
La Bibliothèque des Arts, Paris.
Production Office du Livre, Fribourg, 1983

L'heure qu'il est, les horloges, la mesure du temps et la formation du monde moderne
Harvard University.
D. S. Landes.
Gallimard, Paris, 1983

Dictionnaire professionnel illustré de l'Horlogerie
G. A. Berner
Chambre Suisse de l'horlogerie à la Chaux-de-Fonds, (réédition) 1988

L'Homme et le Temps en Suisse 1291-1991,
Institut l'Homme et le Temps, La Chaux-de-Fonds, 1991

Arts et technique de la montre
E. Introna / G. Ribolini.
Du May, Boulogne, 1993.

Comment habiller le Temps. Un siècle de Design horloger - JUVENIA,
Lausanne - La Chaux-de-Fonds.
H. Marquis.
Éditions Scriptar SA/Juvenia, 1995

The Mastery of Time: Discoveries, Inventions, and Advances in Horology
Dominique Fléchon
Flammarion, Paris, 2011

LITERATURE AND HISTORY

Sparkenbroke,
Charles Morgan
J'ai Lu (paperback edition), Paris, 2004

La Genève de Töpffer
Philippe Monnier
A. Jullien, Geneva, 1914

PAGE 349
Wristwatch, 1921. As with the Driver watches, this 18K yellow gold cushion-shaped timepiece illustrates Vacheron Constantin's freedom in design and the bold style of the Roaring Twenties. The winding crown is positioned at 11 o'clock, extending the 12-6 o'clock axis of the enamel dial, pivoted 45° counterclockwise. Produced by Vacheron Constantin specifically for the American market, this watch was re-issued in 2009 and is still a great success. Inv. no. 11677

PAGE 350
Technical boards of Vacheron Constantin calibers dating from the first half of the twentieth century.

RIGHT-HAND PAGE
Pocket watch, 1923. Referred to as "The Arcadian Shepherds," from the name of the painting by Nicolas Poussin that it reproduces, this exceptional model perfectly illustrates the constant link at Vacheron Constantin between artistic crafts and watchmaking skills (see also pages 277 and 353). Inv. no. 10659

ACKNOWLEDGMENTS

The author and his team wish to express their gratitude to Juan Carlos Torres for welcoming them to Vacheron Constantin with doors wide open.

They would also like to thank Julien Marchenoir for all the light he shed on the company's history.

Special thanks go to their guide at Vacheron Constantin, Anne-Marie Bubanko Belcari, for her invaluable assistance and documentary support.

Lastly, they wish to thank the following people for all their information, advice and willingness to help: Gabriel Angeloz, Dominique Bernaz, Lysiane Blanchet, Marc-Henri Blangero, Armelle Carreras, Muriel Casalotto, François Cely, Julien Chazal, Simeo Da Silva, Élodie Dessimond, Valentine Gérard, Serge Guignard, Vincent Jolion, Vincent Kauffmann, Michel Keller, Yann Lacroix, Alain Lambercy, Yann Le Baillif, Chrystian Lefrançois, Simon Lefrançois, Paulo Lopes, Didier Martin, Patrick Maugard, Jérôme Meier, Sigrid Offenstein, Gilles Osouf, Gérard Paquelet, Jérôme Poencet, Laurent Ramat, Christian Selmoni, Luc de Siebenthal, Johan Strindberg, Christian Thibert, Supachai Wattanakanoktham.

PHOTOGRAPHIC CREDITS

All the photographs reproduced in this book were taken by Bruno Ehrs, with the exception of those on the following pages:
14: © Musée d'Art et d'Histoire de la Ville de Genève, Inv. no. HM 26; *18:* MET; *19:* Frick collection; *25, 32, 41, 42, 50, 59, 61:* Vacheron Constantin archives; *66-67:* © BnF; *70-71:* Dallas Museum of Art, Foundation for the Arts Collection, donated by Nancy Hamon in memory of Jake L. Hamon with additional donations by Mrs. Eugene D. McDermott, Mrs. James H. Clark, Mrs. Edward Marcus and the Leland Fikes Foundation, Inc. Image reproduced with permission from the Dallas Museum of Art; *72, 73:* Vacheron Constantin archives; *74:* Print and Picture Collection, Free Library of Philadelphia; *75, 76-77:* Vacheron Constantin archives; *82-83:* Musée de la chaux de Fonds; *86-87:* Vacheron Constantin archives; *88:* © National Portrait Gallery, London; *89:* © Léon et Lévy / Roger-Viollet; *91, 92:* Eric Sauvage; *94, 95, 99:* Vacheron Constantin archives; *100:* © National Portrait Gallery, London; *102-103:* © Hulton-Deutsch Collection / Corbis; *104:* Vacheron Constantin archives; *109:* © National Portrait Gallery, London; *110:* Rights reserved; *112:* Rights reserved; *121:* © Vacheron Constantin, Photography by Studio Ferrazzini Bouchet Photographies; *124:* State Archive of Bern, FN Jost G 383; *126:* Eric Sauvage; *128:* © Vacheron Constantin Archives; *129:* Eric Sauvage; *136-137:* Hulton archives / Getty images; *139:* © Vacheron Constantin, Photography by Studio Ferrazzini Bouchet photographies; *144-145:* Vacheron Constantin archives; *147:* Eric Sauvage; *149:* © Vacheron Constantin / photography by Studio Ferrazzini Bouchet Photographies; *151:* © Vacheron Constantin, Photography by Studio Ferrazzini Bouchet photographies; *152, 154, 158, 159, 167:* Vacheron Constantin archives; *168:* © Vacheron Constantin Archives; *173:* © Vacheron Constantin, Photographie Studio Ferrazzini Bouchet photographies; *177:* Vacheron Constantin archives; *194:* Eric Sauvage; *195:* Jean-Marc Bréguet; *199:* Jean-Marc Bréguet; *200:* Jean-Marc Bréguet; *202:* © Adagp, Paris 2015 © Jean-Pierre Delagarde; *206:* Jean-Marc Bréguet; *207:* Jean-Marc Bréguet; *208, 209, 211, 212-213:* Jean-Marc Bréguet; *216:* © Fondation Martin Bodmer, Cologny (Geneva),

VACHERON & CONSTANTIN
GENEVE

photography by Hélène Tobler; *223:* Sully Balmassière; *231:* © Denis Hayoun / Vacheron Artists of Time Constantin; *234:* Imagie; *238:* Jean-Marc Bréguet; *240:* M Design; *243:* Sully Balmassière; *244:* © Vacheron Constantin, photography by Lysiane Blanchet; *245:* Jean-Marc Bréguet; *246:* Jean-Marc Bréguet; *247:* © Vacheron Constantin, Photography by Studio Ferrazzini Bouchet phtographies; *248:* M Design; *249:* Sully Balmassière; *251:* Jean-Marc Bréguet; 252: © Vacheron Constantin, photography by Lysiane Blanchet; © Vacheron Constantin, Photography by Studio Ferrazzini Bouchet photographies; *253:* M Design; *268:* © Vacheron Constantin, photography by Lysiane Blanchet; *269:* M Design; *275:* Jean-Marc Bréguet; *277:* Jean-Marc Bréguet; *278:* © Vacheron Constantin, photography by Lysiane Blanchet; *279:* Jean-Marc Bréguet; *280:* Jean-Marc Bréguet; *284-285:* Jean-Marc Bréguet; *290:* Jean-Marc Bréguet; *293:* Zohico Kyoto; *294:* © Vacheron Constantin, Photography by Studio Ferrazzini Bouchet photographies; *298:* Nick Welsh; *304-305:* Jean-Marc Bréguet; *308-309:* Jean-Marc Bréguet.

Chronology Photo Credits:
© Vacheron Constantin, Photography by Studio Ferrazzini Bouchet photographies: Inv. no. 10198 face, 10718, 10302, 10128, 10436, 11324, 10713, 10531, 10536, 10756, 10792, 10655, 10144, 10594, 10237, 11696, 11677, 10840, 10981, 10659 except face, 11131, 11059, 10252 dial, 10405, 10194, 10572, 11243, 10726, Pocket watch once owned by King Fouad, 10794, 103897, 11155, 11164, 11198, 10167, 11182, 10771, 10353, 10795, 10974, 11123, 11056, 10933, 11422, 10416, 11818, 10146, 10984, 11381, 11481, 11671, 10766, 11524, 10150, 10337, 10335, 11497, 11473, 11705, 11374; © Vacheron Constantin, Photography by Dominique Cohas: Inv. no. 10198 open, 10469, 10311, 10329, 10554, 10926, 10803, 10158 mvt, 11035, 10559, 10939, 10184, 10556, 10668, 10659 dial, 10656, 10547, 10157, 10252 closed, 10152, 10120, 10491, 10740; © Vacheron Constantin, photography by Lysiane Blanchet: Inv. no. 10870, 11607, 11744, 10715, 11281, 10155, 11248, 10158 face, 11659, 11527, 11422 side, 11689, 10150 back, 11502; © Vacheron Constantin Photo: Pocket watch once owned by au Fouad I King of Egypt; © Vacheron Constantin, Photography by M Design: *Métiers d'Art Tribute to Great Explorers - Marco Polo Expedition* Wristwatch 2004 (page 269), *Traditionnelle Perpetual Calendar Openworked* Watch 2007 (page 240), *Malte Tourbillon Collection Excellence Platine* Wristwatch 2014 (pages 204 et 248), *Harmony* Wristwatch 2015 (page 180), *Harmony Ultra-Thin Grande Complication Chronographe* Wristwatch 2015 (page 253); © Vacheron Constantin, Photography by Jean-Marc Bréguet: *Saint-Gervais* Wristwatch 2005, *Métiers d'Art les Quatre Saisons* Wristwatch 2005, *Métiers d'Arts les Masques Congo* Wirstwatch 2007 (page 199), *Métiers d'Art la Symbolique des Laques* Wristwatch 2010 (page 292), *Métiers d'Art les Univers Infinis* Wristwatch 2012 (page 275), *Patrimony Ultra-Thin Caliber 1731* Wristwatch 2013 (page 245), *Philosophia* Wristwatch 2009 (page 200), *Métiers d'Art les Dragons* Wristwatch 2009 (page 282), *Métiers d'Art Chagall et l'Opéra de Paris* Wristwatch 2010 (page 203), *Métiers d'Art Hommage à l'Art de la Danse* Wristwatch 2013 (page 279), *Maître Cabinotier Astronomica* Wristwatch 2014 (page 246), *Métiers d'Art Mécaniques Ajourées* Wristwatch 2014 (page 288), *Reference 57260* Pocket Watch 2015 (pages 8, 208, 209, 2011, 238 and 251); © Vacheron Constantin, Photography by Nick Welsh: *Métiers d'Art Lady Kalla Flamme* Wristwatch 2011 (page 298).

FSC www.fsc.org MIXTE Papier issu de sources responsables FSC® C102788

VMXP801893
Printed in Italy